STAGECOACH NORTH

A HISTORY OF BARNARD'S EXPRESS

KEN MATHER

Heritage House Publishing Company Ltd.
heritagehouse.ca

Cataloguing information available from Library and Archives Canada
978-1-77203-309-0 (pbk)
978-1-77203-310-6 (ebook)

Edited by Marial Shea
Proofread by Lenore Hietkamp
Cover and interior book design by Setareh Ashrafologhalai
Cover image from *Transportation: A Pictorial Archive from Nineteenth-Century Sources* (1984), Dover Publications
Maps by Ken Mather
Illustration on page 110 by Jacqui Thomas

The interior of this book was produced on 100% post-consumer recycled paper, processed chlorine free and printed with vegeta-ble-based inks.

Heritage House gratefully acknowledges that the land on which we live and work is within the traditional territories of the Lkwungen (Esquimalt and Songhees), Malahat, Pacheedaht, Scia'new, T'Sou-ke, and W̱SÁNEĆ (Pauquachin, Tsartlip, Tsawout, Tseycum) Peoples.

We acknowledge the financial support of the Government of Canada through the Canada Book Fund (CBF) and the Canada Council for the Arts, and the Province of British Columbia through the British Columbia Arts Council and the Book Publishing Tax Credit.

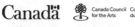

24 23 22 21 20   1 2 3 4 5

Printed in Canada

CONTENTS

INTRODUCTION

F RANCIS JONES BARNARD arrived in the Colony of British Columbia with a scarcity of ready cash and a wealth of hope. Within a few years, his fierce determination would see him build an express and stagecoach business to rival the best in the world. Barnard's accomplishment was made all the more significant by the challenges of fierce winters and great distances that were part of being the furthest-north stagecoach line in North America. Barnard's Express and its successor, the BC Express, would play a key role in the opening up and development of British Columbia as a colony, and later as a province, in the new country of Canada.

Barnard's story was typical of an age that saw millions of young men and women leave their homes in search of a better life. The nineteenth century witnessed an unprecedented international circulation of people, nowhere more so than in western North America. The California gold rush attracted not just Europeans who had immigrated to the United States; Mexicans, Chinese, and people of other ethnicities also found their way to the goldfields. When the gold in California began to diminish from a flood to a trickle, it was no surprise that the masses moved north to "the New Eldorado" when gold was reportedly found in British territory north of the forty-ninth parallel.[1]

An estimated 30,000 gold seekers would come north in 1858. The first wave arrived April 25 on the steamship *Commodore*, inundating the mix of First Nations and a handful of British fur traders in the little Colony of Vancouver Island. Although Governor James Douglas referred to the incredible influx of humanity as "Americans," he pointed out in a dispatch to the colonial secretary:

> Nearly 400 of those men were landed at this place, and have since left in boats and canoes for Frasers River... About 60 British subjects, with an equal number of native born Americans, the rest being chiefly Germans, with a smaller proportion of Frenchmen and Italians, composed this body of adventurers.[2]

This dilemma was not unprecedented. Some twenty years earlier, the British authorities had witnessed an influx of Americans from the east into what was called the Oregon Country, only to lose a vast territory to the wily Yankee negotiators. Unwilling to let this happen again, they did what was done in all their colonial possessions: they sent upper-class English "gentlemen" to add government and legal control to the situation. This few dozen British aristocrats would not have succeeded without the presence of the Royal Engineers on land and the British Navy patrolling the waters. So, for a time, the limited British presence did its best to mitigate the damage that could be done if the "Americans" brought their attitude toward Indigenous people to the First Nations of the Fraser River.

These British colonial officials possessed enough wealth and education to maintain their upper-middle-class or landed-gentry customs and standards. "They had brought with them well stocked libraries; they had kept up their subscriptions to *The Times*; and they contributed scientific articles on anthropology and other subjects to learned periodicals. Politically, they remained the Queen's most loyal subjects."[3] Despite their small numbers, they were able to exert strong influence, and an uneasy power, over the rambunctious "Americans" and may be excused if they occasionally enriched themselves when opportunities arose.

Almost as latecomers to the party came the "Canadians" from the British colonies of Canada East and West, New Brunswick, Nova Scotia, Prince Edward Island, and Newfoundland. I will use the term "Canadians" to describe them, even though citizens of these four colonies would not have used it at the time. What they all had in common was a strong desire not to be "American," even though they were more like their neighbours to the south than any other group. Many of them were descended from United Empire Loyalists, who had left the newly formed United States when the majority of people wanted to form an independent country and were prepared to fight the British to do so.

These "Canadians" were strongly loyal to Britain, but the colonial officials could not figure them out. Unlike the well-to-do British, who lived lives of privilege and comfort, most of the Canadians knew the poverty and challenges of making a home in a new country. Their propensity to count their pennies, even in gold-rich British Columbia, and their oft-stated desire to make their fortune and live in luxury, made one British official comment, "Canada was looked down on as a poor mean slow people who had been very commonly designated North American Chinamen... from their necessarily thrifty condition."[4] This description betrays a racist bias against both the Canadians and the Chinese, whose industry and perseverance were begrudgingly acknowledged by most all who encountered them, miners and colonial officials alike, despite the obvious differences in appearance and dress.

In the Colony of British Columbia, gold was the great equalizer. Everyone wanted the comfort, power, and indulgences it could provide. Everyone had mining "interests" and hoped for fortune's smile. Even the colonial officials could not resist investing in particularly promising mining claims, despite their conflicting role of ruling on mining disputes. As time passed, the power struggle British colonial officials encountered in the new colony of British Columbia was not with the Americans, who for the most part preferred to make their fortune and head to warmer climates, but with the pesky Canadians, who hated social, economic, and political privilege and advocated for such radical ideas as free speech, free assembly, and responsible elected government.

Most of the Canadians who came to the new colony were farmers, merchants, traders, or professional men who arrived with very little and were determined not so much to make a fortune as to live comfortable lives free from the restrictions of class economic dependence. The most vocal of these "rebels" were the newspapermen Amor De Cosmos and John Robson, who used their platforms to attack the power elite of the colonial officials and advocate for representative government. They were joined by other key spokespeople and, eventually, the majority of the Canadians in the colony. Their influence grew, resulting in British Columbia joining the Canadian confederation of provinces.

Francis Jones Barnard was one of these key influencers. His drive and determination, coupled with his business acumen, raised him to a position of respect and responsibility from which he served and guided the colony and province he called home. This book will tell the story of his struggles and successes in the course of making first Barnard's Express and later the BC Express companies into thriving concerns and eventually passing his legacy on to his son and to yet another Canadian, Steve Tingley.

Over the past hundred years, Barnard's story has been told many times, raising it to the level of myth. Unfortunately, errors of fact have rendered that myth seriously flawed. You are about to read an accurate story of this man and his successors and their incredible success in developing a thriving stagecoach and express business. In the process, you will hopefully gain a new and vital perspective on the political and social dynamics that helped to form British Columbia.

$$\equiv 1 \equiv$$

BILLY BALLOU, PIONEER EXPRESSMAN

ILLIAM "BILLY" BALLOU'S first view of Fort Victoria on Vancouver Island in the early spring of 1858 was not encouraging. From the deck of the Puget Sound mail steamer as it entered the Esquimalt harbour, he could see an aging fort centred around an extremely high flagpole flying the British flag. Around its palisades was a scattering of buildings. Not much of a town. As the ship pulled alongside the one and only wharf, Ballou surveyed the handful of passengers who had accompanied him on this trip from Olympia, Washington Territory. This prestigious party comprised LaFayette McMullen, newly established governor of Washington Territory; the territorial secretary, Charles Mason; and John Scranton, who had the mail contract between Puget Sound and Victoria. Together, they were on a fact-finding mission. It was Ballou, a partner in a merchandising business in Olympia, who had alerted the others that miners were bringing excellent gold samples to his store from north of the border. The party was looking for confirmation, aware of the implications that a new gold rush would have for their interests. Although his companions had a vested interest in Washington Territory, Ballou's interests were a little less altruistic.

The party made its way to the fort where Governor McMullen asked to see James Douglas. The guard at the gate took his card, looked the group up and down, and decided that they looked like people who should not be put off.

"Follow me," he said, and led them to a building housing the offices of the Hudson's Bay Company, along with the administrative offices of the government of the Colony of Vancouver Island. For Douglas was not only the chief factor of the company that controlled most of the mainland territory known as New Caledonia; he was also the governor of Vancouver Island, clearly a man who sat in the seat of power. The guard passed through a door and closed it behind him. A short while later, he returned and waved the four men into the inner room.

A large, dark-complexioned man sat behind a desk covered with papers. He sized his guests up at a glance and motioned for them to sit down. The men had heard of James Douglas: that he was the son of a Scottish planter and merchant in the Bahamas and his Creole wife. He had risen rapidly in the fur trade, first with the North West Company and then, after the merger of the two great fur-trading rivals in 1821, with the Hudson's Bay Company (HBC).

Governor McMullen, who had visited Douglas on another matter the previous September, introduced the others and Douglas greeted McMullen warmly. McMullen got directly to the point. He was aware that 300 ounces of gold had been shipped by the HBC from New Caledonia and that there were stories of miners returning to Olympia, Washington Territory, with gold from the Couteau Country in British territory. This region was dubbed the "Couteau" ("knife") by the French Canadian fur traders, a corruption of the Indigenous People's name for themselves, Nicoutameen. It came to designate the traditional territory of the Nlaka'pamux (Thompson) Nation at the confluence of the Thompson and Fraser Rivers. Given the implications to the Territory of Washington, McMullen said he would appreciate denial or confirmation that indications of paying amounts of gold were increasing in the territory controlled by the HBC.

Douglas paused for a moment, wondering whether he should divulge what he knew about the promising amount of gold coming out of the interior. New Caledonia was under the control of the HBC, but already there were indications from the government in London that this would not be for long, given the information they had on the strong possibility of a large influx of miners from the American territories to the south. Douglas would lose little in letting these men in on the news already rapidly spreading through the American states and territories on the Pacific coast. But he did need to emphasize certain points.

"I can confirm to you paying quantities of gold are being found, primarily by the Indian people, in the Couteau country which is in British territory and controlled by the Hudson's Bay Company. I would also like to say that the British government is aware of this and is not prepared to let foreigners enter into the territory without controls and stipulations put in place."

McMullen smiled. "There's little you can do about that. In my experience, the lust for gold is impossible to control and the best you can hope for is to be ready for it when it comes."

It was Douglas's turn to smile. "I agree but will do my best to make sure that many of the atrocities I have heard of south of the border will not be perpetrated in British territory, especially to the Indian people. They have to date benefitted from the gold in what they consider to be their territory and I will do everything in my power to avoid bloodshed. It is a pleasure to meet you and you have my assurance that I will alert you of anything I think you will need to know to assure good governance in Washington Territory."[1]

The men seemed satisfied with this confirmation. As they rose to leave, Billy Ballou stepped forward. A small, stocky man, he spoke with a distinctly nasal quality and an accent that indicated he was from the American deep south. "If there is the rush of miners that I expect you will soon see, it is my intention to establish an express service to deal with their needs. I suppose you are familiar with the service that was provided in California."

Douglas knew very well of the role that "express services" had played in the opening of western North America, where distances were long and organized mail services non-existent. As a young man he had been placed in charge of the express that brought letters, reports, journals, and personnel from the North West Company's Fort George at the mouth of the Columbia River to Fort William at the head of Lake Superior. This trip of about 4,000 kilometres (2,500 miles), mostly by canoe, took three months and, after a short turn-around, the express headed back, reaching the mouth of the Columbia by mid-October. After the HBC and the North West Company merged in 1821, Douglas was involved in developing what was called the York Factory Express, taking similar documents and personnel from Fort Vancouver to York Factory on Hudson Bay. These express trips, the Columbia department's link with the outside world, were not like the regular fur brigades that made their way across the continent. They were all about speed.

The concept of sending "expressmen" at breakneck speed through rugged and sometimes hostile territory was common at this time in the Pacific Northwest. McMullen's predecessor, Governor Isaac Stevens of Washington Territory, had used W.H. Pierson as his expressman. In 1855, Pierson had covered vast distances in a remarkably short time, carrying important letters and documents between Fort Benton in Montana Territory and Olympia in Washington Territory.

Douglas replied, "I am well aware of the express services used in your country and would have no problem with such a venture if such is required." This was what Ballou had come to hear and, once the party returned to Olympia, he began arrangements to set up an express business in British territory.

Ballou sold his assets in Washington Territory and California. In San Francisco, he made an agreement with Freeman & Company's Express, the main California competitor of Wells Fargo & Company, started in 1855 by John M. Freeman. Ballou arranged for them to look after the express business from Victoria to San Francisco and destinations all over the world. This freed Ballou up to operate between Victoria and the mining camps on the Fraser and Thompson Rivers. With his affairs and finances in order, Ballou returned to Victoria. On June 1, 1858, Ballou's Pioneer Fraser River Express was established.

BALLOU HEADS NORTH

Billy Ballou was one of those larger-than-life characters often found on the frontier. American historian H.H. Bancroft referred to him as "a wild waif, a hare-brained adventurer of French descent, who since 1846 had been floating about the mountains and shores of the Pacific."[2] Born in Alabama, he drifted out to California in 1846 and fought in the American–Mexican War, referred to in the US as the "Mexican War" and in Mexico as the "American Intervention." By his own account, he "was in every fight from Vera Cruz to the close of the war with Mexico, and was promoted three times on the battle-field. Have retained a few tokens of respect from the Mexicans; they meant well but they shot carelessly."[3]

In July 1849, at the end of the war, he arrived in California and, in partnership with two others, purchased a cargo of beans from an incoming ship for a quarter cent per pound, shipped them to Sacramento, and sold them for seventeen cents a pound. Next, he went to the Southern California mines and began the first express business on the west coast (or so he claimed), carrying letters and newspapers for four dollars each. He sold out to Adams Express and entered a new partnership with Samuel Langton's Pioneer Express. In both of these enterprises, Ballou was involved in carrying express letters, parcels, and freight that often consisted of large quantities of gold. Because of the increasing bulk and weight of express matter, most express companies owned stagecoaches or wagons to transport their cargo.

During the gold rush in California, expressmen had to contend with more than just rugged terrain and long distances. During one stage trip on the Yuba Express between Marysville and Downieville, Ballou was attacked by a gang of thirteen armed bandits. He and his associates managed to hold off the robbers in a running gun battle that saw a woman wounded in the head and one of the robbers shot in the arm. The bandits were fended off and the cargo of $35,000 in gold was saved. A mounted rider brought the news of the battle into Marysville, where Ballou and his associates were greeted as heroes and presented with gold-mounted pistols and spurs.

In early June of 1858, Ballou made his first trip up the Fraser
River, first from Victoria to Fort Langley by steamboat and from
there to Fort Hope in a canoe paddled by Stó:lō Indigenous men.
On the "bars" above Fort Hope, he found miners at work. (The
term "bar," referring to a low bank of sand or gravel deposited
alongside a river or creek, originated in California and was soon
common north of the border.) At Hill's Bar between Forts Hope and
Yale, he met a group of miners, introduced himself, and explained
his business. James Moore, one of the miners, later recalled, "Of
course we all sent letters and [a] sample of gold to our friends in
the outside world. When these letters and gold dust reached California, [they] helped to cause the great Fraser River stampede of
1858."[4] Other miners in the area gladly sent him away with letters and gold dust to be delivered to California, for which he was
amply paid.

Ballou used his profits to advertise the Pioneer Fraser River
Express. His ad in the *Victoria Gazette* of July 3, 1858, stated:

> This express service runs from Victoria, Port Townsend, Whatcom
> and Schome to Simiamoo City, Nanaimo, Fort Langley, Fort Hope,
> Emory's Bar, Rocky Bar, Hill's Bar, Fort Yale, Sailor's Bar, Foster's
> Bar, the Forks of Thompson and Fraser Rivers, Fort Dallas, Great
> Falls, Fort Thompson [Kamloops], and all points on Fraser and
> Thompson rivers.
>
> Letters, packages, parcels, dust, coin, etc., received and for-
> warded with security and quick dispatch. Commissions attended
> to promptly.
>
> My Express leaves Victoria on the departure of every steamer
> up Fraser River.
>
> Our Canoe line leaves Fort Hope on the arrival of each steamer,
> for up Fraser river in charge of careful messengers. W.T. BALLOU,
> Proprietor[5]

As the ad indicates, Ballou's intentions were ambitious. He proposed to use steamboats running from Victoria to Fort Hope as the

first leg of his express and, from there, whatever transportation was available. He also intended to reach locations on the north end of Puget Sound (Port Townsend, Whatcom, and Semiahmoo), a plan he soon abandoned. On the mainland of New Caledonia he hired men, often from First Nations along the route, to travel by canoe, on foot, or on snowshoes to bring mail, newspapers, and small parcels to the mining camps. As miners were hungry for news from the outside world, the newspapers were snapped up at one dollar a copy. Letters and parcels to Yale cost the receiver a dollar and, for any place beyond, two dollars. To miners, mostly young men, a letter from home was an invaluable link between the goldfields and the outside world. On his return trips to Victoria, Ballou would carry any amount of gold for deposit with Freeman's Express or to be forwarded to any bank or individual, as instructed. To his credit, there is no record of gold being stolen or lost. Almost as important as the gold were the letters from the miners and merchants in the camps. Even though postal rates were low, the government's delivery was hopelessly slow and unreliable, so the express companies took on the delivery of Her Majesty's Mail to the gold camps up the Fraser and Thompson Rivers. Because the government did not subsidize them for this service, they added a surcharge to letters and parcels mailed from the post office in Victoria.

Ballou also catered to the miners' needs in other ways. If a miner in a distant camp needed a pair of boots, a coat, or any other item not readily available, Ballou would make a note and, on his return trip, purchase the item and deliver it to the miner at his claim, charging only the cost of the article plus the ordinary express charge. These services endeared him to the miners and provided an essential service that could not be duplicated.

Apparently, Ballou was not the only one who had seen the potential for business in the British territory north of the forty-ninth parallel. Within a couple of weeks, Sam Knight, bank superintendent of the Wells Fargo Company in San Francisco, arrived in Victoria and rented space in a building at the corner of Wharf and Yates Streets. Wells Fargo had been established in 1852 in the eastern United States but had risen to prominence in California, where it quickly established a reputation for safe, sure, and speedy delivery of mail and packages. Its banking and express services proved to be the first choice of miners. An early advertisement for the twelve California offices stated that it handled "gold dust, bullion, specie [currency money], packages, parcels and freight of all kinds to and from New York and San Francisco."[6] Within a short time, it was concluded that "no one in California mails an inland letter but sends it Express... the miners give their address & power of attorney to the Express agent who takes their letters out of the post office in San F. twice a month and delivers them to every town & camp in the placers."[7]

Wells Fargo had no intention of offering express services to the gold camps. But, since Ballou had connected with Freeman's Express for its Victoria to San Francisco outlet, it is not surprising that, in July, Wells Fargo contracted with Horace Kent and H.F. Smith to service the gold camps in conjunction with Wells Fargo.[8] For a time, both Ballou's Fraser River Express and Kent & Smith's Fraser and Thompson River Express served the mining camps along the Fraser River. As miners began to make the perilous journey through the Fraser Canyon above the "Forks" (the name given by the miners to the confluence of the Thompson and Fraser Rivers), Ballou followed them and soon won the majority of express business. The partnership of Kent & Smith could not compete and dissolved in September. Ballou absorbed their business and later described how Kent & Smith "could not make it pay and hauled off; I connected with them then. I could not make the lower route pay and they could not make the upper route pay; and so we 'joined gibbets.'"[9] Joining with Kent & Smith meant that Ballou could now forward express matter via Freeman's or Wells Fargo Express Companies.

Another early competitor of Ballou's was D.C. Fargo (no connection to Wells Fargo). One of the first miners on the Fraser River, he holds the distinction of having two bars on the Fraser named after him, one below Fort Hope and one above Boston Bar. Fargo began to operate an express business between Yale and Lytton but Ballou outreached him, extending his service as far as Fort Kamloops. Fargo soon realized he had met his match and started working for Ballou. Ballou's battle for supremacy on the Fraser River was off to a roaring start.[10]

PROCLAIMING THE NEW COLONY OF BRITISH COLUMBIA

The influx of gold seekers continued unabated into July 1858. According to John Nugent, the Consular Agent for the United States in Victoria, in May, June, and July of 1858, at least 23,000 persons travelled by sea and another 8,000 overland, making a total of over 30,000 in all. As one writer put it, "The worm-eaten wharves of San Francisco trembled almost daily under the tread of the vast multitude that gathered to see the northern-bound vessels leave."[11]

The British government in London decided it could stand by no longer and watch this valuable territory on the Pacific become another victim to the US "manifest destiny." The new secretary of state for the colonies, Edward Bulwer-Lytton, saw the opportunity to cancel the HBC's trading rights in the territory on the west side of the Rocky Mountains and advocated the establishment of a new British colony in its place. He introduced a bill in Parliament, read for the first time on July 1, 1858, that would put the area referred to as New Caledonia directly under the jurisdiction of the crown. Since a French colony of New Caledonia already existed, the suggested name for the new colony was British Columbia, a choice made by Queen Victoria. The boundaries of the new Colony of British Columbia would stretch from the Rocky Mountains in the east to the Pacific Ocean in the west, from the Peace River and Nass River in the north to the forty-ninth parallel in the south. Vancouver Island was to remain a separate colony. The act received royal assent on August 2, and James Douglas agreed to accept the position of governor of British Columbia, to add to his existing titles of governor of Vancouver Island and chief factor of the HBC.

Bulwer-Lytton recognized the need to select the right officials for the new colony, consisting of "representatives of the best of British culture, not just a police force," but men who possessed "courtesy, high breeding and urbane knowledge of the world."[12] To that end, he appointed Matthew Baillie Begbie as judge and Chartres Brew as inspector of police, among other officers. Bulwer-Lytton sent Colonel Richard Clement Moody at the head of a detachment of Royal Engineers consisting of 150 officers and sappers and appointed him as the first lieutenant-governor of British Columbia and chief commissioner of lands and works. It took months for the new colonial officials to reach Victoria. But, on November 29, 1858, at Fort Langley on the Fraser River, James Douglas read the commission establishing Begbie as judge of the new colony. Begbie, in turn, read Her Majesty's commission appointing Douglas as the new governor of British Columbia. Then Douglas read the proclamation revoking the HBC license of exclusive trade on the mainland. As historian H.H. Bancroft described the event, "Guns were fired, flags flaunted, and amidst a drizzling rain mother England was delivered of a new colony."[13]

NAVIGATING THE FRASER RIVER

When the first shiploads of miners arrived in Victoria, they stayed for only a night or two and purchased provisions, as they were anxious to get to the diggings on the lower Fraser. Unfortunately for them, the HBC steamship *Otter* was at Fort Langley. Unable and unwilling to wait for its return, many set out in skiffs, whale boats, canoes, or rafts, many homemade, to cross the Strait of Georgia, braving high winds and drenching rain. When they reached the Fraser River, their troubles continued. In early May, Governor Douglas wrote to Henry Labouchère, secretary of state for the colonies:

> Boats, canoes, and every species of small craft, are continually employed in pouring their cargoes of human beings into Fraser's

River, and it is supposed that not less than one thousand whites are already at work, and on the way to the gold districts. Many accidents have happened in the dangerous rapids of that River; a great number of canoes having been dashed to pieces and their cargoes swept away by the impetuous stream, while of the ill-fated adventurers who accompanied them, many have been swept into eternity. The others nothing daunted by the spectacle of ruin, and buoyed up by the hope of amassing wealth, still keep pressing onwards, towards the coveted goal of their most ardent wishes.[14]

As miners proceeded up the Fraser River, prospecting the gravel and sand bars, they began to find paying quantities of gold in a bar just below Fort Hope. From there on, every bar yielded paying quantities of gold up to the foot of the Fraser River canyon, where the boom town of Yale sprang into being. At first, Douglas tried to exclude any American steamships from entering the Fraser River, but the HBC steamer *Otter* could in no way handle the demand. Soon, Douglas relented and American steamers such as the *Sea Bird, Surprise, Umatilla, Maria,* and *Enterprise* were allowed on the Fraser. The *Umatilla* had the distinction of being the first steamboat to reach Yale, which remained the head of navigation on the Fraser River below the canyon. While many of the miners found the $25 cost of passage to the Fraser too much to handle and chose to take their chances with their own homemade boats, the expressmen found the steamships the ideal way to get them to Fort Hope, from where they could reach the various mining camps.

The great obstacle preventing further exploration of the Fraser River was the canyon that began just beyond Yale. In his 1859 exploration, Judge Begbie wrote in his report to the secretary to the colonies, the Duke of Newcastle, that "the trail between Fort Yale and Quayome [later Boston Bar], by which we advanced, is by this time, I should think, utterly impassable for any animal, except a man, a goat, or a dog."[15] Many of the miners, looking for an alternative route, began to follow a trail that had been explored by fur trader Alexander Caulfield Anderson in 1846. This route ran from

Yale, at the foot of the Fraser Canyon, was the head of steamboat navigation
and the start of the Cariboo Road. UL_1019_0001, UNO LANGMANN
FAMILY COLLECTION OF BRITISH COLUMBIA PHOTOGRAPHS, RARE BOOKS
AND SPECIAL COLLECTIONS, UBC LIBRARY

the head of Harrison Lake, thereafter known as Port Douglas, via
Lillooet, Anderson, and Seton Lakes to reach the Fraser at Cayoosh
Flat, later known as Lillooet, well above the Fraser Canyon. While
the trail had its drawbacks, involving no less than four boat trips and
three portages over swampy ground, in Governor Douglas's mind
it was the best route into the Couteau Country. With no money to
spend and little authority to spend it, he proposed a solution. He
approached a group of miners in Victoria and asked them to build
the trail without pay and make a deposit of $25 toward receiving
the same amount in supplies when they reached Cayoosh. Surprisingly, 500 men agreed to the terms, no doubt thinking that, when
they finished the trail, they would be in excellent position to prospect the Upper Fraser. They were divided into groups of twenty-five,

each with its own "captain," the first 250 arriving at Port Douglas on the *Umatilla* in mid-July. The second group arrived later in the summer and, by October, the trail was completed and thousands of miners were heading through it, using everything from rafts to whaleboats to get to Port Douglas. Some of these were hauled to Lillooet Lake where they were left, as the men took the "long portage" to Port Anderson, where members of the St'át'imc (Lillooet) Nation would take them by canoe along the lake. Then they proceeded by what was called the "short portage" to Seton Lake, which led to Cayoosh Flat.

By September, those miners making their way through the Fraser Canyon established the little town of Lytton (named after the colonial secretary, Edward Bulwer-Lytton) near the Forks and were beginning to push up the Fraser and Thompson Rivers. In November, Douglas was able to report that "the Forks, where the Town site of 'Lytton' was laid out, now contains 50 houses and a population of 900 persons . . . and the banks of Fraser's River above the Forks are said to afford good dry diggings as far as the upper Fountain, and sluices yield at the rate of 20 dollars a day to the hand." Douglas went on to report that between Bulwer-Lytton and the "Fountain" (meaning the upper Fountain, just downstream from the confluence of the Fraser and Bridge Rivers), approximately 3,000 miners were at work.

Douglas further reported that "many of the miners are leaving the country on account of the want and high prices of provisions, flour being now sold at the Forks at the rate of 4s/2d [four shillings, two pence, or about one US dollar] per pound, and other articles of food being equally high priced, arising from the cost of transport, and the inaccessibility of the country; the land route between the Forks and Fort Hope and Fort Yale being now rendered impassable through the depth of snow in the mountain passes."[16] This meant that Ballou's Fraser River Express was sending its agents farther and further up the Fraser and Thompson Rivers.

Douglas wrote the following figures to give an "approximate idea of the quantities of gold dust, exported and remaining on hand in the country," which indicates the role of express companies in the colony:[17]

Production of gold in the Colony of British Columbia, in ounces, from June to November 1958 (recorded amounts, unless estimates are indicated)

SHIPPED OUT FROM THE INTERIOR	OUNCES
Wells Fargo & Co.—exported	16,593
Freeman & Co.—an estimate	9,462
Ballou & Co.—in deposit	6,250
Hudson's Bay Co.—exported	4,000
Total	36,305
ESTIMATE OF GOLD STILL IN HAND	
In the hands of private parties—exported	30,000
In the hands of miners in British Columbia	40,000
Total	70,000
Total gold extracted (approximately)	106,305

As Ballou's Fraser River Express was supplying Freeman & Company and Wells Fargo with the gold they were exporting, Ballou likely handled over $500,000 in gold during this six-month period. Some miners may have travelled to Victoria to consign their riches directly to Wells Fargo or Freeman's express, but likely the majority of gold was consigned to Ballou, given the incredibly heavy loads the Indigenous men he hired were packing on their backs over the rugged trails.

By the end of 1858, the mining frontier had advanced as far as The Fountain and a handful of adventurers had pushed even further up the Fraser. The only problem holding the miners back was lack of supplies. But by this time, the trail by way of Harrison, Lillooet, Anderson, and Seton Lakes—the Douglas–Lillooet route—was getting more use. It was the preferred way to avoid the Fraser Canyon and access the ever-northward expansion of the mining frontier, even though it involved transferring baggage and freight several times.

INTO THE CARIBOO

The year 1859 began with renewed optimism. Queensborough, the new capital of the Crown Colony of British Columbia—soon to be renamed by the Queen herself as New Westminster—became the main port of entry. But the citizens of this new capital were chagrined that Governor Douglas decided to keep his office in Victoria, declaring it a free port while imposing customs duties on all goods arriving in New Westminster. Greeted with outrage by the people of New Westminster, these duties were specifically earmarked for the construction of much-needed roads in the mainland colony.

The mining frontier was advancing. In January of 1859, one hundred men were reported to be digging around Lytton and averaging eight dollars a day. A large number of miners were heading up the Fraser from Yale to take advantage of the low water level. Most of the sand and gravel bars on the lower Fraser were abandoned, as miners turned their focus to the Couteau Country, north of the canyon. By March 24, the *Victoria Gazette* reported that three hundred boats, carrying an average of five miners each, were working their way through the canyon. When the stream of miners reached the forks of the Thompson and Fraser Rivers, they parted, the majority heading up the Fraser. Throughout the spring, mining was concentrated around The Fountain and Cayoosh. Bridge River, just above Cayoosh, was prospected and found to contain much fine gold. But the general feeling among the miners was that richer diggings would be found further north. By May, miners had penetrated beyond Fort Alexandria on the Fraser and as far as the Quesnelle River (often misnamed the Canal or Quesnel River).

Billy Ballou continued as the primary expressman for the ever-expanding gold country. In July, the Victoria *British Colonist* reported that this "indefatigable pioneer, and enterprising expressman W.T. Ballou sent off from Yale and Hope his first express for Fort Alexander and Canal River... Hereafter it will make monthly trips. N.T. Clark has been engaged as an express agent at Queen Charlotte Island and will accompany the expedition." A few weeks later, the

British Colonist reported that Ballou had brought down $34,620 in gold dust.[18]

Ballou's personal integrity and ingenuity were legendary, as was his chameleon-like ability to transform his personal appearance to avoid recognition. This interesting trait was pointed out by C.E. Barrett-Lennard, who was travelling in the Interior at the time:

> The [Wells Fargo] travelling agent for British Columbia, Mr. Bellew [*sic*], is a man of great courage and resolution. It is his habit, at intervals, so completely to disguise his personal appearance as almost to defy recognition. I have seen him at one time bearded like a Turk, at another close-shaven as a Puritan divine, now adorned with long flowing locks, now close cropped as a round-head. His object in doing is to render his identification as difficult as possible, as being frequently entrusted with large quantities of gold, he thinks it desirable that his person should not be too well or too generally known.[19]

Ballou's record for carrying tens of thousands of dollars in gold remained unblemished. He was later to boast, "I do not know why it is, while I was riding Express I took money and I have been on roads where they have robbed everything of the kind, and through the worst Indian countries alone, or with one man; and I never had any fear, and never had any thought of being interrupted; and I never was interrupted."[20] The miners' confidence in Ballou and his ability to deliver was solid, but competition for the lucrative gold-camp business was not long in coming.

In October of 1859, the *British Colonist* offered "Thanks—To Mr. Wm. Jeffray the obliging and reliable Travelling agent between Victoria and British Columbia, for sundry favors." It is not entirely clear what a "travelling agent" did, but we can assume that he conveyed freight and documents between Victoria and various locations on the mainland. This sounds very much like an express business and, in November, the *British Colonist* began to refer to

"Jeffray's Express" in offering thanks for providing information from the mainland of British Columbia.

The formal establishment of the Jeffray & Company Fraser River Express was announced in early 1860. A "Copartnership Notice," dated March 17, 1860, was published in the *British Colonist* announcing that "the undersigned have this day entered into a copartnership under the style of JEFFRAY & CO., for the purpose of conducting a General Express, to act as Traveling Agents. And to do a Commission Business between Victoria, V.I., and British Columbia." The notice listed William Jeffray and William H. Thain as the owners. Directly below, an ad for the new company stated that, "From the second day of April next, Jeffray & Co will commence and continue to run a regular Express ... connecting with the following places, viz: Fort Hope, Fort Yale, Port Douglas and with all the intermediate landings,"[21] with a list of agents for these places.

Although expressmen other than Ballou had operated on an ad hoc basis before, this was the first serious attempt at direct competition, and Ballou was not long in responding. On April 24, a much larger ad appeared in the *British Colonist*, trumpeting Ballou's Express as "THE ONLY EXPRESS connecting with Wells, Fargo & Co. in Victoria, Batterton & Co. in Yale, and the Pony Express Co. in Lytton City." The ad went on to emphasize its longer reach into the Interior, placing in bold letters its connection with "Alexander, Canal River, Williams Lake, and Horse Fly Creek, weekly."[22]

The mention of Ballou's connection with the "Pony Express" in Lytton is intriguing. In the same edition of the *British Colonist* as Ballou's new ad, the newspaper reported:

BALLOU'S EXPRESS—By an advertisement in another column, it will be seen that this old established company now connects with the Pony Express Company, lately formed to run from Lytton City to Fort Alexandria and Quesnelle River. It is calculated that the trip from Lytton and back can be made in seven days. The Pony Express will prove of great advantage to miners and others in the northern mines.[23]

Obviously, the name "Pony Express" was copied from the American company of the same name. Through its brief eighteen-month existence, from April 1860 to October 1861, the American version of the Pony Express had captured the imagination of the North American public. This new British Columbia express company, operated by Dan Braley, established a vital link for Ballou, allowing him to pick up express matter in Lytton instead of travelling all the way to the gold camps.

By early June 1860, as miners began to find rich gold deposits on the Upper Fraser and Quesnelle Rivers, the Pony Express moved its base of operations to Alexandria. Yet another new company, Myers Express, operated by Samuel H. Myers, appeared in Port Douglas and Cayoosh. Given the ever-expanding mining frontier and the fact that miners were travelling on the Harrison–Lillooet trail as well as up or around the Fraser Canyon, both Ballou and Jeffray had to partner with smaller companies to carry express over sections of the route. The Pony Express connected with Ballou at Lytton and Myers Express carried express over the Harrison–Lillooet route to connect with Jeffray at Port Douglas.[24] Freeman's expresses also vied for the business of the miners and merchants in mining camps all through the interior of British Columbia.

By mid-summer, the mining frontier had advanced up the Quesnelle River to its forks, some 50 miles (86 kilometres) from the Fraser River, an area then being called the "Cariboo," based on a problematic misspelling of "caribou." Governor Douglas, writing to the colonial secretary the next June, spelled it "Caraboo," but, in a later dispatch wrote about the "Cariboo country... though properly it should be written 'Cariboeuf' or Rein Deer."[25] Spelling aside, this largely unexplored region was proving to be the richest yet.

Given the general lawlessness of the country and the ruggedness of the trails, the experienced and well-established expressmen were trusted and preferred by the miners over the Royal Mail carried by the government. Commander R.C. Mayne, who, as lieutenant on the HMS *Plumper*, spent four years on Vancouver Island and in British Columbia, wrote of the expressmen:

All over California and British Columbia, letters or parcels are carried with perfect safety, and, all things considered, very cheaply,
by means of [expressmen]. The organization of some of these
companies is most elaborate. The principal one is Wells-Fargo's,
which has agencies all over the world. The office in Victoria is in
one of the finest buildings there; and their house in San Francisco
is as large as our General Post-office. I have never known a letter sent by them miscarry. The charge for sending anywhere in
California is 10 cents (5d.), and so great is my faith in them that
I would trust anything, even in that insecure country, in the envelope bearing the stamp of Wells, Fargo & Co.'s Express. There are
several minor expresses in different parts of the country—Ballou's
Fraser River Express, Jeffray's Express, Freeman's Express, all of
which appear to flourish; and so great is the trust reposed in them,
and the speed with which they travel, that the miners, as yet, prefer sending their 'dust' by them to the Government escort.[26]

Ballou and Jeffray competed head to head over the next eighteen
months for the express business to and from the Cariboo. Ballou's
advantage was his supporting cast. He had a knack for picking the
most reputable and intelligent agents. His original agent in Yale
was David W. Higgins, later editor of the *British Colonist* and later
yet a member of the legislative assembly. Another agent was Hugh
Nelson, who later became co-owner of the express company that
bought out Ballou and went on to be lieutenant-governor of the
province of British Columbia.

Ballou also established connections with other independent
expressmen, such as Dan Braley of the Pony Express, who had
agents throughout the gold country. After Braley moved his Pony
Express to Fort Alexandria (generally referred to as "Alexander" at
the time), James Batterton became Ballou's expressman, operating
from Yale north to connect with Braley. A second "Pony Express,"
started up by George Dunbar in August of 1860, connected Ballou
with the Similkameen River and Rock Creek diggings in the southern Interior close to the US border. Dunbar was undeterred by the

long trip over the mountains, even in the dead of winter. The *British Colonist* reported that "George Dunbar, the express man, has been crossing all winter, and must have been out in some terrible weather. He deserves great credit for his pluck and perseverance, and may be said to have risked his life each trip. He packed out a train of Indians with provisions almost two months ago, which afforded a seasonable relief to some of the miners on the river."[27]

Ballou also connected with the growing number of Chinese arriving in British Columbia. One of the most powerful was Lee Chang, who was in charge of the Kwong Lee Company in Victoria and set up stores in Yale, Lillooet, Quesnelle Forks, Quesnelle Mouth (today's Quesnel), Stanley, and Barkerville. Known to the non-Chinese population as "Kwong Lee" because of his association with the company, he regularly used Ballou to carry gold from the goldfields, evidenced by a receipt in the Barkerville archives for a shipment of his carried by Ballou's Express. Lee Chang would later partner with Ballou on a number of ventures.

COMPETING TO CARRY HER MAJESTY'S MAIL

Prior to the establishment of the Colony of British Columbia, collecting postage on the mainland was the responsibility of the HBC. While the company was happy to turn this over to the expressmen, the new secretary of the colonies, Edward Bulwer-Lytton, instructed Douglas to "take such measures as you can for the transmission of letters and levying postage."[28]

Despite Douglas's best intentions, the colonial mail service was less than successful. During the winter of 1858–59, Chartres Brew, Chief Inspector of Police, wrote from Fort Yale:

> There are many complaints here of the irregularity and uncertainty of the Mails. Merchants would rather send their letters by Ballors [Ballou's] Express at the cost of half a Dollar than put it in the post at a cost of 5 cents and remain in uncertainty when it

would reach its destination ... At present they may remain at any stage on the route for days awaiting an opportunity of sending them on, and then they are entrusted to the first trustworthy person passing the way willing to be troubled with them.[29]

Clearly, the colonial government could not get along without the expressmen, who could reach even the least accessible mining camps. Governor Douglas believed that, until roads and proper transportation were in place, express operators were the most effective at serving areas beyond the postal service's reach. In recognition of their usefulness, he was open to allowing them to carry mail, subject to a small postal tax, both within and between the colonies and to the United States.

At the urging of the Colonial Office in London, he appointed a former fur trader and colleague, Alexander Caulfield Anderson, as the first postmaster general of the two colonies of British Columbia and Vancouver Island. Anderson decided that "it will be necessary for the protection of our postal interests that I should be empowered to exact from the Express Offices payment of the Colonial postage of five cents per letter upon all letters leaving Victoria through the Expresses."[30] He published a notice in the Victoria *Gazette* on May 5, 1859, stating, "Whereas by the Postal Laws of Great Britain, the conveyance otherwise than by post of letters not exempted from postage is forbidden ... for the convenience of the public, pending the more perfect organization of the Postal System in these Colonies, the conveyance of letters by private Expresses has been sanctioned and allowed under certain conditions."[31] These conditions stipulated that every letter carried by express within the two colonies required a five-cent stamped envelope from the post office or the payment of five cents in cash. Considering that expressmen like Ballou were charging fifty cents for letters to Yale and Port Douglas and as much as two dollars for upcountry locations, as well as Rock Creek, they readily accepted this new demand.

By early 1861, Ballou had been accommodating the colonial authorities and increasing his own prestige for three years by carrying the official mail bags free of charge, and with great difficulty, as far as Lillooet and Rock Creek. So, when reports of the richest-yet gold finds, in Keithley and Antler Creeks in the Cariboo, reached Victoria, Ballou felt it was time to be given a contract to carry the mail. In January, he wrote to Governor Douglas objecting to carrying the government mails up the Fraser River "without a contract or an equivalent for doing the work." [32]

As if in response to Ballou's concerns, the *British Colonist* reported in February, "POSTAL ARRANGEMENTS—There is much complaint from the Upper country in regard to the tardy manner in which the mails are transmitted to the various points above this place. Ballou's Express, as a general thing, is a week in advance of the mails. Such a state of things is very annoying to those in business, and should be remedied without delay." [33]

By then, Warner R. Spalding, a transplanted Englishman like most colonial authorities, had been appointed the first postmaster general exclusively for the Colony of British Columbia. Despite his earnest efforts, the postal system remained significantly slower than the express companies. Nonetheless, he railed against these expressmen for absorbing "what would otherwise be postal revenue." He pointed out that people were dissatisfied with the inadequate postal service and outraged at the exorbitant express rates on letters, newspapers, and gold dust. Spalding urged the governor to suppress the express companies and establish a self-supporting postal service.

Given the fact that, in 1860, the total postal revenue of British Columbia was £121 ($590) and that the express companies were successfully serving the most isolated gold camps, it seemed unlikely that things would turn around in a hurry. The situation remained unchanged through the 1861 gold-mining season, except that yet another express company, Yale's British Columbia Express, entered the field, offering to carry express from Victoria to Douglas, Hope, and Yale on the steamers that ran from Victoria. This was not a bad idea, considering how express companies like Ballou's and Jeffray's were being stretched as the mining frontier advanced further into the Cariboo.

When, during the summer of 1861, Governor Douglas had the bright idea of setting up an armed official escort to carry gold from the mines to the coast, it was suggested that this "Gold Escort" could also carry the mail. Unfortunately, the government would not guarantee delivery of the gold and miners were not in the least interested in abandoning the expressmen. The Gold Escort was a total failure and, after a further attempt in 1863, the deficit to the government amounted to about $80,000.

With the discovery of rich gold creeks near Cariboo Lake in late 1861, prospects for the coming year were quite favourable. Ballou thought it was time to make a stand and, in November, he gave a final warning that he would not continue to carry the mail without a contract. He submitted a tender for the service from Douglas to Lillooet and on to Quesnelle Mouth at the rate of $375 per month. His offer was turned down, and in December Ballou refused to carry the mail any longer.

This standoff between Ballou and the colonial government turned into an opportunity for a newcomer in the express business. In November, Jeffray & Company sold out to Francis Jones "Frank" Barnard. Ballou saw this as a victory over his toughest competitor and would later tell historian H.H. Bancroft:

> Then there was W.J. Jeffries [*sic*]. I ran them all off. All started in opposition to me. I put down letters to three cents and made the custom house business pay me; charging five per cent commission for passing things through the Customs House made that up. I had plenty of money then to pay for goods and they had not. If anybody wanted anything done I would do it and charge neither freight nor anything. It did not last very long. Old Jeffries died hard but he died sure. He was kept up by the Scotch, and they were all clannish. He got in debt $6,000 or $7,000 and then 'busted out.'[34]

Little did Ballou know that this newcomer who had bought out his competitor would hasten the end of Ballou's Cariboo Express.

2

BARNARD'S EXPRESS

THE STEAMBOAT *FORT Yale* was struggling up the Fraser River against the current to its namesake town on a lovely spring afternoon in April of 1861. The purser, Frank Barnard, left his office above the boiler room and headed to the dining room where he joined a table of men, including two other steamboat captains, Grant and Irving. The steamer had just left Fort Hope when the boiler suddenly exploded, shattering the boat to kindling and sending bodies flying. At least a dozen people were killed instantly, including Captain Smith J. Jamieson, master of the boat. Barnard lay senseless on the deck, which was all that was left of the superstructure.

Fortunately, the explosion had occurred just next to a Stó:lō Nation village near Union Bar. Some Stó:lō people launched canoes and began to pick up survivors and bodies from the fast Fraser current. Barnard was brought to shore where he looked at the remains of the steamer and shuddered. There was nothing left of the purser's office. If the accident had happened five minutes earlier, Barnard would have died. He was thankful to be alive, even though his job had disappeared along with the *Fort Yale*.

FRANCIS JONES BARNARD ARRIVES IN BC

Born in 1829 in Quebec City, Francis Jones Barnard was a direct descendent of the Francis Barnard who had settled in Deerfield, Massachusetts, in the mid-1600s and fled north to Lower Canada as a United Empire Loyalist during the American War of Independence. Barnard left school at age twelve, when his father died, to help in the family hardware store. In 1853, he married Ellen Stillman, also of Quebec City, and two years later moved to Toronto, Canada West (later Ontario), where he struggled to make a living with indifferent success. Barnard heard stories of the potential for advancement in the newly founded Colony of British Columbia and headed there in the spring of 1859, leaving his family behind. He travelled from New York in steerage on a steamboat to Panama and then took the Panama Railroad to the Pacific side. From there, he travelled via San Francisco to Victoria, Vancouver Island, where he joined thousands of other gold seekers heading for the Fraser River. Ever hopeful, Barnard boarded a steamboat to the boomtown of Yale, where he arrived with a five-dollar gold piece in his pocket. There was nothing to do but to get to work.

He immediately struggled up the Fraser Canyon where, in partnership with Denis Murphy from County Cork, Ireland, he located a claim just upstream from Yale.[1] Barnard's inexperience as a miner would have handicapped him, but he was quick to learn from the California miners near his claim. At the end of the season, he was able to sell his claim and spend the winter in Yale cutting cordwood in the rapidly disappearing forest and carrying it to town on his back before sawing and splitting it and selling it to local businesses and residents.

In the spring of 1860 Barnard, obviously not a miner by nature or desire, went looking for employment. In June, Governor James Douglas, having decided that a proper trail needed to be constructed though the Fraser Canyon, was in Yale to make arrangements and establish contracts. Frank Way, who ran a hotel and ferry at the mouth of the Spuzzum River, was awarded the contract in

Francis Jones Barnard, ca. 1863.

partnership with J.C. Beedy to build the trail from Yale to Spuzzum. When Barnard implored Douglas to find him a job, the governor referred him to Colonel Richard Clement Moody, commander of the Royal Engineers in the new Colony of British Columbia and suggested that Barnard accompany Frank Way to locate the next leg of the trail, from Chapman's Bar to Boston Bar.

Little did Barnard realize he had inserted himself in the middle of a feud between Moody and Governor Douglas, whose jurisdictions in the new colony overlapped. Aside from being the commander of the Royal Engineers in British Columbia, Moody was chief commissioner and lieutenant-governor. These positions, while quite prestigious, carried less authority than that of governor. This was particularly galling to Moody, who was of the highest social standing and had been appointed by Lord Lytton. He considered Douglas, whose father had been a small land owner in the West Indies and whose mother had been of mixed race, to be socially inferior. The fact that Douglas's wife was also of mixed race outraged Moody's wife, Mary, also a British blue-blood, who wrote in 1859 that "it is not pleasant to serve under a Hudson's Bay Factor, a man on whom you can place no reliance," and concluded that "the Governor and Richard never can get on, it is impossible."[2]

Not only did Moody resent Douglas telling him who to hire, he also viewed Barnard as a "colonial." Nonetheless, he commissioned Frank Way to locate the trail and sent Barnard to work with him. After a few days, Way abandoned the project and went to work on the lower trail. But the town council of Yale was adamant and sent Hugh McRoberts, along with Barnard, to continue mapping out the trail from Chapman's to Boston Bar. McRoberts and Barnard, with the assistance of the local Nlaka'pamux People, were successful in locating the trail and, after walking it with engineer Walter Moberly, McRoberts and William Power were contracted to construct it.

Barnard, however, was dismissed. He awaited payment to cover his pay and expenses, having spent four days with Way, five with McRoberts, and three with Moberly, as well as spending his own meagre money to pay expenses for the Indigenous packers and guides he worked with. In June, he submitted his bill for $116.80, expecting immediate payment. But by October, he had not received anything and anxiously wrote to the acting colonial secretary, W.A.G. Young, "I will feel obliged if you will order the payment of the amt. as it is now due since June last."

Yale's gold commissioner, E.H. Saunders, was not convinced and demanded proof that the employment had been authorized by Colonel Moody who, of course, refused to have anything to do with a Douglas appointee. In December, Barnard wrote again, somewhat desperately, stating that he had witnesses to his work with Frank Way and that he was "much in need of the amt. part of which was for money advanced." Even this was not enough. In late January, Barnard wrote again asking for payment and attaching sworn statements by Ovid Allard and William Power, who were present when he was hired. On February 22, Colonel Moody was authorized to pay the amount submitted, which he did on the 28th.[3] Barnard would not forget his first experience with the British bureaucratic system that controlled the colony. It taught him a valuable lesson he would use to good advantage in the future.

Later that summer, Barnard secured a job as a constable at Yale and was tasked with taking two prisoners in handcuffs to New Westminster. With no steamer available and some urgency in getting the prisoners behind bars, Barnard set off downriver with his two charges in a canoe. He got as far as Hope before he had to stop for the night and take a room with his prisoners. During the night Barnard was awakened by someone tugging his pistol out of its holster. One of the prisoners had slipped his handcuffs and threatened to shoot his guard and escape. A desperate wrestling match took place and Barnard, a stocky powerful man, managed to overcome the prisoner and handcuff him again, this time more securely. The next day, the canoe got an early start and Barnard got all the way to New Westminster, thanks to the Fraser's strong current. But Barnard's career as a constable was short-lived. In 1860, having gained a reputation for integrity and intelligence, he was hired on as purser on the paddlewheeler *Fort Yale*.

The town of Yale, nestled against the mountains at the foot of the canyon, was the head of navigation on the Fraser River. The earliest steamboats on the river at the onset of the gold rush in 1858 were the Hudson's Bay Company's *Beaver* and *Otter*, but in the spring of that year, the *Beaver* was on a trading cruise, not to return until the

end of October, and the *Otter* could not navigate past Fort Langley
from Victoria.

Initially, Governor Douglas sought to restrict navigation on the
Fraser solely to British ships, including the HBC's, but soon saw that
thousands of miners in Fort Victoria were looking for passage up
the Fraser. The first steamboat to navigate to the heart of the gold
excitement in the summer of 1858 was the sidewheeler, *Surprise*.
On June 6, it reached Fort Hope, but was unable to navigate "the
riffle," a shallow place with fast, turbulent water running over rocks,
just above Fort Hope. Even this success could only be achieved by
taking on a Stó:lō pilot, Speel-est, who knew the river. Six weeks
later, the *Umatilla*, a sternwheeler brought in from the Columbia
River, became the first to make it all the way to Yale under Captain
J.C. Ainsworth of Portland, Oregon. Not surprisingly, the ever-
present Billy Ballou was on that voyage.

The hulls of the sternwheelers were designed with flat bottoms,
and would draw no more than two feet of water. Their bows were
"shovel-nosed," with a huge wheel at the stern that drove the boat.
At many of the river and lake landings there were no wharves, so
the steamer simply ran her bow onto the bank, from which a plank
would be laid ashore. Only a reverse churn of her paddles was
required to pull her back into midstream. The deepest part of the
steamer was where the paddlewheel dipped in the water, making it
possible for a resourceful captain, in times of necessity, to actually
"walk" a steamer over a sandbar on its paddlewheel.

Other American steamers, including the *Wilson G. Hunt*, the
Enterprise, and the *Sea Bird,* made trips from Victoria to Hope in
1858. Unfortunately, in September the *Sea Bird* caught fire, with
two hundred passengers on board. Though no lives were lost, the
steamer was destroyed, and no other steamer was able to duplicate
the *Umatilla*'s feat until 1860, when the *Colonel Moody, Hope,* and
Fort Yale made it to Yale consistently, spelling the end of Fort Hope's
distinction as the head of steam navigation on the lower Fraser.

The *Fort Yale* was constructed by a group of merchants in Yale
who had formed the Yale Steam Navigation Company.[4] Having
proven himself dependable and intelligent, Barnard was hired as

purser for the new steamer's regular runs from Victoria. In 1860, with this steady employment, Barnard was able to send for his wife and children. They made the long journey from Toronto to San Francisco via Panama and arrived in Victoria in December. From there they travelled on the *Fort Yale* to Yale, where the family was to live until 1868. Yale had grown to be the largest town on the Fraser River and Barnard was making enough money as purser to support his family and save for future ventures.

Barnard was always quick to spot opportunities. He saw that, with Yale as the new head of navigation on the Fraser, the steamers would need a place to store freight. So, with characteristic boldness, in March of 1861, he wrote to the chief commissioner of lands and works: "The undersigned begs to make application for permission to locate a site to be used for wharfage purposes at Yale with the privilege of collecting wharfage in goods landed at such wharf. With the understanding that he shall be allowed to purchase such site when it is brought into market at the upset price. He is willing to enter into any other reasonable arrangement that may be suggested as he is desirous of commencing operations."[5] This audacious proposition was not accepted by the colonial authorities.

THE ESTABLISHMENT OF BARNARD'S EXPRESS

Though the explosion of the *Fort Yale*, on April 14, 1861, left Barnard without a job, he was of the disposition that when one door closed, another would soon open. He soon obtained a contract to clear and grade Douglas Street in Yale, then began to look for a business in which to invest his hard-earned money. As Yale was the main depot for Billy Ballou's Express, Barnard was well aware of the ongoing controversy between Ballou and the colonial government over mail delivery. That December, Ballou had given notice that he would no longer carry the mail for free.

Barnard also knew of the ongoing discussion about the construction of a wagon road from Yale and Lillooet to the Cariboo, and he saw an opportunity. Even though the mining population was a fraction of what it had been in 1858, he believed that the prospects for the interior of British Columbia were promising. He decided to put together as much capital as possible and purchase the struggling Jeffray & Company Express. According to Ballou, Jeffray was in debt for $6,000 to $7,000,[6] so it is uncertain whether Barnard was able to buy the business outright. He may have arranged to take over the debt, or perhaps he received assistance from some of the many well-off citizens of booming Yale.

Initially, Barnard would continue to operate under the well-known and respected name of Jeffray & Company. He did not want to interrupt the flow of express matter from Victoria and hurried to take out an ad there on December 9 informing customers who may have heard of the sale: "Jeffray's Express. As heretofore the office will be at Mr. Jeffray's Government street, till further notice. Letters may be dropped as usual into the letter box at Mr. Herre's store, Yates Street. F.J. Barnard."[7]

Barnard left on the steamer from Victoria with the express that afternoon, after instructing his agent, Henry Walton, to begin publicizing the business in the new year. On January 6, 1862, a notice was placed in the *British Colonist*, dated December 1, 1861, stating, "I have this day sold to Mr. F.J. Barnard all my interest in the business of 'Jeffray's Fraser River Express,' and solicit for Mr. Barnard a continuance of the favors extended to me. William Jeffray." Immediately below, could be read, "Having purchased Mr. Jeffray's 'Fraser River Express,' I will continue the business thereunto connected . . . and solicit a share of the express business so cordially extended to Mr. Jeffray. Every effort will be made by me to give satisfaction to those who may entrust their business to my care. Immediately on the arrival of the steamer at Yale a messenger will be dispatched to Boston Bar and Lytton. F.J. Barnard."[8]

In the meantime, Barnard lost no time in contacting Jeffray's former agents along the Fraser. By the time the *British Colonist* notices appeared, he had already headed up the Fraser River to encourage a smooth transition by contacting agents and confirming that they wished to stay on. The winter was turning into the worst on record and the trail north from Yale through the canyon was hard going, so it is unlikely that Barnard went any further than Lytton. His return trip to Victoria was even worse. The *British Colonist* reported:

> Mr. Barnard's Express left Lytton on the 28th of December and Yale on the 3d inst. and arrived at New Westminster on the 12th, having been nine days in making the trip between the two latter points. The river was frozen over in many places, and the journey was made mostly on foot. Before Mr. Barnard left for this place, the river was reported frozen from Westminster to Harrison River... [He and five others] arrived in a canoe yesterday noon from New Westminster with a small express. The party left New Westminster at 10 o'clock on Monday morning last, and hauled the canoe over the ice from that place to the mouth of the river, a distance of fifteen miles. They made Plumper's Pass the first night, and on Tuesday night encamped on Orcas Island. The cold was intense, and the party suffered considerably.[9]

During this long and frozen first trip as an expressman, Barnard must have wondered what he had got himself into. Undeterred, he set up his new express office in Victoria with Henry Walton as his agent, and three days later, set off by canoe on the return trip to New Westminster. But the winter continued to break records. The Fraser River remained frozen past New Westminster until late February, necessitating the dragging of the express canoe over ice. In the middle of February, it was reported that "Mr. Barnard of the Express Company, had one foot frozen while making the trip from New Westminster to Yale. He has continued the trip from Sumas on a sledge drawn by Indians."[10]

Much has been made of Barnard "carrying letters and papers on his back and travelling... from Yale to Cariboo, a distance of 380 miles, or 760 the round trip, which he did entirely on foot."[11] This "fact," which first appeared in 1890 and has been repeated in almost every biography written about Barnard,[12] must be questioned for a number of reasons. There is no indication that Jeffray's

Express ever travelled farther north than Lytton, where it connected with other miners and small expressmen. It is also clear that, in the late winter and early spring, Barnard's Express travelled to and from Lytton only from New Westminster and connected with Victoria by steamer. In his advertisement the following summer, he described his express company as "hitherto running between Victoria, V.I. and Lytton, B.C." We are told that, sometime that spring, Barnard bought a pony, which he loaded with express and led, while continuing on foot himself. There is no indication that Barnard ever walked from Yale to the Cariboo carrying express matter on his back. Even his time carrying express to Lytton on his own was short lived.

In fact, none of the expressmen walked the whole way to the Cariboo mines in the gold rush years. First of all, it would have been far too time consuming and, secondly, the sheer weight of gold coming down from the Cariboo made it impossible to carry on foot. All the expressmen used agents on horseback, as Billy Ballou used Braley's Pony Express, and they almost always used Indigenous packers and canoe-men to move express material. From the beginning, Barnard hired Indigenous men to help pack the express matter over the Cariboo and Fraser trails. One of these was Cisco Charlie, named after his Nlaka'pamux (Thompson) Nation village of Cisco (later spelled "Sisko").[13]

Barnard had exhausted his savings in buying out Jeffray & Company and had to run his express business on a shoestring until business picked up in the spring. The incredibly long and severe winter had made travel up the Fraser and beyond almost impossible, and Barnard found himself in serious financial difficulty. His April letter to W.A.G. Young, then acting colonial secretary, explained his situation:

> Sir, In consequence of the severity of the past Winter, and the almost entire stagnation of business for the past four months, an unusually large quantity of goods have accumulated at New Westminster and, as a part of the Express business is to advance for duties until the goods reach their destination, I find it out of my

power for want of sufficient means to conduct that part of the business, and would therefore ask for the following accommodation, viz: To be allowed to pay 50 per cent of the duties in Cash and give the acceptance of one of the Victoria Bankers at 30 days for the balance. This arrangement would facilitate the transmission of Goods to the Upper Country to a very great degree, and will I trust meet with the approval of the Government.[14]

As might be imagined, the colonial government of British Columbia was not favourable to the request. Fortunately, the letters to the colonial government frequently have notations from the various people who viewed them, so we are able to follow the bureaucratic trail. This letter was forwarded to Wymond O. Hamley, the son of Vice Admiral William Hamley, who was collector of customs, another colonial official picked by Edward Bulwer-Lytton, secretary of state for the colonies. He scrawled an extensive note on the back of the letter.

Mr. Young—I think the arrangement in question would be both unsafe and inexpedient. Mr. Barnard is engaged in a business which cannot be carried on (except on a small scale) without ready money always on hand, and I believe his means are very limited. The Bills he proposes could not be negotiated and to accept them at the Custom House would be simply to postpone for a month at a time the payment of a portion of the weekly receipts, the ultimate collection of which I should consider very doubtful as I find people of this class ready to sign anything or to promise anything to get them off of a temporary difficulty... moreover if such a privilege were granted to one person it could not be refused to others and a system of credit would be engendered productive of nothing but confusion and loss of money. W. Hamley, Clinton House, 15 April 1862

The phrase "people of this class" indicates that the British class system was alive and well in the Colony of British Columbia. For outsiders with limited means like Barnard, there was little room for accommodation. The final note on the front of the letter states the decision, "Reply to Mr. Barnard that HC [Head of Customs?] regrets cannot authorize this arrangement."[15] The upshot was that those in the Cariboo mining region, after starving through the worst winter on record, continued without supplies until merchants could make their way to the New Westminster Customs House.

Barnard's financial situation would improve in the months to come. In May, when the trails were open, miners were beginning to find that the Cariboo was the richest goldfield yet. Never one for the status quo, Barnard moved his Victoria office to Yates Street to accommodate increased business and announced he had taken on a new function as "F.J. Barnard Forwarder and Custom House Broker in New Westminster." He informed "shippers and the general public generally that he has opened an Office at New Westminster for the transaction of Customs House business. Parties importing goods to British Columbia can have their Landing Warrants prepared and passed through the Customs without delay, at moderate charges."[16] This new addition to Barnard's Express was in direct competition with Ballou, who was feeling the effects of Barnard's aggressive competition. He advertised that "we have no funds to advance for duties. Permits with the money will be attended to and charges moderate."[17] The battle for express business in British Columbia was on.

Barnard did not stop there. In June, he announced that he had established the "Stickeen River Express." Word of the discovery of gold on the Stikine (as it came to be spelled) River, in British territory, generated another gold excitement that spring and hundreds of miners travelled north by steamboats to take in what turned out to be a short-lived rush. Barnard advertised that he would "send a messenger North on the steamer shortly to be sent to the Stickeen."[18] Although the rush only lasted that season and next, it allowed Governor Douglas to declare British ownership of the region and absorb it into British Columbia the following year.

In the meantime, the colonial government was finally getting a handle on Her Majesty's Mail delivery.

BARNARD CARRIES HER MAJESTY'S MAIL

In December 1861, when Billy Ballou refused to carry the mails any longer without an agreement, Barnard saw an opportunity and offered to carry the mail free of charge. A grateful colonial government agreed and promised to once again look into establishing a mail contract.

The reports coming out of the Cariboo were encouraging. On Williams Creek, the Cunningham Claim recovered as much as 675 ounces in a single day and three month's work returned a profit of $10,000 for each man. On nearby Lightning Creek, Richard Willoughby and his partners recovered 3,037 ounces of gold, worth about $50,000, in less than two months. By the end of 1861, gold returns were over $4,500,000. The Cariboo goldfields were the richest on the continent, even surpassing California in its heyday. In the spring of 1862, the gold rush, which had faded after the initial rush to the Lower Fraser, was renewed in earnest.

Encouraged by the surge of miners to the Cariboo, Governor Douglas saw that awarding a mail contract to an independent business was the only viable way to ensure efficient and prompt delivery. In April, tenders were solicited and received from William Ballou, J. Robertson Stewart, and F.J. Barnard for the conveyance of mail to the Interior. Clearly, Ballou was the most experienced expressman and the one with the best network, connecting via Braley and Company's Pony Express all the way to Quesnelle Forks. Even though his long commitment to carrying the colonial mail for free made him the most deserving, his attempt the previous December to force the government's hand by refusing to carry colonial mail did not bode well for him. The fact that he was not of British background may also have worked against him.

At this time, Warner Reeve Spalding, "bearing high creden-
tials from Downing Street and other prominent persons,"[19] had
been appointed by Douglas as postmaster of British Columbia and
stationed at New Westminster. He reviewed the tenders and recommended Barnard receive the contract at an annual price of £1,500
($7,300). On June 23, 1862, the decision was made public and, on
July 1, Spalding issued the following:

NOTICE TO THE PUBLIC—Notice is hereby given that a
Contract has been entered into with Francis Jones Barnard (Barnard's Express) for the conveyance of the Government mails as
undermentioned:

New Westminster to Douglas, Hope, Yale, Lytton, Lillooet and return

1st April to 30th Novr.	Weekly.
1 Decr. to 31st March	Semi-Monthly.

New Westminster to Douglas, Yale, Lytton, Lillooet to Williams
Lake and on to Antler Creek and return

1st April to 30th Novr.	Semi-Monthly.
1 Decr. to 31st March	Monthly.

The announcement was made less enthusiastically by the New
Westminster *British Columbian*. While stating that "a mail service
has at length been matured and the contract for its performance
awarded to Mr. F.J. Barnard, well known on the river," it went on
to lament the secrecy surrounding the process. "As to the manner
in which the contract was let, the cost to the country, or the details
of the matter we are of course, as all serfs ought to be, in blissful
ignorance." Editor John Robson had long been critical of Governor Douglas, who preferred to carry on governing from Victoria
in the Colony of Vancouver Island. Robson referred to him as "the
absentee Autocrat of James' Bay." While decrying the secrecy of

the selection of a mail contractor, he begrudgingly accepted the recipient.

> And it is a further satisfaction to know that the contract has fallen into good hands. Mr. Barnard is, perhaps, quite unexceptional as regards the requisite qualifications for performing this service in a manner that will give satisfaction to all concerned. He is a gentleman of good business habits, a fair share of energy, and withal, a straightforward, honest fellow. And, so far as he is personally concerned, we shall be glad to see him make a good thing out of it, however much we might censure the Government for letting out so important a contract in this secret and clandestine manner.

After outlining the delivery schedule, Robson went on to mention that "we understand Mr. Barnard intends connecting an Express with it, which will place him in a favorable position for securing a fair share of the Express carrying trade of the Colony. He passed up on Wednesday last with 14 animals and aparahoes for the service, so that the machinery will be in active operation very shortly—by the 1st proximo we believe."[21] The term "aparahoes" was a corruption of the Spanish word *aparejos*, meaning leather cushions stuffed with straw, the preferred saddles for packing mules or horses at the time. The *British Colonist* provided additional information about this new mode of transport by indicating "that the route to the mines will be at once stocked with horses in sufficient number to furnish relays of animals at given points for the use of the express and mail carriers."[22]

At first, the main post office for the Cariboo district was located at Williams Lake; later that it summer moved to Antler Creek, closer to the heart of the Cariboo goldfields. Three years later, after the wagon road was completed, it was moved to Barkerville. Even with these arrangements, the express companies were the preferred method for the miners to send letters. The post offices where the mail could be picked up were often far from the mining camps, and the expressmen were happy to deliver.

Though they were required to pay a colonial postal tax of two and a half shillings for each letter they transported, express agents often ignored this extra cost. The total revenue realized by the new postal system in 1862 amounted to a measly £66 (about $320), largely because express agents were reluctant to charge the postal tax. The government mail service was also slower than the express companies, because the British Columbia and Victoria Steam Navigation Company was the only authorized mail carrier from Victoria to the mainland. And mail carried over the Douglas-to-Lillooet route, although paid for through Barnard's contract, seldom amounted to much because fewer and fewer travellers were using the route. This prompted the New Westminster *British Columbian* to lament the fact that "when mail bags *are* carried over that route it is under the great 'Barnard Contract;' but there is rarely anything in them, as the outrageous postal rates and the disgraceful mismanagement by which the Department is characterized, have completely disgusted the public." The *British Columbian* would later refer to "the bungling absurdity of the notorious Barnard mail contract of 1862." [23]

CONSTRUCTING THE CARIBOO ROAD

Governor James Douglas was a dreamer. He had a vision for this new colony that would extend beyond the first flush of gold excitement into a future of settlement and prosperity. But, for this dream to become a reality, there had to be proper roads through the new colony. He was justifiably concerned that, if he didn't open up the interior routes, the Americans from Oregon, who were coming to the colony via the much easier route along the HBC brigade trail through the Okanagan Valley, would soon corner the market in the "upper country." To build these roads, he needed money, and lots of it.

When the first news of gold in the Cariboo reached the coast in the autumn of 1861, the gold excitement, which had faded over the previous year, was rekindled. The following spring all the idle men in the towns and mining camps rushed to the new goldfields. Miners making good pay on the Fraser River abandoned their claims and headed upriver. Steamers from Victoria and San Francisco were crowded with passengers intent on reaching the Cariboo. Douglas was encouraged by these reports. Significant revenue could be collected by the Colony of British Columbia from customs duties, tolls, miners' licenses, and the sale of lands. When the excitement over the Cariboo goldfields became a frenzy in late 1861, he realized this revenue would allow him to borrow the money needed to undertake his great road-building dream, and he informed Lord Newcastle, the colonial secretary in London, of his intention to proceed.

To provide for the wants of that population becomes one of the paramount duties of Government. I therefore propose to push on rapidly with the formation of Roads during the coming winter, in order to have the great thoroughfares leading to the remotest mines, now upwards of 500 miles from the sea coast, so improved as to render travel easy, and to reduce the cost of transport, thereby securing the whole trade of the Colony for Frasers River, and defeating all attempts at competition from Oregon.

The only insuperable difficulty which I experience is the want of funds: the revenues of the Colony will doubtless in course of a year, furnish the means, but cannot supply the funds that are immediately wanted to carry on these works. I propose, as soon as those roads are finished and the cost of transport reduced, to impose an additional road tax as a further means of revenue, a generally popular measure, and strongly recommended in the several petitions... I have in these circumstances come to the resolution of meeting the contingency, and raising the necessary funds, by effecting a loan of £15,000 or £20,000 in this Country, which will probably be a sufficient sum to meet the demands upon the Treasury on account of these works, until I receive the loan which Your Grace gave me hopes of effecting for the Colony in England. In taking this decided step I feel that I am assuming an unusual degree of responsibility, but I trust the urgency of the case will justify the means.[24]

Douglas was on shaky ground. His urgency was so great that he did not wait for approval from the powers in London. He applied for a loan from the Bank of British Columbia for £50,000 ($243,500) and opened tenders for the construction of new wagon roads.

There is no question that Douglas preferred the Harrison-to-Lillooet route. It had been his idea, in mid-July of 1858, to pay men $25 to work on the road sections of the trail in return for supplies. This emphasis on the Harrison-to-Lillooet route left the miners on the Fraser River above Yale on their own. In 1860, he put the Royal Engineers to work, deepening the channel of the Harrison River and converting what was now called the "Douglas Road" between the lakes, into a wagon road. The following year, he contracted Gustavus Blin Wright and John Calbreath, Americans from Vermont and New York respectively, to construct a road from Lillooet along the east side of the Fraser River to Pavilion and through Cut-off Valley to "The Junction" at the 42-mile post, later named Clinton. But major problems remained with this route. Before Lillooet, it necessitated transferring freight from steamer to or from wagon eight times and, after Lillooet, the trail had to climb over the 4,000-foot-high (1,220-metre) Pavilion Mountain. Nonetheless, in 1862, Wright and Calbreath were contracted to continue from Clinton to Alexandria at a fixed cost of $1,700 a mile and began work on the road.

While Douglas considered converting the Dewdney Trail east to Rock Creek into a wagon road, a delegation from Yale suggested the need for a wagon road through the Fraser Canyon. A similar argument was advanced by Colonel Moody of the Royal Engineers and Walter Moberly, a civil engineer who had worked with Dewdney. Their combined voices managed to convince Douglas that "the Yale-Cariboo route was the best to adopt for the general development of the country and it was imperative that its construction should be undertaken at once."[25]

The previous year, the Royal Engineers had surveyed a possible road and selected a site for a bridge across the Fraser above Yale. So, in May 1862, Captain Grant, with fifty-three sappers from the Royal Engineers and additional civilian labour, began work on the first six

The Cariboo Road at the 17-mile post in the Fraser Canyon shows how
the road was blasted out of the cliff face. UL_1001_0023, UNO LANGMANN FAMILY
COLLECTION OF BRITISH COLUMBIA PHOTOGRAPHS, RARE
BOOKS AND SPECIAL COLLECTIONS, UBC LIBRARY

miles to Pike's Riffle; Thomas Spence was contracted to build the next
seven miles to Chapman's Bar; and Joseph Trutch was awarded the
contract to construct the section to Boston Bar. The section, thirty-
two miles from Boston Bar to Lytton, was given to Thomas Spence.

Although these contracts were in separate names, Trutch and
Spence, both British-born, worked in partnership. Spence had
arrived on the Fraser River in May of 1858, where he was the "dis-
coverer" of Cameron's Bar and had amassed a considerable fortune
before going into road building. Trutch, on the other hand, when
he heard of the Fraser River gold rush, went from Oregon to London to solicit a recommendation from the secretary for the colonies,
Edward Bulwer-Lytton. He arrived in Victoria in 1859 and received

small contracts surveying on the Fraser River and constructing roads on the Harrison–Lillooet route. An additional contract was awarded to a partnership consisting of Oppenheimer Brothers of Yale, Walter Moberly, and T.B. Lewis to construct the road from Lytton to Cook's Ferry on the Thompson River.

The Royal Engineers were assigned the toughest challenges in road construction: the six miles (ten kilometres) of cliffs from Yale to Boston Bar and the nine-mile (fifteen-kilometre) stretch of solid rock cliffs from Cook's Ferry (Spences Bridge) along the Thompson River. In both cases, the road had to be blasted from the face of steep cliffs and some sections built directly over the river on stilts and cribbing. Blasting a road out of sheer cliff faces could be a hazardous business. Bishop Hills, of the Church of England, who travelled through the Fraser Canyon in 1862, was impressed "to see the works being carried out to form a wagon road through the canyon, a narrow gorge of the mountain through which the Fraser converges. A party of Royal Engineers, assisted by others are at work blasting the rocks. The work is one of great magnitude—dangerous and arduous of execution." He was to discover this danger in a very personal way later, as he travelled up the canyon.

> To travel this road while blasting is going on is not free from danger. Sunday, near Chapman's Bar, I was riding along the trail, elevated perhaps 100 feet from the river, and as I arrived on a small bridge over a chasm, an explosion took place immediately beneath my feet. I was enveloped in smoke, and debris were scattered around and over me. My horse happily was quiet, otherwise the least start would have cast me headlong over the edge, which is unprotected, and I should have been dashed upon the rocks below. I of course expected masses of rock to come upon my head. I escaped; and on passing round about thirty yards, found the blasters in a place of safety, they having fled, after firing the fuse, from the very spot which I occupied when the explosion took place. They were not a little surprised to see me."[26]

While the projects through the Fraser Canyon were proceeding without major incidents, the same could not be said for the contract to build the road from Lytton to Cook's Ferry. Walter Moberly, who was in charge of the construction, had great difficulty retaining workers. Once the men had been paid, they abandoned their jobs and headed to the Cariboo, so Moberly hired Chinese and Nlaka'pamux workers, who could be depended upon to stay until the work was completed. By June, the road had been completed for twelve miles out of Lytton but, when the loan from the colonial office was delayed, the project suffered severely from lack of financing. Lewis began to lose confidence in the project and Moberly bought him out. But the problems caused by lack of operating funds only worsened.

Finally, unable to pay his workers and the ongoing expenses, Moberly "called upon Captain Grant [of the Royal Engineers and] discussed the whole matter over in the most friendly manner, and I gave him in writing, my relinquishment of all my charter rights, and also the surrender of all the supplies, tents, tools, etc., on the works (which had cost me upwards of $6,000), for the benefit of the government . . . Captain Grant and myself now proceeded to my different road camps of which I put him in full possession, and when everything was out of my hands, Captain Grant proposed that he should appoint me to carry on the works for the government for the rest of the season. This proposition I was glad to accept for I had not a dollar left."[27]

The Cariboo Road, as it was called, was substantially completed as far as Soda Creek, north of Williams Lake, by the end of 1862. Governor Douglas toured the work that fall and was greatly impressed with the progress. "In smoothness & solidity [the roads] surpass expectation—Jackass mountain. 'The Cleft.' The Great Slides. The Rocky Bridges and other passes of ominous fame, so notorious in the history of the country—have lost their terrors. They now exist only in name being rendered alike safe and pleasant by the broad and graceful windings of the Queen's Highway."[28]

The road north still required the construction of bridges, one over the Fraser River two miles north of Spuzzum and the other over

Alexandra suspension bridge, completed by Joseph Trutch in 1863.
UL_1001_0021, UNO LANGMANN FAMILY COLLECTION OF BRITISH COLUMBIA PHO-
TOGRAPHS, RARE BOOKS AND SPECIAL COLLECTIONS, UBC LIBRARY

the Thompson River at Cook's Ferry. In 1863, the bridge over the
Fraser was contracted to Joseph Trutch, on whose stretch of road
it was required. But it was not until 1864 that the contract for the
bridge over the Thompson was awarded to Thomas Spence.

The Alexandra suspension bridge over the Fraser would prove
to be Trutch's finest work. It had a 268-foot (82-metre) span, sat
90 feet (27 metres) above the river, and had to be built to handle
a three-ton load capacity. When it was completed in September
of 1863 at a cost of $54,000, it was tested with a four-horse team
pulling a wagon loaded with three tons, with deflection of less than
one-quarter of an inch.[29] Considering that it had to be built with the
contractor's money, it was also a source of considerable income for
Trutch—estimated at $10,000 to $20,000 a year—since he was
contracted to collect tolls on it for seven years.

Thomas Spence began his bridge in the autumn of 1864 under the same arrangement of receiving tolls for seven years. In March of 1865, the bridge was completed and Cook's Ferry became known as Spences Bridge. Edgar Dewdney, afterwards lieutenant-governor of British Columbia, visited the completed bridge and later wrote, "I inspected the work and found the bridge a good, substantial structure, and it proved to be so for it stood from 1865 to 1894, when the extraordinary high water of that year carried it away."

THE BRITISH COLUMBIA AND VICTORIA EXPRESS COMPANY

Frank Barnard watched the construction with interest. Now that the wagon road to the Cariboo was at least partially available, he could carry mail there all the way from Victoria. Ever one to take advantage of new developments, he decided to rename and extend his company. The *British Colonist* of June 24, 1862, announced:

NEW EXPRESS COMPANY—A STEP IN THE RIGHT DIRECTION— Barnard's Express, on and after the 1st proximo, will be merged into the "British Columbia and Victoria Express Company" and will make regular weekly trips from Victoria to Cariboo. We learn that a contract for carrying the Royal Mail to and from the Cariboo has been awarded Mr. Barnard by the government, and that the route to the mines will be at once stocked with horses in sufficient number to furnish relays of animals at given points for the use of the express and mail carriers. The express via Douglas and Lillooet will connect with the express via Yale and Lytton at Williams Lake, and from thence will be taken to Antler City, whence carriers will be dispatched to the various mining camps. We have often urged the necessity [of] prompt delivery of mail matter in the sister colony, and confess that, in common with many others, we view with no little satisfaction this . . . awakening of government to [the] importance of establishing a direct postal service between Victoria and the diggings. The new arrangement will

prove of vast benefit to not only the mercantile but also the mining community.[30]

Realizing the vast territory he had to service, Barnard lost no
time in building his network through the colony. In early August, he
announced in the *British Colonist* that "the route above Lytton and Lillooet is under the immediate supervision of Mr. R.T. Smith, formerly
of Fort Hope, who will always accompany the Treasure Express."[31]

Robert T. Smith was typical of the men Barnard hired to make
his express company successful. Born in Ireland, Smith arrived on
the Fraser River in 1858. That September, he was appointed justice of the peace and revenue officer for Fort Hope. In that capacity,
he had the unenviable duty to collect from the miners for licenses.
When he stepped down from his position in September of 1859, the
British Colonist published a letter of appreciation signed by fifty citizens of Fort Hope.

Like most of the poorly paid colonial officials, Smith had to find
other ways of making money and, in the fall of 1861, he organized
a pack train to carry food supplies into Quesnel Forks, where he
stored them in a building owned by Locke and Hart before heading
to the lower country. As the terrible winter dragged on and miners
were desperate for supplies, Locke and Hart claimed that a "leaky
roof" forced them to sell off all of Smith's flour, beans, salt, coffee,
sugar, and other groceries. When Smith returned in the spring, he
launched a lawsuit for £1,800 to replace his supplies. After receiving
a meagre £280, he was obliged to take up Barnard's job of overseeing the vast system of trails and roads from Lytton and Lillooet.[32]
Like most of Barnard's agents, he was a man above reproach and,
in 1866, he constructed the last piece of the Cariboo Wagon Road
from Soda Creek to Quesnelle Mouth. He would serve as a member of the legislative assembly of BC for Yale from 1871 until 1878.

Along with the large number of miners coming to the Cariboo in
the summer of 1862 came lawless individuals who took advantage
of the long, isolated trails to prey on well-to-do miners and merchants returning from the gold camps. Not surprisingly, considering

the riches coming out of Williams Creek, robberies became frequent. In the spring, notorious American outlaw Boone Helm was reported to be in the Cariboo. Jack Splawn, who had driven cattle all the way to Lightning Creek, reported meeting Helm there. "Who had not heard of Boone Helm? The very name spelled blood and crime... His was the most revolting face a man ever had, the look in his eyes was indescribable—something like that of a fiery vulture..." Boone offered Splawn an opportunity to join him, claiming they "could make a big haul and split." Splawn turned him down but later heard of atrocities Boone probably committed.[33]

Governor Douglas sent Judge Begbie to the Cariboo in June to "wave the flag" of Great Britain and make it clear that law and order would be fiercely enforced in British territory. Begbie's presence, though welcomed by the miners, did not prevent one of the most atrocious murders in Cariboo history from taking place.

On July 26, two Jewish merchants, David Sokolosky and Harris "Herman" Lewin, along with their French Canadian packer, Charles Rouchier, went missing on their way from Keithley Creek to Quesnelle Forks. A young man, William Tompkins Collinson, who had been travelling with them, reported them missing when he arrived at Quesnelle Forks and found they had not arrived. A search party was sent out and their bodies were found where they had been dragged off the trail. All three had been shot to death and robbed of their gold, estimated at a value of $10,000 to $20,000, as well as their watches and even their hats. When the bodies were brought in to Quesnelle Forks, the search party found town constable Phillip Coote quite drunk, and gold commissioner Thomas Elwyn away at Williams Creek registering claims. Residents of Quesnelle Forks formed two committees, one to "take it upon ourselves to arrest all suspicious persons" and the other to form a four-man posse to pursue the murderers.[34] But in spite of these efforts and the arrest and jailing of a number of men, no one was ever convicted of the murders.

It is noteworthy that the same edition of the *British Columbian* reported two other Jewish merchants arriving in New Westminster, "Mr. Levi, and Mr. Goldstone, bringing down between them 245 lbs., equal to about $50,000." For this amount of gold, the express companies, which guaranteed safe delivery, were the most acceptable means for miners to get their gold to the coast. Although it was possible for express agents to be robbed, the companies were insured and guaranteed full repayment for any gold lost through theft or other problems.

A few weeks later, more vicious murders in the Cariboo were discovered. The *British Colonist* reported that "the rumor with regard to the finding of the bodies of Benjamin Fish, Victor Durand, and a Chinaman, near Beaver Lake is reasserted. They were all murdered (it is said) by highwaymen for their money, and the remains when discovered in the bushes were in an advanced state of decomposition."[35] These murders were likely perpetrated around the same time as the murders of Sokolosky, Lewin, and Rouchier. Once again, no one was ever arrested or convicted.

Of particular concern to Barnard was the fact that the *British Colonist* article went on to report the possible murder of one of his expressemen, "Alexander Stenhouse, (late of Victoria) of Barnard's Express whose horse is said to have dashed riderless into the town of Williams Lake. Blood was found on the saddle, and Mr. Stenhouse had not appeared at latest dates."[36] No further details follow up this article, but one notes with relief that presumably the same Mr. Stenhouse shows up in an article later that year as a juror in a Victoria case. Nonetheless, the murders (and apparent murder) would have encouraged Barnard to step up security for his expressmen.

THE END OF BALLOU'S EXPRESS

Through the summer of 1862, Billy Ballou competed head-to-head with Barnard. The loss of the mail contract had dealt him a severe blow, giving Barnard an edge in the competition. Ballou had an answer for that, advertising that Ballou's Express "having no Mails to delay us, we go to every Camp." Ballou's ad went on to state, "Owing to the enormous advance on Government Postage, we only add the same to our charges on Letters and Newspapers, less

10 per cent, to all points above New Westminster." Even this "discounted" price meant that Ballou had to charge more than the Post Office rate, whereas Barnard carried the mail under his well-paid contract. Ballou did have the advantage of being the Wells Fargo connection in Victoria, a fact that featured prominently in his ad. In contrast, Barnard's ads for the British Columbia and Victoria Express Company emphasized "carrying Her Majesty's Mails" and that "traders ordering goods... handed to any of the messengers will be executed by Mr. Barnard personally, who has had considerable experience in the Victoria Market, and will make every effort to purchase on the most favorable terms."[37] This indicates that, even by summer of 1862, Barnard was carrying the express from Douglas and Yale to Victoria via steamships.

The express situation in British Columbia changed once again in October. On the 27th of that month a notice appeared in the *British Colonist*: "Ballou's Express—I have this day sold to Messrs. George Dietz and Hugh Nelson all my right, title, interest and goodwill in the above Express from Lillooet Flat, Douglas, Yale, Hope via New Westminster to Victoria. W.T. Ballou—New Westminster, Oct. 1st, 1862."

Immediately below was another notice, "Messrs. Dietz & Nelson having purchased the above business, notice is hereby given that I have this day withdrawn in their favor, connecting with them at Yale and Lillooet, from which points I will continue to carry Express to Cariboo and the Northern Mines, as heretofore. F.J. Barnard, New Westminster, October 15, 1862."

Below that was yet another announcement: "In reference to the above notices the undersigned beg to state that they will hereafter conduct the Express business, in all its branches, between Victoria, V.I. and Lillooet and Yale, BC, under the name of Dietz & Nelson's British Columbia and Victoria Express, connecting with Wells, Fargo & Co., for California, Eastern States and Europe. George Dietz, Hugh Nelson, Victoria, Oct. 24th, 1862."

Still another notice was placed below: "Barnard's Express. The Subscriber, thankful for past favors, begs to announce that he will, under the new arrangement, carry on the business of an Express in

all its branches between Lillooet and Yale and Cariboo, connecting with Dietz & Nelson's British Columbia and Victoria Express.
F.J. Barnard, Victoria, Oct. 25, 1862."[38]

A few things can be assumed from these notices and ads, all
obviously placed by the same person. First, as indicated, Dietz
and Nelson did not buy out all of Ballou's operation. They merely
purchased his business from Yale and Lillooet to Victoria and left
Ballou's Express with the business from those points to the Cariboo mines, meaning Ballou continued to compete with Barnard for
business to and from the Cariboo. This is indicated by an ad in the
British Colonist in December 1862 and January 1863, stating that
Ballou's Express "will leave Lillooet January 5 for Williams Lake,
Beaver Lake, Forks of Quesnelle and Williams Creek. And return
by Mouth of Cottonwood."[39] Also, Ballou was listed as the *British
Colonist* agent in Lillooet from January until the end of June 1863.
The *British Columbian* went on to lament "the retirement of the veteran Ballou from the Pioneer Express" and eulogized him for his
contribution.[40] So it would appear that, although greatly weakened
by Barnard's lucrative mail contract, Ballou used his good reputation and extensive network to compete with the upstart Barnard for
a few months before finally conceding defeat.

From the outset of Dietz and Nelson's express business, they
were in partnership with Barnard's Express, taking over the leg of
his company from Yale and Lillooet to Victoria. This is significant
for being the first example of Barnard setting up a sub-contract with
other parties—independent owners of their own businesses who
were in a loose partnership with Barnard—to look after portions of
his express network. In this way, Barnard could keep his finances
independent from the new company, while still having a control
over what business they did. By encouraging Dietz and Nelson to
buy Ballou's Yale-and-Lillooet-to-Victoria leg, he also, through
them, became the agent for Wells Fargo & Company in Victoria,
which had used Ballou up to that point. Barnard would have also
sublet to Dietz and Nelson the Yale-and-Lillooet-to-Victoria leg of
the colonial mail contract through a private agreement with them,
while maintaining control over the contract.

George Dietz was a miner turned entrepreneur who, in 1859, began construction of a "ways" to transport boats and freight around the Grand Falls just upriver from Yale. Completed in February of 1860, this portage was lauded by the *British Colonist*: "The Ways at the Grand Falls have now been completed at a heavy expense by Mr. Geo. Dietz, and boats are now taken over without trouble or danger. They are also fitted up with cars on wheels to carry the goods. The enterprise should be well patronized."[41] Dietz was granted a five-year charter to charge a toll for transporting boats and freight, and would have amassed a fortune, given the traffic along the Fraser over the next two years. But the construction of the Cariboo Road through the Fraser Canyon in 1862 forced him to look for a new investment opportunity.

Hugh Nelson, born in Larne, Northern Ireland, mined in California before coming to British Columbia in 1858, arriving on the Fraser River early in the gold excitement. Instead of mining for gold, he decided to mine the miners, setting up a business in the booming town of Fort Yale. In 1861, he was secretary of the Yale Steam Navigation Company, and the next spring, he constructed a warehouse in Yale capable of holding 500 tons of merchandise. Nelson would go on to greater things, eventually becoming a member of the Canadian Senate and then lieutenant-governor of British Columbia from 1887 to 1892.[42]

In 1863, when Billy Ballou continued to run his express business to the Cariboo and remained the *British Colonist* agent for Lillooet, he met William Wentworth-Fitzwilliam, Lord Milton, and his travelling partner, Doctor Walter Butler Cheadle. Dr. Cheadle described the encounter: "We had a severe time of it going down [from Victoria], every one pressing us for a drink. Amongst others the noted Billy Ballou, a regular Yankee, formerly had the Express & I hear showed wonderful energy & perseverance in carrying on the communications in the old time of no roads & hard trails almost impassable in the snow. At first sight a loud-talking rowdy, [with] nasal twang excessive."[43]

At this time, as his business dwindled and Barnard's grew, Ballou was looking for other opportunities. In August of 1862, he made a proposal to the minister of lands and works to "build or cause to be built a good Waggon Road, sixteen feet wide on solid earth from opposite the Coquihalla from Hope to the opposite side from Yale of the Fraser River to include all Blasting & Bridging."[44]

Ballou does not appear to have received a favourable response, but in December, in partnership with Lee Chang of Kwong Lee & Company, he submitted to Colonel Moody a "survey of the work we propose to do on the Pemberton road & wish to employ our men immediately." The strength of this proposal was in the fact that Kwong Lee & Company were involved in bringing in great numbers of Chinese men who, as payment for passage to British Columbia, were obliged to work for the company. This is the first mention of using Chinese labour in road construction, a practice that would become common in the years to come.

The first proposal was followed in January 1863 with another one, to "build a road 18 feet wide that will be accepted by Government for ($16,000) [marginal note: £3,200] from Yale to Emory's Bar."[45] The proposal seems to have been seriously examined by Colonel Moody, but was not accepted. Undeterred, Ballou and Kwong Lee & Company followed up with another proposal to repair and rebuild the road near Pemberton on the Harrison-to-Lillooet route. None of these proposals was accepted, but the partnership between Ballou and Kwong Lee & Company, for which Kwong Lee was able to provide an excellent source of cheap labour, continued. The following July, the *British Colonist* reported, "At Long Bar, 9 miles above the mouth of Quesnelle, Wm. Ballou with Kwong Lee and others had a party of about 120 Chinamen at work which they expected to increase shortly to 500, and as soon as they could succeed in bringing water, it was expected that great results would follow."[46]

This partnership appears to have been short-lived as Ballou left British Columbia in the fall of 1863 and headed to Montana and Idaho in search of new opportunities, and later spent time in California. Eventually, he ended up in Seattle, where in 1878 he was interviewed by H.H. Bancroft, who described him as "much broken in health when I took his dictation... and died shortly afterward.

His information was certainly as varied as that of any man I ever met, and he gave it to me in good faith, yet while I have no reason to doubt his word, before placing implicit confidence in an important statement, I should prefer to see it verified."[47]

Ballou was a character larger than life and his wanderings through the frontiers of western North America were typical of a generation of men and women who went west in search of fame and fortune. Ballou found both and his legend lives on. His somewhat premature eulogy in the *British Columbian* is worth quoting.

> Mr. Ballou, more familiarly known as "Billy Ballou" came to this country with the memorable rush of '58, since which he has been through hair-breadth escapes and innumerable hardships, in all of which Ballou never failed to "connect." And so intimately does his name stand connected with the past history of this Colony that it has emphatically become a household word. His humorous and familiar face is known and welcomed on every Bar and in every cabin. Always ready with a word of encouragement to the discon- solate, and a dollar or two to the strapped miner, he has succeeded in becoming a general favorite, and almost making one feel that the Colony could not get on without him. We are not aware of his destination or intentions, but only express general sentiment when we say that we wish him well wherever he goes. As for his successors, all we know of them is that they are honorable and responsible men, respected and esteemed where they are best known. The best wish we have for them in their new avocation is that they may be as successful, efficient and popular as their pre- decessor, "BILLY BALLOU."[48]

BARNARD STRUGGLES TO RULE THE ROAD

Even though Barnard had secured a partnership with Dietz and Nelson to look after the Yale-and-Lillooet-to-Victoria route and no longer had to compete with Ballou, he was not prepared to rest. In the fall of 1862, he submitted a new proposal to carry mail bags to the Cariboo much more frequently than he was obliged to under his existing contract. A letter he wrote in November to Attorney General H.P.P. Crease mentions his suggested terms for an amended contract that took into account the new Cariboo situation and gives a good picture of his ambitions for the future:

> Sir, I was much surprised to learn from you today that you had not heard from Victoria respecting my proposal to amend the mail service contract. I must really beg to be informed at the earliest period whether my proposal is accepted or not as I am being put to a very serious loss & to my great inconvenience at being kept in a position I am now in. As you are no doubt aware I have abandoned the Express business on the lower river so as to be in a position to pay more attention to the mail service but the recent action of the Government in stopping a portion of the mail matter so as to reduce the cost of carrying has rendered the contract a losing concern to me and must ere long embarrass me completely. Will you please represent my case in the proper quarter and by so doing you will confer a favor on Your Most Hmbl Serv F.J. Barnard.[49]

What the government was doing "in stopping a portion of the mail matter so as to reduce the cost of carrying" is uncertain, as the terms of the contract are unknown. But the government was apparently limiting the amount of mail heading into the Cariboo to keep its costs down, implying that Barnard was being paid for the amount of mail carried. More significant is Barnard's statement that the current mail contract was "a very serious loss" and a "losing concern." This reflects Barnard's determination to negotiate changes in the existing and future contracts, as he continued to do through the winter. On January 1, 1863, he wrote to W.A.G. Young, the colonial secretary:

> Some time since at the request of the Post Master General I sent in a proposition for carrying the mail next spring under the

supposition that a more extended mail service would be required.
I should like very much to know whether my proposition was
likely to be accepted or not. In the event of it being accepted I can
make arrangements for placing light wagons or Dogcarts on the
route in which case I could carry 150 lbs if necessary without any
extra charge. It is most necessary that I should be advised of any
change at the earliest moment so as to make such preparations
as will ensure the carrying out of the contract with energy and
efficiency. I have been a loser by this year's contract but some of
the loss has resulted from inexperience and from having had an
opposition to contend with. Should the Government wish a weekly
service to Williams Creek it can be done at a small advance on the
price named in my proposal. I have the honor to be Sir your most
obedient servant, F.J. Barnard.[50]

Though he mentions that he had "been a loser by this year's contract," Barnard admits that "some of the loss [had] resulted from
inexperience and from having an opposition to contend with." He
was prepared to accept some responsibility for the problems with
the contract, but he also pointed to Ballou, who was making every
effort to drive him out of business. Had it not been for the mail
contract, flawed as it was, he would no doubt have been out of business. Interestingly, this was the first time he was considering using
wagons or dogcarts on the trails where possible and extending his
service to Williams Creek, the most promising creek in the Cariboo
at the time.

In 1863, the colonial government made a concerted effort to
ensure that postage was paid on all letters carried by the express
companies, and that year lower postal rates were established. To
help overcome the delays in transporting the mail, Barnard agreed
to convey the mailbags more often than required by the contract. As
the Harrison–Lillooet route was more or less abandoned, mail for the
Cariboo was all forwarded via Yale after the middle of May. Despite
the improvements in mail delivery, express companies like Barnard's were still the preferred carriers, with the government's total

income from postage in 1863 amounting to only £750 ($3,650).[51] While Barnard was not making a substantial profit on the contract, he did use the fact that he was carrying Her Majesty's Mail to good effect. In May, he wrote to the colonial secretary complaining that he was being charged twelve dollars for the ferry at Lillooet for crossing the Fraser and asking, "Will you please inform me whether a mail carrier is liable to pay ferryage any more than a Constable on Her Majesty's Service." He went on to report that "the mail is now carried in light wagons and we are obliged to cross for repairs and attending to animals. The charge is enormous & I would like to be relieved from it."[52] While the use of light wagons involved a financial outlay for equipment and horses, Barnard clearly saw a time approaching when the completion of the Cariboo Wagon Road would make horse-drawn transportation the best means of moving the express matter and perhaps even passengers.

Despite the ongoing concerns with the mail contract, the year 1863 proved to be the best yet for gold mining and Barnard saw his finances take a turn for the better. In a letter written in July of 1863 to George Gowdie, a former merchant at Quesnelle Forks, who was now in the east, Barnard outlined his situation:

> Business since you departed has improved materially. We have brought down from $10,000 to $21,000 each trip and about 150 letters each way beside a very fair commission business and quite a stack of packages to carry... I leave myself on Tuesday for Rich-field with $25,000 in coin for a new bank. The establishing of the Bank by Macdonald & Co will increase the business very much. The Bank of British Columbia have established themselves.[53]

Barnard went on to describe the contract situation. "The mail contract is out July 7th on application for a change. I was told to go in as of old or drop it. They have no time to devote to it just now and I will be told in time what their intentions in the matter are. My idea is there will be no change till the road is completed so that we carry the mail *next winter*." Because of the difficulty of carrying mail and express in the winter, Barnard asked Gowdie to purchase in the east:

> 3 largest size Indian sleighs or tobogins [*sic*] the best quality. They are made in Quebec and made by the knife not sawn as lumber is. Be careful in this respect. They ought to be at least 2 feet or 2 feet 6 in. wide very thoroughly tied with gut. Should you not go to Quebec you might take means to have them sent to New York for you. Henderson & Co of Montreal Farriers deal in the article but the kind mostly sold there now are sawn not split. Split are the best and toughest. Price is no object if the best can be had. They ought to be 7 or 8 feet long.

At the same time, he ordered "1 doz. pairs of what are known in Upper Canada as Beef Boots (in Lower Canada as moccasins) with calf skin tops knee high. They must be large size say 13 & 14 inch. If you have time have them made to order of the best quality of leather." [54]

In a cover letter to his brother James, attached to the above letter, Barnard asked that, if Gowdie was unable to buy the sleighs (actually toboggans) and boots, would James buy them and send them via Wells Fargo. He admitted that it "will cost a small mint of money coming thru that way but it is the only quick way and there is nothing in this country that will suit my purposes so well."

Barnard, as the above letter indicates, was planning for the future. His situation would be greatly facilitated by the ever-growing network of trails and roads that were appearing in the colony and, in short order, he had graduated from packing express on his back to using horses extensively. The transition to wagon transportation was just beginning.

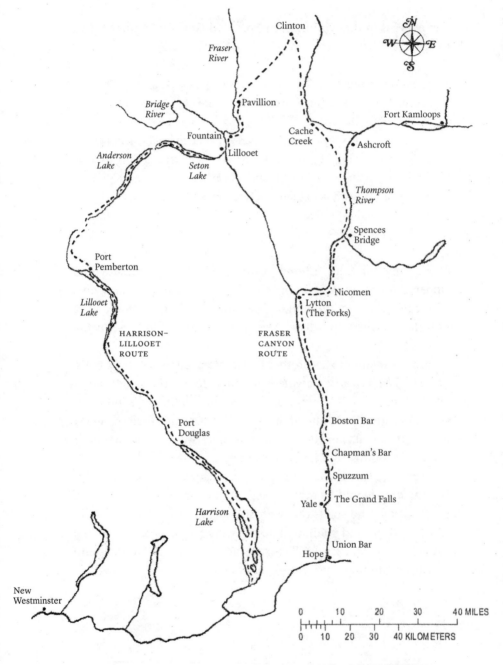

Two routes through Lower BC to Clinton: the original "Douglas Road"
connected Harrison with Lillooet along the Harrison River, while the new
"Cariboo Road" connected Yale with Lytton through the Fraser Canyon.

3

BRITISH COLUMBIA'S FIRST STAGECOACHES

STEVE TINGLEY was tired. Making and repairing harnesses kept him busy from dawn until dusk. And now that the road to the Cariboo was completed through the Fraser Canyon, Yale was the place where everybody started their journey on horseback. He admitted that he made good money, mostly in the form of gold, the currency of the day, and he kept his fat poke of gold dust and a scale to weigh it in his harness shop. Of course, the real fortunes in the previous year, 1862, were being made in the Cariboo. He continually heard of miners coming down from there with tens of thousands of dollars in Cariboo gold. Sure, he had tried his hand at gold mining in 1861 and '62, but for every man who made a fortune there were fifty who straggled back with nothing to show for their efforts. He was one of those men. Good thing he'd learned a trade as a saddler at home in New Brunswick. But there must be a better way to make a fortune in this land of opportunity.

A shadow appeared through the wide doors of the harness shop and a man walked in—probably another person who wanted his harness resewn. Tingley looked up and recognized Frank Barnard, the expressman. He had been in a few days before to order complete sets of harnesses for a four-horse hitch, a big order. Even in the bustling town of Yale, people had time to talk, and he and Barnard had chatted a while. It turned out the two of them had both come from the eastern part of British North America, Barnard from Quebec City in Lower Canada and Tingley from the adjoining Colony of New Brunswick. This time, Barnard got right to the point.

"I'm looking for men who can drive a four-horse team. I plan on starting up a stagecoach run from Yale to the end of the Cariboo road construction."

Tingley responded, "I'm a pretty good teamster and my friend James Hamilton, who's also from New Brunswick, has lots of experience too. But where are you going to get enough horses? Good stage horses should be trained from scratch."

"I hear that there are horses for sale in Oregon," Barnard said. "The Nez Perce cayuses aren't big enough, but in the Willamette Valley they're breeding good-sized pulling horses. What do you think?"

"You'd have to drive them through the interior into British Columbia and up through the Okanagan Valley," replied Tingley.

"Are you up for it?" asked Barnard, "I'll pay you good money to go down there and buy 160 head, and drive them up here and distribute them along the road. Then I'll hire you on full-time as a driver."

Tingley asked to think on it overnight. He'd been offered a good price for his harness shop and could probably still work at it when he wasn't driving. But, in his four years in British Columbia, he had seen express businesses come and go. Who knew how long Barnard's Express would last? Still, the thought of driving a stagecoach up and down the new road appealed to him.

In the morning, he found Barnard at his Yale express office, walked up to him, and shook his hand. "When do I leave for Oregon?"

Sometime in the summer of 1863, Tingley took the steamer to Portland to look for horses. This new job would challenge and empower him for the rest of his life.

BARNARD'S EXPRESS ADDS PASSENGER STAGES

Barnard was not the first one to think of operating a stagecoach line to the Cariboo. Since the fall of 1861, passengers could travel by stage and steamboat on the Douglas-to-Lillooet route with the British Columbia Royal Mail Company, which didn't actually carry the Royal Mail. When the road was completed from Lillooet to Clinton, the *British Columbian* reported that the company had "a line of stages . . . now making a weekly trip as far as Williams Lake, and would extend to Frank Way's [Deep Creek House, about ten miles northwest of Williams Lake] as soon as the road was completed to that point." The same article mentioned that "Mr. Barnard has express waggons running on the same route, carrying passengers and light freight."[1]

It didn't take Barnard long to do his best and eliminate the competition. In August, he set up a regular express wagon with room for passengers from Quesnelle Mouth to Boston Bar, with a fare of $75 per passenger. The *British Colonist* remarked, "The line is likely to be well patronized. The fare seems to be very reasonable. In addition to this he has relays of horses every 25 miles for the express, which has been running on the finished portion of the road some 60 miles a day. The enterprise deserves encouragement, and every effort on his part to make the communication between this distant place and civilization shorter, will be fully appreciated by the miners of Cariboo."[2] Barnard realized that the Douglas-to-Lillooet route was in decline now that there was a continuous road from Yale instead of the road-to-lake-to-road required on the Harrison–Lillooet route. By early November, the British Columbia Royal Mail Company was in receivership and in January auctioned off its horses, stagecoaches, and harness in Victoria, Lillooet, Pemberton, and 100 Mile House. No doubt, Barnard bid successfully on many of these assets.

With the competition out of the way, Barnard began in earnest to plan for a stagecoach line that would eventually run all the way to Barkerville, which was rapidly becoming the heart of the Cariboo goldfields. Though Barnard had already sent Tingley off to purchase horses in Oregon, he knew he could use more. He needed strong, fast horses, preferably ones that could be broken for harness only, that had not been used for any other purposes. In February, he wrote to Governor Douglas, asking, "Having understood that the Government intend discontinuing the Gold Escort and as I will require a number of horses for intended increased communication between the Cariboo mines and the heads of navigation on Frazer River [sic], may I request to be informed whether it is the intention of the Government to dispose of Escort Horses and if so, whether I could have the privilege of purchasing by private contract. May I beg an early reply, as it is necessary that I should have the horses on hand to feed with grain preparatory to the commencement of business early in March." Governor Douglas noted on the back of the letter, "Direct the acting Com[missioner] of Lands and Works to enter into arrangements for the sale of the Escort horses & inform Mr. Barnard accordingly."[3] Douglas's prompt and favourable response indicated that he was willing to help anyone attempting to make good use of his beloved Cariboo Road.

Little is known of Tingley's 1863 Oregon expedition, but his well-documented 1868 trip provides clues. On that trip, he went directly to The Dalles to contact William Connell, who lived in Rockport, directly across the Columbia, and who "offered to assist in buying."[4] Connell had travelled over the Oregon Trail in 1846 and had originally settled in Wasco, just south of The Dalles, moving north across the Columbia into Washington Territory in the late 1850s. It is possible he assisted Tingley in 1863 to purchase horses in the Willamette River valley. At the time, there was an abundance of horses in the valley, most of which were a cross between the small, agile cow ponies the Indigenous people of Oregon had been raising for decades, and the larger breeds of horses used to pull wagons or carry people over the Oregon Trail. Though less agile, these mixed-blood horses were strong and able to sustain a good pace over long distances.

The financial success of Barnard's 1863 express business meant he could purchase the best stagecoach horses. Tingley negotiated a price for about 160 head of horses and hired some men to help

Barnard's Express stage, starting from Yale, 1866. Note the canvas roof on
the stagecoach, typical of the first stagecoaches in BC. UL_1001_0018,
UNO LANGMANN FAMILY COLLECTION OF BRITISH COLUMBIA PHOTOGRAPHS,
RARE BOOKS AND SPECIAL COLLECTIONS, UBC LIBRARY

him drive them to British Columbia. The logical move was to take
the trail being used to drive thousands of head of cattle into British Columbia, either through the Yakima Valley or via Walla Walla,
joining the abandoned HBC brigade trail at Fort Okanagan. From
there the usual route was through the Okanagan Valley. Customs
records at Osoyoos show large herds of horses passing the customs
house in June and August of 1863. Tingley needed a place to pasture the horses as he trained them for pulling wagons. It is unlikely
he would bring them to the Fraser or Thompson River areas, where
feed and pasture were at a premium. We can surmise his actions
from what he did five years later, when he brought horses up from
California, pasturing and breaking them at Stump Lake on the
old fur-trade brigade trail in the Nicola Valley. Likely, he did the
same with those first horses through the winter of 1863-64, until
spring came and he could bring them to the stopping places on the
Cariboo Road.

That spring, Tingley had the job of distributing the horses to the various way stations, some south through the Fraser Canyon and the rest north to the stops on the way to Soda Creek. Barnard's agent, Robert T. Smith, reported meeting the stage horses at Lytton in mid-March.

Barnard had hired four men to drive the route between Yale and Soda Creek: Steve Tingley, driving from Yale to Nicomen; John Haskell, from Nicomen to Clinton; James Hamilton, from Clinton to Lac la Hache (111 Mile House); and Bill Freeman, the final stage to Soda Creek. Each man would drive the stage about sixty-five miles, a long day's drive.[5]

The first stage left Yale on Monday, March 21, but Tingley was still up the road distributing horses. So the honour of being the first driver on the new line fell to Charles Major, who was not actually a stage driver. He ran a pack train to the Cariboo and, on March 20, he was in Yale packing horses and mules when he was approached by Robert Poole, who ran express for Barnard from the Cariboo and asked if he could drive a four-horse team the next two days through to Clinton. Major agreed and, at seven o'clock the next morning, the four horses were hitched to the stagecoach, with nine passengers on board, including Mrs. Florence Wilson, who Major described as "a married lady from the States. I remember she looked quite delicate for that wild country." Florence Wilson was headed to Barkerville, where she would open a saloon and become an important figure in the cultural life of the city as its first librarian and a member of the Cariboo Amateur Dramatic Society, which performed in the Theatre Royal.[6]

Of course, the horses for that first run were quite "green" too, not entirely broken to pull heavily loaded stages, as Major was to find out. Just as they were ready to start, one of the horses decided to lie down. A "touch" with the whip got the horse not just up but on the run and, with a jerk, the stagecoach was off, making good time all the way to Boston Bar. On the next stretch, all went well until they reached Jackass Mountain, which had seven miles of the steepest grades on the entire road. Major recalled:

At Jackass mountain we were going fine until, at a narrow turn, we met an empty pack train coming down. I couldn't hold my horses in time, and the first two pack horses of the train backed in between my leaders. Then they commenced bucking—which is very inconvenient on a narrow road with a drop on one side of three thousand feet [a slight exaggeration] to the Fraser river. The brake wouldn't hold 'em on the down grade and my brutes went ahead full tilt with the two horses of the pack train stuck between 'em. An' they travelled!

We made that grade with the two cayuses buckin' an' kickin' all the time, but we made it, tangled up as up we were. Fortunately, at the bottom we ran into soft ground and I managed to get 'em checked. Then I looked over my shoulder. I'd been kind of occupied up to then. There wasn't a soul in that coach but Bob Poole, and he was as pale as a ghost. We'd shed the rest in the rush.

Major's nightmare drive wasn't quite over. From Nicomen, where the stage over-nighted, to the Cornwall brothers' ranch, called Ashcroft, only three horses were available. The gap was filled at Ashcroft with a half-wild horse. Once again, Charlie's memory was vivid:

At Ashcroft I was given a wild cayuse as a fourth ... and some of the passengers undertook to get him into the traces. I didn't help 'em. I didn't want my brains kicked out; I needed 'em for drivin'. Well, sir, they got him in at last, but the harness was so big he could almost jump through the collar. Finally we had to put him alongside a pole next a big steady fellow [horse] that could hold him in. I climbed on the box. It took six or seven men to get him to that pole, but they did it, and then had some fun hitching the traces. How he did kick! They shouted "Are you ready?" I yelled "Let 'em go!"—and they did. That cayuse went as far as from here to across the street—an' then lay down. It was a beautiful down grade with fine gravel. I cracked the whip at the other fellows and away they went and dragged him on his side for four hundred yards. By that time he'd had enough, and got up, but there wasn't a hair left on one side of him! By golly, he was a sight! But we had a good trip the rest of the way.[7]

By the time Major had finished this historic run, Steve Tingley had finished distributing horses to the stopping houses along the line and so was available to drive for the trip down from Soda Creek.

TRUSTED TO CARRY GOLD, MAIL, AND EXPRESS MATTER

In March of 1864, the *Government Gazette* announced, "Notice is hereby given that a Contract has been entered into with Francis Jones Barnard, (Barnard's Express) for the conveyance of GOVERN-MENT MAILS." There followed a schedule of deliveries, including "From 1st April to 30th November: From New Westminster to Douglas, Hope, Yale, Lytton and Lillooet and return weekly." Following that was a list of the same places with "Williams Lake and on to Antler and return semi monthly." From December 1 to March 31, delivery to the first list was reduced to semi-monthly and the second to monthly.[8] The mail contract signed the previous year with Barnard was still in effect until the end of May.

In the meantime, Governor James Douglas retired and his successor, Frederick Seymour, whose jurisdiction was solely the mainland Colony of British Columbia, was installed. One of Seymour's first official acts was to announce that he would proceed with passing a postal ordinance for British Columbia. The original postal contract with Barnard, probably never officially signed, was declared null and void and, in May, new tenders were called for by the postmaster general for the colony, Warner Spalding.

Before any decision was made on the new contract, the postal ordinance was passed by the Legislative Council on May 2 and received assent from the new governor two days later. Among its many regulations, the Act stipulated that "the private carriage of letters and other mailable matter, without the previous payment of the full rates of postage prescribed by the Ordinance, was made punishable by fine," but the postmaster general's sole and exclusive privilege of conveying the public correspondence was not insisted upon.[9] In layman's terms, this meant the government insisted in taxing all mail matter but would not interfere with express operators carrying the mail. Express agents and private persons had to prepay and put postage stamps on all mail, ensuring the government some income. Anyone who informed the government of a breach in this law was entitled to half the fine of from £5 to £50 ($25.34 to $253.40).

The new postal ordinance also provided for new post offices at Clinton, Lac la Hache, Soda Creek, Quesnelle Mouth, and Van Winkle in addition to the Cariboo head office at Williams Creek. Constables and other government officials acted as postmasters.

Together, Barnard and his new partners, Dietz and Nelson, had a virtual monopoly on the express business in British Columbia. In early June, it was announced that they were awarded a twelve-month contract for carrying the mail at a rate of £5,000 ($25,340). The *British Colonist* gushed, "The high position all three have obtained in this colony as honest, enterprising and active business men is a sufficient guarantee for the faithful performance of the service."[10] Under the new contract, the mail was carried from New Westminster to Hope, Yale, and Douglas twice a week, to Lytton and Lillooet once a week, and to Williams Creek via Clinton and Quesnelle Mouth three times per month from March through October, and once a month the rest of the year.[11]

While this is the schedule by which mail was carried, express letters, which all had to have postage stamps, were carried by every stage going up and down the Cariboo Road and over the trail to Williams Lake twice a week. Envelopes with "Barnard's Express" in one corner could be purchased for one dollar at any stage stop along the way, and express envelopes were still the preferred method of mail delivery, faster than regular mail. Since Barnard's Express was making two trips a week all the way to Williams Creek, this advantage did not go unnoticed. The grand jury, convened in Richfield on Williams Creek in November to advise the colonial government, noted the discrepancy. While complimenting Barnard for having "faithfully performed the conditions" of the contract, the jury concluded "that better arrangements might have been made" and, "on Mr. Barnard's contract expiring, which it does in the early part of next summer, that great care should be taken so as to ensure the public the advantage of having the mails brought to the creek at the same time, and as often as the Express." They had "reason to believe that there is an un-necessary delay somewhere... which induces the public to patronize the Express in preference to the mail, with letters from Williams Creek to Victoria and intervening points."[12]

Barnard was not long in replying to the grand jury. In a November 18 letter to the editor in the *British Colonist*, he clarified his position:

> The mail contract called for a service three times per month to Williams Creek... The Victoria and New Westminster steamers, the up-river steamers to Douglas and Yale, and the steamer from Soda Creek, made two trips per week; the stages over the portages to Clinton, and from Yale *via* Clinton to Soda Creek, also made two trips per week, so that a regular semi-weekly communication was kept up between Victoria and Quesnelle Mouth. Now, it appeared to me preposterous that so regular and frequent a communication should exist to within fifty miles of the principle business place of the colony [Williams Creek], and no further. I, therefore, determined to complete the line by running a semi-weekly newspaper and package express from Quesnelle Mouth to Williams Creek. To have refused to carry letters would have been an act of injustice to the business community, who are my chief supporters, and indeed it needed the letter business to render it at all remunerative. Thus, then, the express arrived semi-weekly, whilst the mail only arrived semi-monthly. The presumption on the part of a few individuals was, that the mail was held over to serve the purposes of the express. This was not the case as I am prepared to prove.[13]

Of course, Barnard was right. He had no need to "tip the scales" in his favour because the contract already did that. By contract, he had agreed to supply the regular mail to Williams Creek three times a month, but he ran an express business there twice a week. The customer's choice was clear.

The arrival of the express was always an event at the stopping houses on the Cariboo Road. Everyone knew when the stage arrived and there was a rush to the agent's office to check for mail. The agent would stand behind the counter, open the bundle of Barnard's Express envelopes, and begin reading the name of each recipient out loud. There would be a loud cry of "Here!" and the agent would spin the envelope through the air, leaving the excited recipient to recover the letter from wherever it landed. This routine was the same at every express office, from Victoria to Williams Creek.

In 1863, the "official" returns of gold recovered in the Cariboo amounted to a staggering $3,913,563, and that did not account for the gold carried out by individual miners, which probably represented another 3 million dollars. Transporting this gold safely was an ongoing concern and, that year, Governor Douglas tried for a second time to establish a Gold Escort of fifteen men. But, as Barnard pointed out in a letter that summer, "The Bank of British Columbia... send all dust & coin by the Gold Escort which was principally established on their account. This same escort is going to be a grand fizzler. It will need $600,000 in treasure each trip to pay their running expenses. This they cannot get... Their price is about $3/16$ per cent. Ours now is $2\frac{1}{2}$ to 2 from Richfield to Vic."[14] Despite the government's more favourable rate, it was not able to guarantee safe delivery of the gold as could the express agents, so the miners still preferred the express companies. It was suggested that the Gold Escort should carry the mail as soon as Barnard's contract expired, but the escort to Williams Creek and back took six weeks, much too slow for the mail. The Gold Escort made four trips from Williams Creek that year. The first brought down about $40,000 in gold, which seemed impressive enough until compared with the $103,000 that Barnard's Express carried down in the same period. Altogether, the four trips carried $281,000 in gold at a cost of $60,000 and revenue of $9,000.[15] Having lost a significant amount of money in a misguided attempt to provide a service that was already available, the government left the field to Barnard.

In the same letter mentioned above, Barnard related an incident that occurred that summer:

> There has been no murdering this season so far. A report of two men being stopped [by suspicious men] above Mitchells Bridge at the North Fork [was reported] at the Forks of Quesnelle and made some of the boys quake. They were brave enough however to send word to me by a man going out, to keep a sharp watch... The message reached me at evening 3 miles from the bridge and I was bound to make the Forks that night. I offered to engage men but no go. I had 75 lbs. dust with me and felt a kind of weakening in the pins, at last succeeded and got the Capt. of the *Emily Harris* [steamship] to come in with me. We walked along pistol and shot gun in hand and made the Forks at 10 p.m.... The party had described a villain that had been at the forks for a week or so. I saw him as I went up [toward Williams Creek]. I concluded not to let him near me or meet me on my way down. He left the Forks three days after me and was seen two days later at the bridge. I did not meet him at all and missed him by turning off the trail round Cariboo Lake to Louke's House [on Cariboo Lake]. He was met on the direct trail at the same time. He was in luck that I did not see him first for I would have fired on sight. He was an old jailbird and I knew it. I was in luck that he did not see me or he might & likely would have let me smell his powder. This thing of taking a peep down the barrel of a six shooter... I am down on it. Ugh!![16]

Of the literal tons of gold that were carried by Barnard's and Dietz and Nelson to Victoria in 1863, their record was near perfect. The gold from the Cariboo was carried by Barnard's Express as far as Yale, where it was consigned to Dietz and Nelson, who shipped it by express on a steamer to Victoria. There, it was deposited with

Wells Fargo. On September 11, 1863, the steamer *Reliance* was pulling away from the dock at Yale when the Dietz and Nelson express agent realized he had not handed the leather express bag over to the purser of the *Reliance*. In a panic, the agent grabbed the express bag, ran to the dock, commandeered a canoe, and paddled out to the steamer, which was just in the process of turning to face downriver. The captain of the *Reliance* shouted down to the deck and someone ran to connect with the canoe. As the express agent teetered in his canoe reaching up to the deck of the steamer, the express bag slipped from his hand and, weighted down by about twenty pounds of gold, sank quickly to the bottom. It was later learned that there was $3,700 worth of gold in the bag. George Dietz was quick to assure all concerned that "the amounts will be promptly paid over at their office in Victoria the same as though no accident occurred." It was estimated that the Fraser River was thirty feet (nine metres) deep at the point the bag had been dropped. So Dietz waited for the water level to fall and, in the meantime, looked for some way of searching the murky bottom of the river. In Victoria, he located what the local press called "sub-marine armor," probably an underwater diving suit, consisting of a metal helmet attached to a heavily waxed canvas body that was supplied air from a pump on the surface, used for marine salvage work. In early November, when the Fraser was slightly lower and clearer, Dietz went down into the water in search of the elusive express bag. Unfortunately, he was unable to ascertain exactly where the bag had been lost and, after a week of searching the bottom of the river, he abandoned the search. The bag, containing about $300,000 at today's prices, probably still rests deep in the mud of the Fraser River bottom some 150 years after being lost.[17]

The following year Barnard, in an effort to make the trip safe for the "treasure," had his stagecoaches equipped with massive steel strongboxes, described in detail in the *British Colonist*:

Acting upon the suggestion of one of our most prominent merchants here, Mr. Barnard has fitted an iron, burglar proof safe into each of his wagons, and bolted it securely to its bed. Not resting content with this precaution he has had the chests constructed with detonating powder in the interstices. The safes are also fitted with combination locks, known only to the principals at each termini, and no amount of intimidation exercised on a captured Expressman could force from him a secret which had not been entrusted to him. The skill, labor, ingenuity and perseverance with which the whole scheme has been elaborated, and the well known partiality which the miners entertain for their plucky friend, warrant us in believing that Francis Jones Barnard will in a few years be one of the most important men in that rising Colony.[18]

In February, Barnard wrote to Governor Douglas, suggesting that "a mounted police of four men be established in the Cariboo district from the Mouth of Quesnelle to Williams Creek."[19] After serious consideration, the government decided that Barnard's Express should provide this security. Barnard reluctantly agreed and on one of the first trips from Williams Creek to Quesnelle Mouth, he provided "an escort of eight armed men" and carried out $150,000 in gold dust. Four of the men were provided with double-barrelled shotguns that Barnard had obtained from the former Gold Escort.[20] The Cariboo correspondent for the *British Colonist* declared that "this escort is a new feature in our express business, and the result predicted last year that private enterprise would supplant the efforts of the Government in this direction, has been verified."[21]

For the stagecoach trip down from Soda Creek, Barnard provided a guard armed with a rifle. The first man to fill that position was named Ormandy and he was succeeded by James Reid, who afterward became the Barnard's Express agent in Quesnelle Mouth. No one was fooled into thinking an armed man, even with a loaded rifle, could protect a well-filled treasure box from an attack by a gang of robbers. But, probably due to the isolation of the road and the limited paths of escape, no holdup took place for the next twenty years. In the first year of operating the four-horse stages from Yale, Barnard's Express had established itself as a reliable and efficient business, prompting the New Westminster *British Columbian* to sing its praises:

> It only remains to give a few figures, in order to afford the reader an idea of the present magnitude of the institution, and the success with which it has met under the able management of Mr. Barnard and Messrs. Dietz & Nelson. The number of miles traveled during the present year is 110,600. Number of men employed, exclusive of agents whose time is not entirely devoted to the Express, 38. Number of horses employed in the Express service, 160. Number of Expresses despatched from the head office in New Westminster during the present year, 450. Total amount of treasure during the present year, $4,619,000.[22]

Barnard's 1864 contract required mail delivery to Williams Creek once a month from the end of October until the end of February, and during those winter months the express earned its wages in full. One of the most difficult trips ever recorded took place that winter. When Barnard's expressman Robert Poole set out from Williams Creek on December 12, the thermometer read –26 degrees Fahrenheit (–32 Celsius) and the snow lay a foot deep, with cold so intense that all mining on the creek stopped. The trip over the mountain to Van Winkle on Lightning Creek was through two feet of snow. From Cottonwood House, Allen Smith, who operated the roadhouse, had managed to keep a good sleigh road open all the way to Quesnelle Mouth. With a sleigh and horses, Poole arrived there on the fourteenth, when the thermometer stood at –18 (–28 Celsius). After taking the steamboat to Soda Creek, he set out again by sleigh, the snow and cold making a coach impractical. He arrived at Felker's 127 Mile House stopping place at the north end of Lac la Hache, where the temperature had fallen to –38 (–39 Celsius). From there to the Fraser Canyon, Poole made reasonable time but the snow kept falling and avalanches made travel through the canyon almost impossible. Again and again, Poole had to dig out a passage through the snow wide enough for his horses and sleigh.

The Steamship *Enterprise* docked at Soda Creek before travelling north to Quesnelle Mouth. LIBRARY AND ARCHIVES CANADA, MIKAN 3308377, C-004965

When he arrived at Yale on December 27, the snow had reached a depth of three feet and continued to fall. The *British Colonist*, in recounting this epic fifteen-day journey, called it "perhaps the greatest amount of hardship ever experienced by an express messenger on the route."[23]

BARNARD LINKS TO BARKERVILLE WITH THE CARIBOO STAGE COMPANY

In 1864, the Cariboo Road was completed from Yale and Lillooet to Clinton, where the two roads connected. From there, the single road ran as far as Soda Creek, where travellers and freight were loaded on the steamer *Enterprise*. The steamer had been constructed by Gustavus Blin Wright, who had also overseen construction of the wagon road from Lillooet to Soda Creek. The *Enterprise* travelled to Quesnelle Mouth, later known as Quesnel. From there, the trip to Barkerville, the booming heart of the Cariboo, had to be completed on foot or horseback. The heavily travelled trail was horrible—one hundred miles of mudholes and fallen trees. Despite its greater distance, the well-used pack trail via Quesnelle Forks and over the Snowshoe Plateau was preferred by many miners and packers. In the summer, the plateau had abundant grass for horses, and in winter it was easier to pack goods into Beaver Lake and transport them by sleigh or on backs by snowshoe.

In 1865, Barnard saw an opportunity to control transportation through to Barkerville. He wanted a service over the entire Cariboo Road, so he arranged for three of his employees, William Humphrey, Robert Poole, and Aaron Johnson, to organize the Cariboo Stage Company. Commonly referred to as Humphrey, Poole and Johnson, it would cover the route from Quesnelle Mouth to Barkerville.

Poole and Humphrey had been Barnard's expressmen for the Cariboo and had played a vital role in the success of his business. Dr. Cheadle, the Englishman who was accompanying Lord Milton across the continent in 1863, had met both of these expressmen two years earlier, when they had been in charge of the express wagons from the Cariboo to Yale. They had paid to ride from Davidson's Lake Valley Ranch (150 Mile House) as passengers on Barnard's two-horse express wagon with Poole as driver. Three days later, they reached the 79-mile post in a snowstorm. The wagons and drivers were changed and they rode the rest of the way to Yale with Humphrey. The trip was not without incident. After three days on the road, the wagon broke down near the bridge at Spuzzum. Fortunately, the express wagon from Lillooet, driven by W.T. Smith, was just passing by and Humphrey hitched a ride to Yale, leaving Milton and Cheadle to guard the express. Cheadle described the trip through the canyon in darkness:

Humphreys [*sic*] returned with other waggon & extra horses which
we hitched on in front. Humphreys had brought a bottle of brandy
& was greatly exhilarated, had never driven 4 in hand before. Off
we went, however we went rattling down hill along the edge of
precipices at an awful pace. Humphreys holding the reins, Smith
sitting beside, whipping up & passing the brandy. Milton and I
were in a funk at first, but seeing that the leaders took all the turns
to perfection without guiding, felt relieved & half dozed into Yale
where we arrived at ½ past 10, having come the 14 miles in about
two hours.[24]

The third owner of the Cariboo Stage Company, Aaron Johnson, had looked after the express wagon from Lillooet the previous
year. As the road from Quesnel to Cottonwood had been completed
the previous summer, Johnson was to drive a stage on that stretch.
Humphrey was in charge of the pack trains to Barkerville, and Poole
the saddle trains. The *British Colonist* reported:

A company comprised of these three young men will possess an
amount of energy and practical experience which can hardly fail
to ensure success. The *Reliance* carried up yesterday a splendid
new stage built by Duck & Sandover of Victoria, and is calculated
on a pinch to seat sixteen persons. For the present the coaches
will be run twice a week between Quesnelmouth and Cottonwood,
connecting with the steamer *Enterprise* at the former place, and
with a saddle train to Williams Creek at the latter place.[25]

TRAVELLING UP THE ROAD IN 1865

James Buie Leighton, who was to spend his life in British Columbia—
much of it in employment with Barnard's and the BC Express
companies—first travelled up the Cariboo Road as a young man.
Despite being only thirteen years old at the time, Leighton would
retain and record vivid memories of this trip.[26] His account of the

stagecoach run provides an excellent overview of the early days of Barnard's Express.

Leighton left Yale on June 2, 1865, at six o'clock in the morning on a stage packed with mail and passengers, Steve Tingley driving. The first leg of the journey was a run of some eighteen miles to Chapman's Bar, where the horses were changed out at William Alexander's "Chapman's Bar House." Originally from Indiana, Alexander had been there since the booming days of 1858.[27] Another seven miles brought the stage to Boston Bar, where they stopped for lunch at the International Hotel, run by "Boston Bar Alex" Coutlie, considered one of the best stops on the road.[28]

After an excellent lunch, the well-fed passengers piled into the stagecoach for the next leg. Horses were again changed, at George and William Boothroyd's "Forest House," named not for the surrounding forest but after the maiden name of George Boothroyd's wife.[29] The stage laboured up and over Jackass Mountain, covering only eleven miles before reaching Kanaka Bar, so named after the Native Hawaiians who had worked for the Hudson's Bay Company during fur-trade times. Kanaka Bar House was operated by Eugene Combe and Charles Sadoux, who "opened a stopping house and had a liquor license as they all did along the Cariboo Road. They sent home to France for alfalfa seed and planted it at Kanaka. By 1865, they had a good field of it. They supplied the stage horses, also the freight teams that stopped overnight."[30]

But the stage only stopped there to change horses and head up the Fraser to Lytton, which was reached between five and six o'clock and where supper was taken at the Globe Hotel, owned by Louis Vincent Hautier, a Belgian.[31] At Nicomen, sixty-nine miles from Yale, drivers as well as horses were changed up. Tingley handed the whip over to John Haskell and waited to take over the stage from Soda Creek and drive it to Yale.

Haskell drove the eleven miles from Nicomen to Spences Bridge, previously been known as Cook's Ferry, where Mortimer Cook ran a ferry across the Thompson River and kept a roadhouse. But Thomas Spence had completed construction of the bridge the previous

March and Cook had sold out to T.G. Kirkpatrick, who now operated the stopping house. Once again, the horses were changed. Twelve miles on, at the 92-mile post, the horses were again changed in what Leighton would describe as "a rather peculiarly constructed stable. At this point there was a high culvert on the road and this the B.X. had boarded up to make their stable!"

By then the long spring day would have turned into night and the stage kept on in darkness. Passengers, already tired and cranky from a full day, had no opportunity to stretch their legs without contacting another tired individual, whose response would be less than charitable. As Leighton put it, "travelling all night in a stage coach is dreary work." The best that could be hoped for was to sleep in snatches and pray for dawn. This being June, the night was short and at six o'clock in the morning, long after daybreak, the stage pulled into Ashcroft House at the 104-mile post from Yale, built by the two Cornwall brothers two years earlier. There the passengers enjoyed a substantial breakfast before facing a new day of travel. Fresh horses were hitched up and changed again at Hat Creek, at the 117-mile post, and then at Kay's 129 Mile House. All mile posts described the distance from Yale but, once Clinton was reached, a new set measured the distance from Lillooet, the start of the original trail to the Cariboo.

At Clinton, the 47-mile post from Lillooet, "all hands were allowed several hours for rest, this respite being given on account of this place being the meeting station of the up and down stages. During our period of rest the stage came in from Cariboo, driven by James Hamilton." As the drivers and agent arranged freight on the two stages, passengers from both had an opportunity to eat lunch at the Clinton Hotel.

"When all was ready fresh horses were hitched up and we left Clinton about 4 in the afternoon with Hamilton handling the ribbons." Hamilton drove through the night, changing horses at the 59-, 74- and 88-mile posts, before heading down the hill to 100 Mile House, also called Bridge Creek House, named when cattle-drover brothers John and Oliver Jeffries first used the area for holding cattle

Northbound and southbound stages meeting at Clinton.

and built a log structure there as a stopping house and store. The stage pushed on from 100 Mile House to the 111-mile post, where breakfast was taken and Bill Freeman took over the reins for the remainder of the journey to Soda Creek. After four more changes of horses, the stage pulled into Soda Creek, some 266 miles and sixty-two hours travelling from Yale—the end of the stage ride, but far from the destination.

At Soda Creek, passengers were transferred to the steamer *Enterprise,* described by Dr. Cheadle as "built on the river, all the timber sawn by hand, the shaft in 5 pieces packed on mules, cylinders in two, boiler plate brought in the same manner. Boat cost $75,000!"[32] Mail and express packages were loaded on deck alongside piles of freight and the passengers, once they had stretched their cramped legs, headed for whatever sleeping arrangements they had made, even though the steamer did not cast off until three o'clock in the

morning. It was slow work against the Fraser River current but, with
Captain Gustavus Blin Wright at the wheel, the steamer pushed
upstream. It was not until four o'clock the next afternoon that it
reached Quesnelle Mouth.

Once again, the passengers boarded a stagecoach, this one operated by Humphrey, Poole, and Johnson. With Aaron Johnson driving,
the stage made its way to Cottonwood House, where the passengers
were greeted at a new two-storey log stopping house built for Allen
"Cottonwood" Smith, so called to distinguish him among the multitude of Smiths along the road. Unfortunately, all was not well with
Mr. Smith's new roadhouse, as he had defaulted on his short-term
mortgage and would lose the house on July 1.[33] In spite of this news,
the passengers enjoyed an excellent night's sleep in the new house.
As Cottonwood was the end of the wagon road, the final stretch to
Barkerville was over a rough trail on horseback. Thirteen-year-old
James Leighton was somewhat disappointed when they reached
Halfway, or "Pine Grove," House, operated by Edward F. Edwards.
His description of the occasion is worth quoting in full:

> While on the stage between Quesnel and Cottonwood, the writer
> heard his fellow passengers talking about someone whom they
> called Bloody Edwards, and this aroused his curiosity. Before
> leaving Cottonwood, Pool [sic] told the writer to stop at Bloody
> Edwards' place at Pine Grove for lunch. Bloody Edwards! The very
> name conjured up visions of a man covered with blood, and the
> desire to see this strange spectacle overcame every other feeling.
> When the writer arrived there he expected to see a man dripping
> with gore, but instead saw only a small, mild-mannered man
> without a sign of blood about him! Taking his horse to the stable
> the writer went into the house and found several people gath-
> ered there. He made enquiries for this Bloody Edwards and then
> learned that Edwards was so-called because he had the habit, like
> so many of his class, of an indiscriminate use of the word bloody:
> every article he spoke of had the adjective "bloody" prefixed to it.
> This explanation knocked on the head all the preconceived ideas

of what this formidably-named hotelkeeper would look like, and the writer was intensely relieved. Judge Begbie was wont to refer to him as "Sanguinary" Edwards.[34]

Leighton elaborated on his short stop at Edwards's Halfway House: "For his lunch at Pine Grove the writer paid $1.50 and $1.50 for the feed of hay for his horse. The charge for beds was the same figure, $1.50. There was one uniform form of dessert served at that time all along the Cariboo road, dried-apple pie; sometimes it had currents in it. This uniformity obviated a difficulty in deciding on the question of what seat to have!"[35]

Edwards's stopping house had the distinct disadvantage of not being in a location conducive to raising its own produce and animals. This lack was exacerbated when traffic on the trail lessened the following year. He had to sell his house for a song and the reign of "Bloody" Edwards came to an end.

The horseback travellers spent one last night at Van Winkle on Lightning Creek before arriving at Barkerville on the morning of June 10 at ten o'clock, having taken five days and four hours to travel from Yale to Williams Creek.

James B. Leighton, as the only youngster in Barkerville, was called "The Boy" and went on to spend the next twenty-nine years on the Cariboo Road. He was a telegraph operator at various stops along the road and spent sixteen years with the BC Express, successor to Barnard's Express, as "special" driver, purchasing agent, and express agent before becoming superintendent for eight more years.

STAGES COMPETE FOR THE BIG BEND RUSH

By 1865, a significant change had taken place in gold-mining techniques. This was especially true on Williams Creek, considered the heart of the Cariboo, where the gold "lead" was found deep in the overlaying gravel. No longer could a single miner with a gold pan or a rocker box expect to make a fortune. Throughout the Cariboo mines large companies were now required to extract the gold—companies with enough capital to build flumes, waterwheels, shafts, ditches, and tunnels. For this reason, the mining season in 1865 got off to a slow start. The usual rush of miners from San Francisco never happened. Warehouses in Victoria and New Westminster remained crowded with imported goods, and merchants who had extended credit to prospective miners struggled to survive.

Therefore, the news that gold had been discovered on the "Big Bend" on the Columbia River was greeted with enthusiasm. The first mention of this discovery reached the *British Colonist* early in the year and, on May 1, the paper reported that "great numbers of people are making their way up the Columbia towards Big Bend, in boats and canoes."[36] The government of the Colony of British Columbia, no longer under the leadership of James Douglas, saw the new discovery not as a benefit but as a new problem. The gold-field had been discovered by miners proceeding up the Columbia River from the Wild Horse Creek area in the Kootenays and was populated almost entirely by miners from the United States. The government saw the necessity, once again, to stay a step ahead of the Americans and provide a transportation network to the Big Bend. This involved further expenditure in building a road from Cache Creek along the Thompson River to Savona's Ferry and, from there, providing steam navigation on Kamloops Lake, the South Thompson, and Shuswap Lake. Pressure was added when businessmen from Portland, Oregon, announced their intention to put steamers on the Upper Columbia River.

As usual, Barnard viewed the new discovery as an opportunity and, as early as mid-May, Barnard's Express advertised that "passengers for the Great Bend Diggings on the Columbia River can take these stages to Cache Creek, foot of Lake Kamloops, 110 miles above Yale. Awaiting the completion of the Hudson Bay Co.'s steamer, small boats will ply over Lakes Kamloops and Shuswap to within sixty miles of the Great Bend Diggings!"[37]

Barnard extended his express service to the new mines, placing his first express in the hands of W.S. Stone. When Stone first returned from the new mines, he wrote from Clinton on August 7 that, because of high water, the miners were idle. Stone found about 120 men on the different creeks, "a large number of whom are Fraser River fifty-eighters." Because the miners were awaiting low water, the express did not meet with success. Stone reported:

> I arrived here after an absence of three weeks, during which time I have been employed in carrying Barnard's Express on its first trip to the mining camp on the Columbia. It is needless to say that, as an express messenger, I was well received: joy filled the hearts of the hardy fellows who had struck their tents and made for so desolate a region. As there was not a cent in the crowd, the express trip, financially was a failure, so I made the best of it by giving the boys a free read of what was going on in the outer world. I found all hands in excellent spirits, none were dejected or cast down and confidence was as fully maintained in the richness of the diggings as it could be... I believe it is Mr. Barnard's intention to send out another express about the 1st of September. The Columbia is not navigable for steamers for 100 miles below the diggings. Yours truly, W.S. Stone.[38]

Throughout 1865, much was made of the potential of the Big Bend area and word spread through the Pacific Northwest, where miners would rush to the next "big discovery" in hopes that it would exceed all others. By the end of the year, the editor of the *British Colonist* proclaimed that "the news which we publish today from Big Bend is the most cheering of any intelligence yet received in the colony, not even excepting the announcement of the discovery of Cariboo."[39]

The great road-builder Gustavus B. Wright was contracted by the government to construct the road from Cache Creek to Savona. Walter Moberly was contracted to construct a thirty-five-mile wagon road to connect the head of Shuswap Lake with the Columbia River, and this was completed by year end. The Hudson's Bay Company, not wanting to miss out on the excitement, constructed a lake steamer, the *Martin*, at Savona's Ferry to carry passengers as far as the proposed new town at the north end of Shuswap Lake. The town was originally called Ogden, but later renamed Seymour City after the new governor. Not to be outdone, Oregon and Washington interests began the construction of their own steamer, the *Forty-Nine*, on the Columbia at Marcus, Washington. With the year 1866 shaping up to be "the Year of the Big Bend," competition over the best route to the new mines grew fierce. Ads were published in the *British Colonist* pointing out that the distance to the Big Bend from Victoria was 473 miles (766 kilometres), compared to the distance from Portland of 752 miles (1,218 kilometres).

As the only carrier from Yale to the Big Bend connection at Savona's Ferry, Barnard was in an enviable position. Like any wise businessman, he kept his fares high and made three stage runs a week from Yale to Savona's Ferry (regularly spelled "Savana's" in the press), all operated at capacity. But his monopoly didn't last. On April 30, an advertisement appeared in the newly established Yale *Tribune* for what was called the "Opposition Line of Stages—Savana's Ferry! Stages will leave Yale on the arrival of steamers for Savana's Ferry, carrying passengers and express freight at REDUCED RATES. Jacob Davis, Proprietor."[40] Clearly, this new stage line had only one competitor.

Throughout the 1866 mining season, Jacob Davis's Opposition Line went "head to head" with Barnard's Express to transport passengers to the Big Bend. Barnard was quick to respond to the challenge and dropped his fares to $25, only to have Davis drop his fares even lower, causing the *Tribune* to report, "During the past week fares on the stages from Yale to Savana's Ferry were only $15. As a matter of course they were well patronized by the miners."[41] These fares were prohibitively low and did not even cover costs, probably more to the detriment of Davis than Barnard. Within a few weeks, both competitors settled for the very low fare of $25 to Savona's Ferry.

The battle proceeded to play itself out in the pages of the *Tribune*. Davis had the support of George Wallace, who published the *Cariboo Sentinel* in Barkerville with the support of Victoria entrepreneurs;

he sold it and then started publishing the *Tribune* that spring. He saw fit to publish a letter in successive editions of the *Tribune* to cast Barnard's Express in the worst light.

> We, the undersigned passengers by Davis' Stage Line from Savana's Ferry to Yale, beg to inform the public, through the medium of the press, that in our late trip down from the mines to this place, we received the best treatment from the proprietor of Davis' well conducted line of stages ... We think the people should support a line of stages that carries passengers for $15, in opposition to a monopoly line that, when it had the power in the beginning of the season, before Davis' line went on, extorted $40! from the helpless traveler for the same trip ... As it is for the interest of the country to break down the monopoly of the staging in this colony that has kept up fares to an extortionate height, and to keep up a healthy competition in this as well as other branches of business, we would urge all persons going up or coming down from the mines to give Davis' line support on account of its cheapness, rapidity of conveyance and comfort.[42]

Barnard's reaction was to cancel all advertising in the *Tribune* and increase his advertising in the New Westminster *British Columbian* just down the river, owned and published by John Robson. Initially, Robson published a balanced article on the two rival stage lines: "Barnard has a stage running, and there is an opposition stage, fare by either $25; Barnard's runs night and day, stopping only for meals, making it a most trying and fatiguing journey of 36 hours. The opposition stops for the night on the road, starting at 4½ or 5 in the morning, and is some 10 hours longer on the road, arriving in ample time for the steamer."[43]

Insult was added to injury when, at the end of July, Davis announced his establishment of "Opposition Stages to Cariboo!" His first advertisement in the *Tribune* went into great detail.

> Who will the Public Support? The man who charged $80 to Soda Creek when he had a Monopoly, or the man who brought down the

fares to $40? The UNDERSIGNED has well appointed Stages on the road to Soda Creek, which are guaranteed to make faster time than any other line. He has brought down the fares to $40 and the public ought to see that it is [in] their own interest to support and maintain a cheap and efficient Opposition... The line through to Cariboo will shortly be in operation. Jacob Davis.[44]

Since that spring, the American steamer the *Forty-Nine* had been travelling from Marcus, Washington, just above Kettle Falls, through the Arrow Lakes to the foot of Dalles des Morts (Death Rapids). Not to be outdone, by July the HBC's *Martin* was picking up passengers from Barnard's Express stagecoaches at Savona's Ferry and taking them to Seymour City. Barnard also ran a regular express to the Big Bend and his "large express canoes were making regular trips, and were well patronized" with passengers wanting to find a cheaper way to the new goldfield.[45] In its extensive promotion of the British Columbia route to the Big Bend over the route from the US, the *British Colonist* advertised "the following Statistics, respecting the probable Time and Expenses in Travelling from VICTORIA TO BIG BEND... compiled by Mr. F.J. Barnard, the well known British Columbia Express Agent and Stage Proprietor"[46]:

Victoria to Yale by stagecoach, distance, time, and cost

	DIST.	TIME	RATES	MEALS
Victoria to Yale	175 mi.	24 hrs	$4	$6
Yale to Kamloops Lake	133 mi.	24 hrs	$40	$5
Over the Lakes	120 mi.	15 hrs	$10	$4
Head of Lake to Columbia River	35 mi.	18 hrs		$9
Total number of hours travelling	81 mi.			
Total cost	**$78**			

Once the snow was gone on the road from Seymour City to the Columbia, the miners flooded in. Between eight and ten thousand miners were estimated to have travelled to the Big Bend. In June, Walter Moberly laid out a townsite for French City on French Creek, and the small town of Kirbyville sprang up on Goldstream Creek. Other towns appeared on McCulloch Creek and at Wilson's Landing, boasting the usual stores, saloons, billiard halls, and other businesses. By fall, most of the creeks had been tested and the shallow diggings exhausted. But the large volume of water in the creeks and the many boulders meant there was little chance of extracting the gold from deep diggings.

By the end of 1866, the Big Bend gold rush was over and only a handful of miners remained. In 1869, H.M. Ball, in his report on the mining activities in the Kootenay area, reported only about thirty or forty miners on French Creek and none on the other creeks.[47] Despite its short lifespan, the Big Bend excitement is estimated to have yielded about 3 million dollars in gold in the two years of activity.[48]

After the initial Big Bend rush, Barnard hired Moses Lumby to continue carrying the mail to Fort Kamloops and on to the Big Bend. From 1867 to 1871, he carried a large sack of mail and express matter on his back, and walked from Cache Creek to Savona's Ferry. Then, as the steamer *Martin* lay idle due to costly freight rates and expensive repairs, he rowed the remaining 127 miles (204 kilometres) to Kamloops and then beyond, to Seymour City at the head of Seymour Arm. Lumby eventually became the government agent in Vernon.

When traffic to the Big Bend diminished, so did the threat of Jacob Davis and his Opposition Line. While he had invested heavily in hopes that the Big Bend traffic would continue, he lacked the necessary stagecoaches and horses to match Barnard, especially on the long route to Barkerville. Once again, Barnard had the field to himself.

THE ROAD TO BARKERVILLE COMPLETED

In October of 1865, the newly established *Cariboo Sentinel* announced that "the new road from Cottonwood is now open for traffic. Whilst the road appears to be generally well made, yet there are spots which are even worse with mud than the old trail. It would seem as if the drainage, which is so essential to the making of a firm road, had been greatly neglected. We are apprehensive that it will be a long time before waggons can pass over it." The editor of the *Sentinel* expressed concern that there would be only one mail and express delivery a month to the Cariboo. He also noted that "we feel it only due to the mail contractor, Mr. Barnard, to state that he has carried out his contract during the summer to the entire satisfaction of the public in this district. We have not heard a single complaint against him during the season, which is highly creditable to the contraction. It is only justice to Messrs. Humphrey, Pool [*sic*] and Johnson, who carry the mail from Quesnelmouth, to state that they have performed their part with promptitude and efficiency that is highly commendable. On their part of the road not a single mistake or delay has occurred." [49]

Through the following winter, Barnard was able to deliver mail and passengers with sleighs. The winter turned out to be a hard one, with heavy snows making the roads impassable through most of the Cariboo. By March of 1866 the snow was so deep in the Fraser Canyon that Barnard had to provide passengers with saddle horses to get through from Yale to Boston Bar until the road from Yale was open. [50] Late in the spring, the snow still lay deep in the Fraser Canyon and at higher elevations in the Cariboo.

When the hot weather finally arrived, it brought flooded creeks and rivers throughout the colony. At the beginning of June, the bridge over the Bonaparte River at Cache Creek was washed away and portions of the Cariboo and Savona roads were washed out. [51] A few days later, Barnard's Express lost two of its fine stage horses, together with their harness, when attempting to ford a flooded part of the road in the Fraser Canyon near Rombrot's roadhouse,

Barnard's Express office in Barkerville, ca. 1867.
LIBRARY AND ARCHIVES CANADA, MIKAN 3306727, C-088919

sixteen miles from Yale. The floods also washed out portions of the
road north of Yale, forcing Barnard to reduce his stage trips through
the canyon to one a week until repairs could be made.

Early in 1866, Barnard "bought out" the Cariboo Stage Company that was run by the partnership of Humphrey, Poole, and
Johnson, which had operated the transportation from Quesnelle
Mouth to Williams Creek. Given that all three had been employees of Barnard and had received the sub-contract for mail delivery,
the arrangement had probably been a temporary one, with all three
offered employment with Barnard's Express. Poole later became the
Barnard's Express agent at Barkerville and, in 1869, married Elizabeth Hamilton, whose father ran the Halfway House on the road to
Barkerville between Cottonwood and Van Winkle.

In May, Barnard's agent John Lovell moved the office of Barnard's Express to Barkerville from Richfield, in recognition of its

role as "capital" of the Cariboo. Lovell advertised that the stage would leave once a week "carrying Treasure, Letters and Valuables to all parts of the world." The ad specified that the stage would "connect with the steamer 'Enterprise' at Quesnelmouth and the stages from Soda Creek."[52] This is surprising, as all accounts indicate that the road from Soda Creek to Quesnelle Mouth was complete and open to traffic, but the stage connected with the *Enterprise* all that year. Barnard also arranged for Joseph Spooner to set up a branch express business to visit the gold camps at Grouse, Stevens, Begge, Antler, Cunningham, and Keithley Creeks to pick up and deliver express matter in connection with Barnard's Express.

Barnard had not only won the transportation competition with Jacob Davis, he had established his express as the only reliable mode of travel up the Cariboo Road. At the end of the 1866 season, the *Cariboo Sentinel* mentioned that, beginning on November 2, there would be only one mail delivery to Williams Creek a month and noted that "there is now good sleighing from this creek as far as Edwards' Ranch ... the snow is 17 inches deep. Barnard's Express was brought in on a sleigh last trip." Elsewhere in the same edition, the editor wrote that "it is only due to Mr. Barnard to state that he has carried out his contract during the past summer with the greatest regularity, and to the entire satisfaction of this community."[53]

Finally, in May of 1867, Barnard's Express advertised that it would make the whole trip from Barkerville to Yale by road. This meant that the stagecoach run from Yale to Barkerville would cover 356 miles (572 kilometres) one way and 712 miles (1,146 kilometres) round trip, allowing some to boast that it was "the longest stage line in the world." This impressive statement is tempered by the end of the long stagecoach runs south of the border in 1869, when the Union Pacific Rail Road was finished. The most notable of these runs had been the Butterfield Overland Stage, which covered 1,920 miles (3,090 kilometres) from St. Louis, Missouri, to San Francisco between 1858 and 1861. A few years later, the brief-lived Butterfield Overland Dispatch covered 592 miles from Atchison, Kansas, to Denver, Colorado, in 1866 and 1867, until the railroad rendered it obsolete. So Barnard's Express and its later configuration, the BC Express, could claim the distinction of being, at least for a time, the longest stage run in North America. Meanwhile, Barnard, with his business on firm ground, began to think of other things.

BARNARD EXPANDS INTO POLITICS AND PROPERTY

In the mid-1860s, the colonies of British Columbia and Vancouver Island were carrying a heavy debt load, largely due to investments in building infrastructure to handle the huge influx of gold seekers and related factions. As the revenue from the mining sector dropped, the loans taken out to pay for this infrastructure increased and both colonies found themselves in dire economic straits. British Columbia's Governor Seymour argued that the best way to strengthen the British presence on the Pacific and solve the economic crisis would be to merge the two colonies into one. Pressure from the colonial office in London for the amalgamation of the two colonies grew intense and, despite the general antagonism and ambivalence from both sides, on August 6, 1866, the two colonies united under the name of British Columbia. The institutions and revenue laws of British Columbia were superimposed on Vancouver Island, and the capital city and legislature was located in Victoria. Governor Seymour, returning from Great Britain with a new bride, was installed as governor over the new single colony and Governor Kennedy of Vancouver Island, never popular, was recalled.[54]

In 1866, when George Wallace, editor of the *Cariboo Sentinel* and later the *Yale Tribune*, resigned as a member of the Legislative Council for Yale, he left a vacancy that needed to be filled. Initially, Dr. Black, a well-known physician, ran for the empty seat, strongly supported by the New Westminster *British Columbian* under the editorship of John Robson. Black's fitness to serve in the position was strongly questioned by the *British Colonist,* which found him so "favorable to the lower river interests as to be a thorough Westminster man" and suggested that "Mr. Barnard, of the Express, is understood to have aspirations for the vacant seat; but is said to have come too late into the field." Ten days later, the *British Colonist* announced that "Mr. Barnard has consented to stand for the Yale representation," adding that he "is a clever and energetic business man, a '59 pioneer, has large interests in the Colony, and will make a good and intelligent member." Barnard's eligibility was questioned by the rival *British Columbian* because he held a mail contract with the government, but the *British Colonist* pointed out that council member W.T. Smith had held a road contract with the government at the time he was elected, and the editor of the *British Columbian* sold advertising space to the government all the time.[55]

When the votes were counted on election day, January 26, 1867, Barnard, with 171 votes to Dr. Black's 20, became a member of the Legislative Council. To avoid any suggestion of favoritism, he had Dietz and Nelson bid on the mail contract that year. It was announced in May that, "the contract for the interior mail service has been awarded to the well known firm of Dietz & Nelson, which of course includes the Hon. F.J. Barnard. This will be gratifying intelligence to the people of the interior inasmuch as it is a sure guarantee that the work will be done faithfully and well."[56]

As the Yale representative on the council, Barnard was expected to attend regular meetings in Victoria and to represent the government in Yale and the Interior. When Governor Seymour arrived in Yale on May 16, he was received by Barnard "with firing guns, flying flags and general demonstrations. The party started out for Boston Bar at 10 o'clock the following morning, some in carriages, some on horse-back and others in Mr. Barnard's coach, who was driving six-to-hand."[57] The account makes clear that Barnard himself drove the six-horse team pulling his stagecoach, no mean feat for the boss of the outfit.

Barnard's new responsibility was more onerous than heading the express company, as he had to deal with the financial problems that plagued the new colony. One result of the tight budget was the colony's inability to maintain the Cariboo Road, its main organ of transportation. In June, it was reported that the toll road between the 150-mile post and Deep Creek was impassable and Barnard had to put his passengers on saddle horses to take them on the round-about route through Williams Lake. The *British Colonist* reported that spending some of the road toll income on road repairs would be logical, but the majority felt it more important to pay the salaries of its employees. This decision by members in the legislature brought the editor of the *Cariboo Sentinel* to declare, tongue in cheek:

> The official salaries must be paid, but it is not absolutely neces-sary to repair the roads. Mr. Barnard may grumble because he has to use half a dozen yoke of oxen to drag his empty wagon through the mud, and indolent passengers may feel aggrieved because they are compelled to wade through mire like so many ducks, but it only shows the want of consideration on the part of these people.[58]

Despite his political duties, Barnard had a productive business year. In May, he filed a pre-emption on an abandoned 160-acre lot at the 134-mile post of the Cariboo Road six miles north of Lac la Hache.[59] This was an ideal location for a horse ranch and stage-coach depot, but there was a hitch. The farm had originally been pre-empted by Peter Eddy in 1862 as a roadhouse and, as traffic on the road declined and Eddy fell into debt, he mortgaged the land to a Mr. C. Fulton. When Barnard filed his pre-emption, Fulton sued him for the cost of the mortgage. In magistrate's court held in Rich-field, Fulton was found to have a rightful mortgage on the property and had to be paid out by Barnard, raising the price of his Cariboo Road stage depot.[60]

Even with dwindling traffic on the Cariboo Road, Barnard's mail contract and the lucrative express business kept his finances in good order. As his situation became more secure, he decided to buy out Dietz and Nelson, who were operating the express business from Yale and Lillooet to Victoria. On December 2, the sale was finalized and Barnard controlled the express business and mail contract for the entire colony.[61]

Dietz and Nelson had already, in 1866, formed a partnership with Sewell Prescott Moody, who had a sawmill on Burrard Inlet. The capital realized from the sale of their express business probably enabled them to build a new steam mill in 1868, equipped with the latest machinery. The firm, referred to as Moody, Dietz and Nelson by 1870, continued to prosper until the fall of 1873, when the mill was destroyed by fire. Operations resumed the next May and, following the death of Moody in November 1875, Nelson managed the company until his retirement from business in 1882. Nelson was a delegate, along with Barnard, to the Yale Convention and a strong advocate for Confederation with Canada. He was lieutenant-governor of British Columbia from 1887 until 1892.

Barnard's bright red and yellow stagecoaches and sleighs would travel the Cariboo Road from Yale to Barkerville for the next twenty years, until the completion of the Canadian Pacific Railway made the Fraser Canyon impassable for coaches and the express moved its headquarters to Ashcroft. By this time, the stage and express line was affectionately referred to by miners and settlers alike as the "BX." The BX would remain a much-loved icon in the Cariboo for the next half-century and beyond.

— 4 —

STAGECOACHES, DRIVERS, AND HORSES

A S STEVE TINGLEY guided the stagecoach up and over Jackass Mountain, the steepest grade on the Cariboo Road, the pretty young lady passenger perching on the seat of honour beside him peered nervously over the side. All she could see was the river far below, a white torrent from which came a roar she could hear from her seat on high.

"Mr. Tingley," she nervously asked, "What would happen if our outside wheels should go over the bank?" Never taking his eyes off the horses in front of him, Tingley deadpanned, "Well, that would depend, my friend, upon the sort of life you had led."

The road had been blasted out of the rock cliffs, and in places it hung on log cribbing far above the river that ran like a white ribbon far below. A stagecoach ride over the Cariboo Road through the Fraser Canyon was not for the faint of heart.

BX STAGECOACHES DESIGNED FOR THE CARIBOO ROAD

A stagecoach was a closed four-wheeled, horse-drawn coach used to carry passengers and freight. The name comes from the coaches

Cariboo Road at China Bar Bluff in the Fraser Canyon where
the road was not for the faint of heart. LIBRARY AND ARCHIVES
CANADA, MIKAN 3306727, C-088891

travelling in stages between stops where horses could be changed
up for fresh ones. Stagecoaches were used in Great Britain as early
as the thirteenth century, with regular stagecoach routes by the
early 1600s. The highest class of British stagecoaches were those
that carried the Royal Mail over the network of macadamized roads
across England and the south of Scotland.

Because the roads of North America did not lend themselves
to English stagecoaches, a new design was developed in Concord,
New Hampshire, by Lewis Downing and J. Stephens Abbot in 1826.
These "Concord" stagecoaches were stylish and durable, utilizing
"thorough braces" for suspension, a design that had been long abandoned in Britain. The thorough braces were wide strips of leather
cured to toughness and strung on either side, so that the entire body

of the stagecoach rested on them. These braces allowed the coach to rock back and forth, absorbing the shocks of rough roads and sparing horses and passengers. Concord stagecoaches were used extensively as the American frontier spread west. But, with an empty weight of two-and-one-half tons and a cost of approximately $1,400 US dollars in 1857, they were not ideal for the long-range stage runs like those travelled by John Butterfield's Overland Stage Company.

Butterfield designed the much lighter and more rugged "Celerity Wagon" (celerity meaning "swiftness of speed") to cover the 2,238-mile (3,200-kilometre) route from Tipton, Missouri, to San Francisco. The Celerity cost about one-third of the Concord and was used for most of the route, especially for the more rugged sections. With its much lighter weight, it could negotiate sand and mud and was often referred to as a "mud wagon."[1]

There was no mistaking a BX stagecoach at a distance. The coaches of all BX stages were painted bright red and the wheels and running gear yellow. The company name was in lettering on both sides in yellow, just under the driver's seat. The BX used a variety of vehicles, ranging from the two-horse thorough-braced "jerky" to the six-horse stagecoach and, in the winter, sleighs of all sizes, including those that could carry fifteen passengers. By far the most common coach was the Celerity, which had wide steel "tires," so-named because they "tied" the wooden spokes of the wheel together. The wide wheels were designed for better "floatation" through sand and mud. Initially, the wheels were a standard five feet two inches (1.574 metres) apart, from one side to the other, to give better stability and balance, lessening the danger of the vehicle turning over. But in later years, as the Cariboo Road was improved and stagecoaches were adapted to maximum carrying capacity, the distance between wheels was increased to five feet ten inches (1.778 metres). Instead of having a heavy wooden top common to the Concord stagecoaches, the first Celerity wagons had a light frame structure with a thick canvas duck covering.

The running gear was designed to suit the variety of conditions along the Cariboo Road. The back wheels, larger in circumference than the front ones, were fixed firmly to the solid steel axles on each side and held in place with steel nuts threaded onto the ends of the axles. The smaller front wheels were made so they could turn ninety degrees maximum for hard turns. Heavy chains were attached on each side of the axle tree near each front wheel that, in turn, were attached to the pole or "tongue" of the wagon. The chains hung loosely enough to enable each wheel to turn about forty-five degrees before becoming taut so the stagecoach could not be over-steered. This meant that a turn of more than forty-five degrees could not be accomplished without driving the stagecoach back and forth a few times. The front wheels could be easily detached from the wagon in case of trouble.

The front wheels were fastened onto the axle with steel nuts in the same way as the rear wheels, unlike the freight wagon wheels that were held on by linchpins. To construct a proper wheel required a skilled wheelwright with many years of experience. Each wheel comprised four main parts: the hub that fit on the axle; the spokes radiating out from the hub; the felloes, curved wooden sections of the rim; and the tire, which was a steel band shrunk around the felloes. Each of these four parts was essential to the integrity of the wheel unit. The spokes were "tenoned" into the hub, secured with steel bolts, and mortised and tenoned into one of the felloes at the outside end. A four-foot wheel had six felloes and a five-foot wheel had seven. In many instances, the steel rim or "tire" of the wheel, which held everything else in place, was put on red hot and then doused with water to make it shrink on tight. In the hot summer days of travel on the Cariboo Road, the wood spokes and felloes would dry out and cause the metal rim to become loose, and drivers would stop at a creek crossing to soak the wheels in water to swell the wood and make it tight to the rim.[2] All wheels were "dished" so the spokes flared outward from the hub. Based upon the principle that each spoke had to be able to hold the entire load on the wheel, this had the effect of forcing the wheel hub inwards toward the axle and preventing the nut that holds the wheel in place from loosening.

The stagecoach's suspension system of thorough braces consisted of five layers of long leather straps about five inches wide attached to the undercarriage directly above the axles. The body of the stagecoach was slung on these leather straps and attached with metal brackets. The straps both cushioned the ride and allowed the driver to use the weight of the stagecoach to modify how hard the wheels hit an obstacle in the road. By rocking the body of the stage-coach back, he could take the weight off the front wheels, and by rocking forward, take the weight off the back wheels.

Most historians who have written about the BX have stated that Barnard's "first Concord thorobrace stages were purchased in California."[3] This does not appear to have been the case. In 1862, even before Barnard first conceived of going into the stagecoach business, there were two excellent carriage builders in Victoria, Bunting & Dodd and Duck & Sandover. In October of that year, at the Victoria Agricultural and Horticultural Exhibition, the *British Colonist* reported that "Messrs. Bunting & Dodge [*sic*] exhibited a large spring-cart, manufactured at their wheelwright establishment on Yates street, as well built as any vehicle ever imported to this Colony. It deservedly took the prize." As well, "Duck & Co's two wagons of the same description were honorably mentioned." The same edition also reported that Bunting & Dodd had bought out John Kane and intended "carrying on every description of Carriage and Wagon work."[4]

Further information was provided in a *British Colonist* article in late 1863, at the time when Barnard was preparing to establish his stagecoach line for the following year. A lawsuit was reported concerning "a pair of thorough braces made by Gibbon for Bunting & Dodd. Plaintiff [Gibbon] alleged that he had delivered them, according to order. Defendants said that they had ordered [the thorough braces] to be stitched through, whereas they had been sent home unstitched; the braces were for Barnard's express wagon, and it was alleged on behalf of the defendants that [thorough] braces

Three-seated stagecoach, 1911, loaded for the Swannell survey expedition.

IMAGE I-58117 COURTESY OF THE ROYAL BC MUSEUM AND ARCHIVES

when used for light carriages were usually stitched, yet for heavier wagons they were as often used unstitched."[5] This clearly reveals that Barnard went to Bunting & Dodd to construct his first express wagons and that they were thorough braced.

A little over a year later, in January of 1865, Bunting & Dodd sold out, auctioning off their "entire stock-in-trade and tools" in their "carriage and wagon manufactory, consisting of heavy and light Team Wagons, Express Wagons, Carts & Trotting Sulky."[6] This left Duck & Sandover as the main carriage manufacturers in Victoria and they were not long in getting orders from Barnard. In April, it was reported that "the *Reliance* carried up yesterday a splendid new stagecoach built [for Barnard's subsidiary, the Cariboo Stage Company] by Duck & Sandover of Victoria, and is calculated on a pinch to seat sixteen persons." It is doubtful that Barnard would bother ordering and paying shipping for stagecoaches from California when he could obtain excellent models in Victoria. This misconception that all of Barnard's early stagecoaches were manufactured by

Blacks of San Francisco likely arose because Blacks was contracted to make the Dufferin coach for the visiting Governor General, Lord Dufferin, in 1876.

The earliest photographs of BX stagecoaches show that they were built to the specifications for similar coaches in California. Over the years, though, one major adaptation of the Celerity wagon was added. Unlike the early stagecoaches used in California and by Barnard's, which had tops of treated canvas over a light frame, the later coaches were constructed with sturdy flat roofs supported by wooden slats and covered with canvas, to allow passenger seating and extra baggage and freight storage. The variety of vehicles, probably all manufactured in Victoria, included thorough braced two- and three-seat stagecoaches and jerky wagons, along with sleighs of various sizes and descriptions. These vehicles were still being manufactured by Duck & Sandover in 1873, when "a handsome express wagon built by Duck & Sandover for F.J. Barnard & Co. for use in this city was driven through town." [7] It is probable that Barnard's and, later, the BC Express used stagecoaches constructed by Duck & Sandover until the company constructed a large shop at the 134-mile post, where their own skilled craftsmen could construct coaches from scratch. In 1886, these shops would be moved to Ashcroft along with the head office, after the completion of the Canadian Pacific Railway the year before.

BX DRIVERS, THE "ROCK STARS" OF THEIR DAY

Stagecoach drivers were called "whips" because they all carried this necessary tool with them at all times—not to punish horses (perish the thought!) but to give them a touch when needed. To be a "crack whip," as Steve Tingley was called for many years, was to be acknowledged as the best among these extremely adept drivers. They were also called "jehus" (pronounced "yay hoos") after the Biblical prophet Jehu, son of Nimshi, of whom it was said, "He drives furiously." To be able to control six horses by six thin reins as the stagecoach careened through the Fraser Canyon and up the Cariboo Road to Barkerville was considered a feat few on the frontier could duplicate.

The best stagecoach drivers were generally considered to possess three essential "tools" of their trade.[8] The first was what could only be called "horse sense," an ability to read the signals the horses were sending. The second tool, tied closely to the first, was "light hands," as the reins in the driver's hands connected directly to the bits in the mouths of the horses; a "heavy hand" on the part of the driver would result in a hard-mouthed horse or team. A good driver communicated through the reins and the horses signalled back.

On a six-horse coach, there were three pairs of horses, each with different characteristics and temperament because each pair had a specific role to play. The "lead" team was required to be the most alert, responsive, and agile. From his perch behind and above the team, the driver had to focus on the movement, or lack of it, of the horses' ears. An unhappy or uncomfortable horse would usually give itself away by laying its ears back on its head, indicating that it was more interested in what was going on behind it. The driver needed to recognize this as a sign to check the feel and look of equipment or hitching. Normally, a lead horse would flex its ears forward and back, one at a time or both together, showing it was relaxed and attentive. It would move its head back and forth to a limited extent, but carried to excess this could cause a horse to stumble or shy, requiring that blinders be put onto each side of the bridle to control the horse. These signs were communicated as much through the "lines" or reins as by the driver's vision. The advance signal would be the movement of the lead pair's ears, something that a good driver would feel in his hands. The driver could also reassure the animal through a gentle movement of the lines.

So, from up on the box of the stagecoach, always seated on the right, a good driver would have the lines and the horses' ears to detect whether things were proceeding normally. Even in semidarkness, the horses' ears would be visible to the driver and his hands would pick up their signals. When drivers talked about "talking to the horses through the lines," they were not exaggerating. The best drivers were aware of the conditions on the road ahead because they could read the subtle reactions of the lead horses, which an inexperienced passenger would be totally unaware of.

Because most drivers worried that they would lose "the feel" of the reins if they wore gloves, they drove with bare hands, even in the coldest weather. The coordination of man and horses was crucial and a failure could result in tangled harnesses, stumbling horses, or even upset stagecoaches. To an ordinary passenger, the work of driving a six-up of horses would seem easy, with the horses doing all the work. But sending six loosely hitched horses into a turn, with each pair turning at just the right moment, was an intricate and skilful achievement.

The third most important tool in a driver's kit, next to his eyes and hands, was the whip. Used at exactly the right time, the driver's whip was an essential communication tool, alongside his reins and his voice. It's worth repeating that the whip was not designed for punishment. The driver had both hands full just managing the six lines, and any animal that needed to be regularly whipped would not be accepted for the BX. The typical driver's whip was about twelve feet long. The first four feet were stiffened but not to the same extent as a regular buggy whip. The remaining eight feet were of soft but durable leather, usually buckskin, which could be coiled up in the driver's hand. Since at that length whips were about ten feet short of reaching the lead team on a six-horse hitch, these horses were controlled by the reins alone.

Whips were most often cracked alongside a horse's head to send a message to the horse to move to one side or the other or to swerve around some obstacle. At other times, the driver would use his whip to "touch up" a lazy or uncooperative horse by giving it a gentle smack on the flank. The horse would know exactly what this meant and respond accordingly. The whip became especially useful when a driver picked up a fresh relief team of horses at daybreak. The frisky horses would require all of his attention as they would take

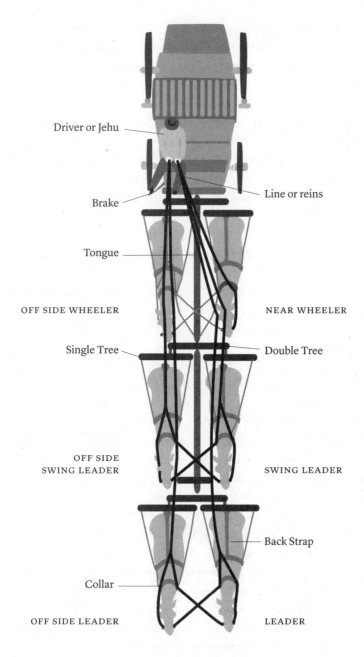

Holding the reins of six-horses.

a while to settle down. Whips were seldom abused or used in jest, implying their important role as a tool.

All stagecoach drivers considered their whips extremely valuable and some had them ornamented with silver ferules around the handle. Author Walker Tompkins described the relationship between drivers and their whips: "Whips were considered a part of the driver, who kept the lashes well-oiled and as pliable as 'a snake in the sun.'"[9] Because each driver had his own whip, he usually carried it with him wherever he went, as a badge of status. Stagecoach whips were lighter than bull whips and could easily be coiled in one hand. The whip identified him as a driver, a "whip" or a "jehu," and usually resulted in deferential treatment in a society where stagecoach drivers were high on the social ladder. Selling, trading, or even loaning a whip was unheard of. Drivers always hung their whips up instead of resting them in a corner, to prevent the stock from warping. They avoided wrapping the lash around the handle as this might curl the thongs.

The Barnard's and BC Express drivers were professionals who made their living from driving stagecoaches. Because of their unique ability to control a six-horse stagecoach along the often perilous Cariboo Road, they were unquestionably the "rock stars" of their day, While they made good time and cared for the freight and passengers, their primary responsibility was getting the most out of their horses while making it easiest on them. The distinction has been made between ordinary drivers and those who had achieved the distinction of being "reinsmen." According to Captain William Banning, considered the last active six-horse stagecoach driver, "a reinsman was a master driver who, by virtue of his exceptional skill, was able to drive each span of his complement wholly independent of the other."[10] Banning made this distinction based upon the way the teams were harnessed: "With breast-straps (pole-straps) and traces drawn taut, or nearly taut after the old English mode, there was a team so hitched that it could not possibly be 'reined'—the separate spans could not be driven independently... The animals could scarcely move without moving either the pole or the vehicle proper...

The drivers of these strapped-up teams, however well they drove, *were not reinsmen.* And they sacrificed, along with certain elements of grace and certain practice in the most delicate sort of fingering and brake work, a great deal of efficiency to include power, speed, endurance, and ofttimes much hide from their wheelers' necks." Banning goes on to say, "It was a happy team whose driver was a reinsman. His horses showed it; he could let them show it; he would permit the romping of any animal, knowing that the others would not be taxed by it, though they might be reminded they were free to join in the dance." Banning's conclusion is worth quoting at length:

> Where the mountains in America were loftiest and most rugged, where the roads were most narrow and threatening, there, above all places, was the greatest demand for the whip who had learned to "rein," the driver who had mastered the most difficult of modes of driving. His was strictly a triplex power plant of duplex units operating on twenty-four hoofs; and if, by means of his six lines and his brake and whip, he could exact from all of its parts and potentialities a maximum degree of efficiency at all times, then he was a master of masters. He was a reinsman indeed. He was one in a thousand.[11]

A ROUGH RIDE FOR PASSENGERS

In the first year of operation, from March 1864 to the end of April 1865, the BX carried 1,500 passengers and was by far the quickest way to get from Yale to Barkerville and the Cariboo goldfields. Between 1865 and 1867, except for a brief competition with the Opposition Stage Line, the fare was set at $125 to Barkerville from Yale. Then, to encourage passengers, Barnard dropped his rates to $85 in the spring of 1867. Throughout its many years of operation, thousands of passengers, regardless of class, gender, or race, travelled together in the tiny space inside—or, even more challenging, perched on the roof—of Barnard's stagecoaches.

The place of honour was always the seat beside the driver, and woe to the individual who assumed that his or her high status made the place theirs. They would be subject to the displeasure of the driver, who would remove them and leave them to suffer the sneers of their fellow passengers for the duration of the trip. The driver would choose his own seat companion and, if there was only one woman on the trip, she would automatically be chosen, regardless of whether she was a woman of the night or a duchess.

Travellers on the BX were classed as either "through" passengers, going the full distance between Yale and Barkerville, or "way" passengers, travelling only part of the distance. Other than the seat of honour next to the driver, passengers chose their seats on a "first come, first served" basis. The typical stagecoach had two seats facing each other, situating the passengers practically knee to knee. But on crowded runs, a longer coach would often be used, one with a third row of seats in the middle so nine passengers could sit inside. The middle row, facing forward, would be slightly offset to the rear to give more room to those facing each other. This row of seats was in three sections, with the centre seat bolted to the floor and the two side seats hinged to allow passengers to access the back seat. Most often, the back rest for this centre seat was merely a broad harness that fit the small of the back and was suspended from the roof by straps. The harness could be unsnapped to allow the side seats to be lifted and, if the coach was not full, the back of the middle seat could be unsnapped and folded down to allow one person at a time to stretch out and take their chance to sleep on the middle seat of a bouncing stagecoach.

Either way, inside passengers were placed three to a seat, shoulder to shoulder, unless the stage was not full. Each passenger had fifteen inches to call their own. In the case where they sat knee-to-knee with the passenger across from them, it was necessary for these six people to dovetail their knees. Since most coaches had room for only ten of the twelve interlocked knees, a foot could often be seen dangling outside the coach near the wheel, desperately seeking support.

The story is told of a particularly rotund woman and a Fraser River steamboat captain who had ended up on the middle seat facing her in a BX stagecoach. When the captain asked politely whether she would "dovetail" with him so that they could accommodate each other's legs, she screamed for the driver to stop the stage as she was insulted by his proposition. She left the wagon and took refuge in a wayside house muttering, "Dovetail with me will he! The nerve!"

Large items of luggage were stored in the boot (the canvas-covered rear of the stagecoach) or on the roof. But most passengers carried a bag, blanket, hat box, coat, basket of food, or bottle of water or other "beverage" on their laps or in the limited space underneath the seat. Once the inside of the stagecoach filled up, passengers could climb up to the roof, where there was a seat for three behind the driver and others could sit as best they could among the luggage and freight.

The thorough braces on BX vehicles could have a decided effect upon the passengers. Veteran passengers knew to take the seat inside directly behind the driver, even though this meant they would have to face backwards as they travelled. They would graciously offer the forward-facing seat to the inexperienced riders, knowing that the motion of the stagecoach body would be much more pronounced at that point. If the boot was filled with heavy trunks or freight, people in the front seats would have to lean forward, but they would be content. Then the old-timers could watch with amusement as the newcomer's face gradually whitened and eventually turned to green with the onset of "stage sickness," which was strikingly similar to seasickness. As the BX rolled on through day and night, the swing and sway of the stagecoach produced a nausea that only compounded the crowding and dust that were natural parts of this mode of travel.

Since summer dust and heat and winter cold were uncontrollable, each BX stagecoach had canvas curtains to enclose all or part of the inside of the coach. Still, the conditions of travel were, at best, barely tolerable. Passengers might find their seatmate an overweight man, a woman with a crying baby, or a miner deep in his cups. Fatigue and uncomfortable conditions would make passengers wonder if speedy arrival at their destination was worth it. Sure, there were regular brief stops to change horses and three longer stops every twenty-four hours, but stagecoach travel was a trial at the best of times. The following advice to passengers published in the *Omaha Times* in 1877 was relevant for travellers on the BX.

- The best seat inside a stagecoach is the one next to the driver... When any old "sly Eph"... offers through sympathy to exchange his back or middle seat with you, don't do it.

- Never ride in cold weather with tight boots or shoes, nor close-fitting gloves. Bathe your feet in cold water before starting...

- When the driver asks you to get off and walk, do it without grumbling... If a team runs away, sit still and take your chances; if you jump, nine times out of ten you will be hurt.

- In very cold weather, abstain entirely from liquor while on the road; a man will freeze twice as quick while under its influence.

- Don't growl at food stations; stage companies generally provide the best they can get. Don't keep the stage waiting; many a virtuous man has lost his character by so doing.

- Don't smoke a strong pipe inside especially early in the morning. Spit on the leeward side of the coach. If you have anything to take in a bottle, pass it around; a man who drinks by himself in such a case is lost to all human feeling. Provide stimulants before starting; ranch whisky is not always nectar.

- Don't swear, nor lop over on your neighbor when sleeping. Don't ask how far it is to the next station...

- Never attempt to fire a gun or pistol while on the road, it may frighten the team; and the careless handling and cocking of the weapon makes people nervous. Don't discuss politics or religion, nor point out places on the road where horrible murders have been committed.

Stagecoach horses were superbly conditioned and well groomed.

IMAGE C-082229 COURTESY OF THE ROYAL BC MUSEUM AND ARCHIVES

- Don't linger too long at the pewter wash basin at the station. Don't grease you hair before starting or dust will stick there in sufficient quantities to make a respectable 'tater' patch. Tie a silk handkerchief around your neck to keep out dust and prevent sunburns. A little glycerin is good in case of chapped hands.

- Don't imagine for a moment you are going on a picnic; expect annoyance, discomfort and some hardships. If you are disappointed, thank heaven.

THE POWER OF HORSES

"Horsepower" in the stagecoach business used individual animals with varying capacities and personalities to propel its vehicles over long stretches of road through all sorts of conditions and terrain. Though two-horse open wagons, sometimes called "jerky coaches," were used, especially on the branch lines, the typical BX stagecoach team was either four or six horses. We will take a look at the six-horse teams common on the Cariboo Road for fifty years.

The six-horse team consisted of the "lead" pair in the front, the "swing" pair in the middle, and the "wheel" pair closest to the stagecoach. For each pair, the horse on the left was called the "near" horse and the one on the right the "off" horse. Generally, the wheel horses were heavier and stronger, and were accustomed to pulling backwards at the command of the driver. The swing horses needed to have control and balance and were steady and responsive, but not necessarily as strong. The lead horses had to be agile and obedient with an ability to move sideways quickly. Each member of the "team" had a different role to play and there was a difference between the lead, swing and wheel pairs and between the near and off. Each horse had a separate personality and capability, and it was important to place it in a position appropriate to its nature. Once positioned, a horse would always be hitched in the same spot.

All six horses had collars made out of leather stuffed with excelsior ("wood wool" made of wood slivers) or straw. As most of the pulling was done from the collars, this furnished necessary padding. Over time, as the collar became broken in and fitted to the shoulders of the horse, it was essential that the horse use only that collar. An unfitted collar could cause "gall" sores on the shoulders, which would render the horse unusable until healed. The hostellers who cared for the horses made every effort to keep the complete set of harness for each horse separate.

On the outside of each collar, fitted on each side, were wooden pieces called "hames" to which the pulling harness was attached. Each horse also had a bridle with a simple snaffle bit, a mouthpiece with rings on either side to exert pressure on one or the other side of the mouth. A single rein or line was attached to the metal ring on each side of the bit and ran through a ring on the hames and connected with the same side of the rein on its partner horse. From there, a single rein ran to the hand of the driver, so that he had two reins for each pair of horses, one for the near side control and one for the off side.

Attached to the centre of the hames on either side of each horse were the traces, or tugs, that ran through a loop on a side strap and attached to a "single tree" made of solid oak slightly wider than the width of the horse. The last few feet of the tug was a chain that could be adjusted to hook on each side of the single tree. Each single tree was attached to a double tree, which was in turn attached to the tongue or pole that extended out from the front axle of the coach like the handle on a child's wagon. Each horse of the wheel team had a strap from the hames to the front of the pole to hold it up. In a six-horse hitch, there was a "false pole" that attached to the main pole and ran between the swing team that had a similar neck strap to hold the false pole up. Once the tugs were hooked on the single tree, a continuous force was exerted from the collar of the horse through the single tree to the double tree and to the stagecoach.

Unlike the foremost two pairs, the wheel horses had different harnesses and were hitched to a double tree. This was because the wheel team alone had the job of backing up the stagecoach. The major difference in harness was a heavy leather strap around the buttocks suspended from a back strap. This extra harness was the breeching, often called the "britching." Under normal forward pulling, the breeching would hang slack, but if the stagecoach had to be backed up, the wheel horses would back in tightly to the breeching and put all their weight into pushing backwards on the coach.

As the only means of locomotion for the BX stagecoaches, wagons, and sleighs, properly trained horses were essential. So, as his stagecoach line grew in size and coverage, Barnard knew he needed the finest horses available. The BX purchased only horses that had not been previously "broken" so they could be trained exclusively for pulling stagecoaches. They would soon learn what was expected of them and, in the hands of a good driver, they could be depended upon to pull the stage safely to the end of its run. Regular drivers had a certain number of horses on their section of the road and were carefully attentive of their condition. No one else was allowed to drive them. A good stage horse was highly prized by the BX and no price would be considered for their sale. Hostellers at the various stopping and hitching places had to be excellent farriers, as the feet of the horses had to be in perfect condition. They were usually old horsemen who knew horses and their care and feeding and who would vie with each other to see who could turn out his horses in the finest condition. One hosteller even made it his practice to blacken and polish the hooves of his horses for special effect.

The regular mail stage took four days to travel the 280 miles of Cariboo Road between Yale and Barkerville. Stations were an average of eighteen miles apart, except in the Fraser Canyon, where they were closer due to the long climbs. The stage travelled on level ground at a steady trot but the average speed of six miles an hour factored in walking the horses up the steep hills.

Willis J. West, who worked for the BX in its latter years and was superintendent from 1903 into the 1920s, described the horses as he knew them:

> These stage horses were never really broken. They were trained for staging alone and had to be handled in a way they would understand. To illustrate this the custom observed in preparing a stage and its horses for leaving a station had to be carefully and expertly carried out to ensure a safe departure. When the mail, express matter and baggage had been loaded and securely lashed into the stage, the passengers were requested to take their places. Then the driver with his treasure-bag took his seat and all was in readiness for the horses to be brought from the stable. First the wheel team was led out by the hostler who backed it into position on either side of the stage pole and passed the lines to the driver. After this team was ready with harness and rigging adjusted to the satisfaction of the driver, the swing team appeared and the same procedure was followed. Finally the two leaders, the freest and most spirited horses in the six-horse team, were brought out and after the horses had indulged in much restless prancing, the hostler would eventually succeed in completing the 'hooking-up' of the team and would then quickly back out of the way. At this moment the driver released the brakes and the horses lunged forward starting the stage on its way to the next station.

Some teams when leaving the station at the beginning of their drive would behave in a most alarming manner and fill timid passengers with fear. The horses would stand on their hind legs and would seem to be so wildly entangled that a serious accident appeared inevitable. They would continue these antics until they had travelled about 100 yards and then they would settle down to a brisk trot. In their natural health and vigor they could not refrain from these exuberant demonstrations.[12]

If, for any reason, these stagecoach horses strayed or were lost, they had a built-in homing instinct and would head for their home ranch, be it in the Okanagan or Nicola Valley. When a description of the horse and its brands was distributed, the horse would inevitably be located somewhere between where it was lost and its home range.

WELCOME TO THE STOPPING HOUSE

Horses had to be changed an average of every eighteen miles (twenty-nine kilometres) because they were bred for speed, not distance. At these stopping places, the hostellers would have fresh horses ready to hitch to the stagecoach when it arrived. As most of these changes were accomplished quickly, little time was lost. But, when the stops occurred at a mealtime, longer stops were necessary for the well-being of the passengers. The stopping houses and hotels that supplied meals and beds were carefully chosen for their hospitality, beds, and meals; though not owned by the BX, they were integral to the success of the stage line. These stopping houses were usually operated by families, often lonely settlers, eager to learn whatever they could about the travellers. Payment was not generous, but for the settlers struggling to make a living, it was important.

The food was almost always excellent, and when it wasn't, another nearby stopping house could take its place, for any ranch house in the Cariboo would welcome travellers day or night. At the ranch houses where women were doing the cooking, the quality and quantity of the food was usually outstanding. In some cases, the ranches would be fifty miles from the nearest store, so nearly every dish was produced on the ranch. Often, large gardens supplied fresh vegetables and root cellars provided a year-round supply. Every ranch had its milk cows and was able to supply fresh beef, pork, chicken, or duck. The standard rate for a meal or a bed was fifty cents, except for the stopping houses beyond Quesnelle Mouth, where the charge was increased to seventy-five cents. Breakfast, lunch, and dinner looked pretty much the same, except that breakfast always included oatmeal porridge and a jug of rich yellow cream. All meals included thick steaks, fried potatoes, and eggs. Some cooks supplied fresh-baked pies, even for breakfast. One roadhouse was famous for always serving three kinds of hot meat for the midday meal, augmented with vegetables, at least three kinds of pie, pudding, two kinds of cake, and amenities like relish and cookies—all for fifty cents!

Winter travel over frozen roads made stopping houses like this one even more welcome. The proprietors had five lovely daughters, and on cold winter nights, the girls were roused from sleep to warm the beds that awaited the travellers. Wherever travellers spent the night, beds were equipped with a "pulu" (a silky fibre obtained from a Hawaiian tree fern) mattress for ultimate comfort. Most roadhouses had fireplaces, wood-fired cook stoves, and kerosene lamps or candles as sources of heat and light. Fire was always a concern and most were caused not by human error but by hot stovepipes coming in contact with dry shake roofs.

Before the motor car became popular on the Cariboo Road, around 1910, the roadhouses were an institution. Their reputation for hospitality, food, and accommodation made every traveller look forward to the stagecoach stops.

THE VITAL ROLE OF INDIGENOUS PEOPLE

The Barnard's and British Columbia Express stage lines not only passed through the territories of the Stó:lō, Nlaka'pamux, Secwépemc, and Dakelhne Peoples, but would not have succeeded without the help of these people. Barnard's very first job in British Columbia was to find a route from Chapman's Bar to Boston Bar, with Nlaka'pamux guides. When the *Fort Yale* steamboat blew up with Barnard on board, it was Stó:lō people who canoed out and saved him. On his first trip as an expressman, in the terrible winter of 1861-62, Barnard hired Indigenous people to take him from Yale through the ice floes by canoe.[13] His next trip was even worse and, once again, Indigenous people came to the rescue. The *British Colonist* reported, "Mr. Barnard of the Express Company, had one foot frozen while making the trip from New Westminster to Yale. He has continued the trip from Sumas on a sledge drawn by Indians." In those two instances, it was Stó:lō people who helped Barnard but, time after time, especially in winter, it was the Nlaka'pamux who helped get the express matter and stagecoaches through the Fraser Canyon. In his earliest days of packing the express on foot, Barnard hired and travelled with a Nlaka'pamux man, Cisco Charlie. When the canyon was snowed in and no one else could find their way through with the mail and express, the Nlaka'pamux found a way. This happened so often that it was seldom reported, but there was no doubt that Barnard depended upon their help.

Recognizing that the Indigenous Peoples along the road through the Fraser Canyon knew how to move around in such harsh winter conditions, Barnard proposed to Joseph Trutch, Chief Commissioner of Lands and Works, in 1866, "to employ 2 Indians at each ranch [Indigenous village] to travel to the next ranch & back, after every fall of snow, they should be yoked by means of a light stick, & compelled to travel say 4 ft. 6 in. apart, thus breaking a double track in the middle of the road its entire length, once a double track is open both lines will be used equally by the Indians and foot men, and the track answering to the gauge of the sleighs in use will enable travel to be kept up all the season... The number of Indians to be employed I plan at 12. They could be hired at say $10 per month as the work would be light and the employment steady for the winter."[14] Barnard had worked extensively with Indigenous people, especially in the Fraser Canyon, and would have considered his proposal mutually beneficial; his employees would receive an income and his sleighs would be better able to navigate the snowy canyon. There is no indication, however, that Trutch adopted the suggestion.

It is important to note that, in 1871, when British Columbia joined Confederation, there were a mere 8,576 Caucasians and 1,548 Chinese, with Indigenous people comprising seventy per cent of the province's population, at 26,661 people.[15] When stagecoach robberies occurred over the next two decades, it was Indigenous men who formed the posses to hunt for the perpetrators. In an 1894 holdup, a posse from the Esk'etemc First Nation at Alkali Lake captured the bandit and Basil Eagle brought him in to Clinton (see chapter eight for details).

Clearly, in the days of expressmen and stagecoaches on the Cariboo Road, Indigenous people, who formed the majority of inhabitants in British Columbia, played a significant role in the development and infrastructure of the Colony and Province of British Columbia.

RULES OF THE ROAD

In 1861, a letter to the editor in the *British Colonist* requested information on travelling on the roads of the colonies of Vancouver Island and British Columbia. "Suppose I am driving a wagon, and meet or pass a vehicle, which side of the road must I take?" The editor replied, "Our correspondent must turn to the left if he *meets* a vehicle; if he overtakes one and desires to *pass* it, he must go to the right. This seems to be the rule generally adopted here. As they say in England

> The rule of the road is a paradox quite,
> In riding or driving along;
> If you go to the *left* you're sure to go *right*;
> If you go to the *right* you go *wrong*."[16]

This clearly indicates that the system in effect in Great Britain for centuries also applied in its colonies. Historians have determined that the Roman conquerors of Britain drove their chariots on the left-hand side of the road, which meant that, if a stranger passed you on the right, your right hand would be free to defend yourself. Traffic congestion in eighteenth-century London led to a law being passed to make all traffic on London Bridge keep to the left to reduce collisions. This rule was incorporated into the Highway Act of 1835 and was adopted throughout the British Empire. In British Columbia, this system was adopted in the Road Act of 1866. The decision to change to the right-hand side to conform with the rest of North America did not come into effect until the 1920s.

After the Cariboo Road was substantially completed and Barnard introduced his new stagecoaches, he wrote a letter to the colonial secretary, Arthur Birch, in Victoria.

Sir—I beg to present that there is need of the publication of some order, concerning the right of way on the Wagon Road in the Upper Country. At present the mail and Express wagons are at times delayed and often placed in such a position as to render it dangerous to the lives of passengers, owing to the want of some published rule on the subject. I would respectfully suggest that the right of way and choice of side be given to the Mail Express wagons. To show the necessity of some such regulation, I beg to call your attention to the following facts.

In the month of August last while the Mail Express wagon was travelling thro [sic] the "Big Canyon" the driver noticed his leaders running off toward the precipice, [the driver] having a tight rein at the time, they were swung back to the opposite side. On an examination it was found that a packer had camped on the Road and to prevent his animals from straying had made fast a rope across the road. If the driver had not had a tight rein at the time, 12 persons would have been thrown over the precipice and much valuable property destroyed.

In October last, a man engaged in putting up a Mile Post on the Lytton and Alexandria wagon road, left a small hand cart on

one of the bends of the Road leaving but sufficient room for the
Mail Wagon to pass. The leaders on coming to the spot, and seeing
such an unusual object, took fright and jumped up on a Bank and
upset the wagon, which was full with passengers and had it not
been for a particular arrangement of the wagon which allowed
the fore wheels to become detached as the wagon overturned, life
would have been sacrificed, as the horses ran away. The driver was
slightly injured... All of these occurences [sic] render it dangerous to travel by stage. On one occasion supplied by Mr. Sanders of
Yale, representation to place <u>placards</u> making known the law and
offered to post them up at points on the Road. He referred me to
you, stating that, if I could bring the parties before him, he would
fine them for obstructing the highway.

I would respectfully request your attention on this matter, as
it is of very great moment to the safety of passengers who travel
by the Stages.

This letter received serious attention, as was indicated by two separate notes, one on the back and the other on an attached sheet.
The first read, "Express to Barnard that this letter shall be considered when the road bill... is being drawn up [at the spring sitting of
the legislature]. Ask... the opinion of the [Attorney General] ... I
cannot despite expressed opinion see the patent absurdity of giving
the mails the right of the road in the narrow and dangerous roads
through the Canyon."

Since there was no room on the back of the letter after the above
note, a separate sheet was attached. The next reply wrote,

There is no law here known familiarly as the 'rule of the road.' Tho
it could be easily imported under the act of 19 Nov. 1866 by any
magistrate. Mr. Barnard's application for power to choose sides is
absurd as tending to utter confusion. His other complaints the law
as it is can at once remedy if the facts be as he states without his
calling on the Legislative justice to help him. It may be wise to pre-
scribe the rule of the road in the proposed road act. HPP Crease,
[Attorney General].[17]

The subsequent Road Act confirmed the traditional regulations about keeping to the left side of the road and not obstructing the public roadway, but fell short of giving the mail contractor the "choice of side" he could pass on.

The stagecoach was the main means of public transportation in British Columbia for fifty years and Barnard ensured that he had the finest equipment and horses available. As he solidified his business, he began to think of a future that would include a transportation network from coast to coast in the British North American possession. He could see a day when the stagecoach would be used to span the vast prairies and he wanted to be the man to make it happen. His vision, considered preposterous by some, would require thousands of horses.

5

BARNARD'S EXPANDING VISION

TRAVELLING UP THE Cariboo Road in the depth of winter was never a pleasant experience. In the early days, Barnard's Express did not offer robes or blankets so passengers had to make their own arrangements to keep warm. On one occasion in 1870, in the dead of winter, the Express sleigh was making its way from Cottonwood to Barkerville with the horses ploughing through deep snow. The thermometer stood at –20 Fahrenheit (–29 Celcius) but, as is frequently the case in that part of the Cariboo, there was no wind, which made the cold somewhat tolerable.

The sleigh pulled into Pine Grove House, previously owned by the legendary Edward "Bloody" Edwards but by then owned by John Hamilton. Hamilton's wife and their daughter, Elizabeth, prided themselves in providing excellent accommodation and good food, and his son, John Junior, helped with the stagecoach horses. The sleigh was carrying a woman passenger, appropriately bundled up for the weather, who dashed into the house when the sleigh stopped. The other passengers assumed this was a short stop and went in to warm up and have a bite to eat.

When all passengers were called to get back in the sleigh, the woman passenger didn't appear. The driver began to fret, as he was

One of a wide variety of sleighs used by the BC Express Company.
IMAGE D-00746 COURTESY OF THE ROYAL BC MUSEUM AND ARCHIVES

still a long way off from reaching Barkerville by nightfall, but John Hamilton came out from the house and quietly spoke to him. The driver responded, "Well I'll be darned!" Then he turned to the other passengers and said, "She will be out in an hour, so we'll just have to wait." An hour later, the horses were hitched up again and the driver was waiting, a little impatiently, when the woman emerged, carrying a little bundle. She climbed into her place with her newborn baby, and rough but caring hands tucked her in with plenty of robes around her. She thanked them and smiled weakly. And away went the sleigh, carrying one extra passenger.[1]

STEVE TINGLEY'S EPIC HORSE DRIVE OF 1868

Barnard watched with interest as the Province of Canada, consisting of Upper and Lower Canada, later Ontario and Quebec, joined with New Brunswick and Nova Scotia to form the new Dominion of Canada on July 1, 1867. As a visionary, Barnard immediately saw the inevitability of the new dominion spreading across the continent and taking in the Colony of British Columbia. This was a vision he shared with the majority of British Columbians, most of whom lived on the mainland and came from those original colonies. In Victoria, feelings were quite different. The extensive government hierarchy, consisting mostly of the British upper classes who preferred colonial status, feared they would lose their jobs if BC joined the Canadian Confederation. And up against both of these sides were the many American businessmen who favoured union with the United States.

On December 1, 1867, just five months after Confederation, Barnard wrote to a friend that British Columbia would inevitably join the Canadian union:

> Among other items it may interest you to know that I have bought out Dietz & Nelson and now run through from Barkerville to Vic. It is a novelty to see Concord coaches running into Barkerville but I am sorry to say that I make but one trip a week. I find it pays better than two. I am ambitious enough [to] look still for a daily line and even further. I propose going this winter to lower California to purchase a Band of Mustang mares & to work raising BC Stock preparatory to running a coach from Yale to Lake Superior. Don't put me down for crazy. The [speculative venture] is safe for horses are always in demand in BC and will yield a fine profit if our own land route is not opened for ten years. I am ready to wager money that the route will be opened by the time my colts (in prospective) are 5 years old.[2]

Barnard was dreaming big. At a time when the little Dominion of Canada was a cluster of former colonies on the eastern seaboard and everything from British Columbia to Lake Superior was British territory, he was planning a stagecoach line to stretch some 1,800 miles (2,880 kilometres) to connect BC with Canada. Nonetheless, he was right that horses were in demand in BC and, even if his project failed, he would make a profit.

Not surprisingly, Barnard turned to Steve Tingley, who had established himself not only as the "crack whip" of the BX but also as the best judge of stagecoach horses in the colony. He approached Tingley about travelling to California and told him the company would cover all expenses and the cost of whatever good horses could be obtained, as he had done when Tingley purchased horses for him in Oregon in 1863. Numerous historians have stated that Barnard sent Tingley to Mexico or New Mexico, but the primary sources do not bear this out.[3]

Originally, Tingley saw an opportunity to purchase horses for himself and drive them back to British Columbia along with the BX horses. He discussed this with Barnard who, after some thought, replied:

> Dear Sir. I have been turning the subject of our last conversation over and can hardly make up my mind as to what is right but this is as near right as I can get it. When you reach San Francisco I will telegraph you to go on or not. If you go and buy on my account only, I will pay wages while you are at work for me and the expenses as low as you would if traveling on your own account. Should you conclude to buy any Stock on your own a/c in connection with me, they must be all bought together & the division to take place when brought in and the amount advanced by you to be liable to the proportion of the whole amt of stock and expenses. For instance, if you put in $2000.00 and I put in $4000.00 your proportion will be ⅓ (one third) of the whole cost of Stock and expense and the division to be made here.
>
> If you propose going in you must let me know at San Francisco before starting out.
>
> As yet I cannot say whether the cash will be forthcoming in time but can tell you by the time you get to Frisco.
>
> Expecting to hear from you by telegraph on your arrival. I am yours truly, FJ Barnard[4]

Tingley must have thought about the possibility of making a profit for himself but ultimately decided to stick to purchasing

Steve Tingley. IMAGE B-04915 COURTESY
OF THE ROYAL BC MUSEUM AND ARCHIVES

horses for the BX. Fortunately, Tingley's diary for the trip, despite
its cryptic nature and semi-legible writing, provides a day-by-day
account of the epic journey.[5]

Tingley left Victoria on January 1, 1868, and travelled by steamer
to Monticello on the Columbia and then to Portland, Oregon. After
talking to William Connell, who is believed to have helped him on
the 1863 trip to Oregon, he went by steamer to San Francisco. On
January 31, he was in San Francisco and sent a letter to Barnard via
Wells Fargo. Then he travelled by train to San Jose, by stagecoach to
San Luis Obispo, and then on to Santa Barbara, where he found that
"wild horses range from 10 to 30 dollars according to catch men and

quality of stock." [6] Tingley visited first the Rancho San Julian, which had recently come into the hands of Albert and Thomas Dibblee, where he was "gathering and looking at horses. Nothing as to price yet think $15. Best stock have seen yet but will not give more." That same day he visited the Rancho Dos Pueblos, originally a Mexican land grant amounting to 15,535 acres that in 1842 was awarded to Irish immigrant Nicholas Den. Den had died in 1862 and his huge holdings were being disposed of by his descendants. [7]

Between the two massive ranchos, Tingley could obtain 300 head of horses, comprising an equal number of mares and colts, for $15 each. On February 12, he recorded, "Returned to Santa Barbara and agreed with Dib [Albert Dibblee] and Den [probably Manuel Den] for 300 head mares and colts for $3150 at no expense until stock start. 150 head very fine mares." [8] The agreement was conditional on the approval of Barnard, so Tingley had to return to San Francisco by steamer and telegraph Barnard for approval. As the lines were down somewhere near New Westminster, it was not until March 3 that Tingley got the telegraph from Barnard confirming the deal and authorizing the money. Tingley travelled overland to Santa Barbara and began organizing his long horse drive north. On March 16, Tingley sent two men ahead with the "grub wagon," agreeing to pay them $30 a month. The next day he "left Dos Pueblos Ranch with Band of three hundred horses and five men." [9] What was probably the longest horse drive in North American history was begun.

We can get an idea of the origins and backgrounds of the men Tingley hired to drive his horses from their names and the places where they joined the drive. At the start of the drive, he hired five men to accompany the herd in addition to the two sent ahead with the cook wagon, a full complement to handle a herd of this size. Not surprisingly, given that he was hiring them at the Rancho Dos Pueblos, these men were mainly of Hispanic origin. Names like José Romero, Gabrillo Romero, Spaniard Theodore, Oliver Farra, Manuel, Hosa, and Antoine occur early in the drive and a few of them appear to have stayed until the end. Some of these were trained horsemen out of the long *vaquero* tradition of horsemen in

California. It is significant that Tingley was paying one dollar a day to most of his men but agreed to hire José Romero and Theodore at $2.50 and Gabrillo Romero for $2, indicating that they were experienced *vaqueros* who could oversee the herd in Tingley's absence. Hired men were leaving and more arriving throughout the drive and, as the herd progressed into northern California, men like George Turner, Morgan, Simpson, Woodruff, and Allen joined the drive. In the vocabulary of the day, all of these men would have been called "drovers," as the term "cowboy" was not yet in common usage west of the Rocky Mountains.

Driving horses is different and more difficult than driving cattle. As Tingley's herd consisted of mares and foals, the pace had to be slower than with a herd of mature horses. The drovers would have to ride around the herd during the night and turn back horses if they drifted away. Tingley also made frequent mention of the difficulty of driving horses along roads through unfenced grain fields.

Thanks to Tingley's diary, we can trace his route northward. He headed the herd through San Luis Obispo and by April 7 was camped in the foothills east of San Francisco. Leaving the horses and men in camp, he spent two days in San Francisco paying bills and obtaining supplies. After rejoining the herd at Stockton, he had the men and horses ferried across the San Joachin River from Antioch to Collinsville. A few days later they were on the Sacramento Plains near the gold rush city of that name. From there, they headed north through Red Bluff and then veered east to Millville, gaining altitude steadily as they entered the Sierras.

The next leg of the journey would be the hardest, through the mountainous terrain where the snow was still deep. The trail brought them over a low pass through three feet of snow to the Cayton Valley, which they reached on May 10. For the rest of May, Tingley would leave the horses to rest and struggled ahead on his own to find a way through the snowy and rugged country, occasionally finding grassy valleys where he could rest the stock before another push through a snowy pass. Progress was painfully slow, and where the snow was gone, the trails were so rocky that the horses' hooves were badly damaged. Finally, they reached the Klamath River and crossed it before proceeding into Oregon and on to Klamath Lake where they camped on the Williams River, north of the lake. It had taken Tingley's party over fifty days to travel the 300 miles from Sacramento to Klamath Lake, but the worst was over.

Just north of the lake was Fort Klamath, established in 1863 to deal with Klamath, Modoc, and Northern Paiute people who were attacking travellers. When Tingley passed through in 1868, the area was relatively peaceful, but the US Army was concerned that a large herd of horses passing through would be an open invitation for trouble. So Tingley was offered an escort of seven soldiers and two officers to accompany the horses and men as far as the Crooked River, which runs into the Deschutes River south of the Columbia. To assist in finding the route, three Klamath men went with the party. Tingley could finally see his way clear to British Columbia and recorded in his diary, "Things going lovely."[10] Of course, two days after that, the herd of horses was spooked on the trail and stampeded and five horses were lost. The soldiers turned into horse hunters, found four of the missing horses, and headed back to be greeted by the warm thanks of Tingley and party.

The party took its time from the Crooked River to the Columbia, allowing the horses to rest and recuperate. They reached the south bank of the Columbia on June 27 and found the river very high, presenting them with yet another obstacle. Tingley went to The Dalles and waited four days for an express from Walla Walla bringing him $250 from Barnard. A few days later, he received an additional $500, which he hoped would carry him through the final leg of the journey. But The Dalles was the stopping point for some of the crew who had been with him for a long time. He paid $119 to Hosa, $168.50 to Antoine, $70.50 to George Turner, and $50 to Simpson, leaving him short for the trip north. So he borrowed $160 from William Connell.

On July 6, the herd was successfully swum across the Columbia at The Dalles, with only one horse drowning. The horses then started out on the overland trail that had by then been used by thousands of head of cattle, by way of Fort Simcoe and the Yakima Valley. When they reached the Kittitas Valley, Tingley let the horses graze for three days and recorded, "grass good but flies bad."[11] The drive reached the upper Columbia across from Moses Coulee, which Tingley, like many others before him, identified as the "mouth of the Grand Cooley."[12] Two days later the herd swam the Wenatchee River and Tingley paid an Indigenous man for rafting over their food and assisting their crossing. On the last day of July they reached a point seven miles from the customs house at Lake Osoyoos, ready to cross into British Columbia.

While Tingley was making his way north, Barnard had been busy preparing for the arrival of his large band of horses. On March 11, before Tingley had even left Santa Barbara, he wrote to the colonial secretary:

> Sir I have received advice from California that a band of about 200 head of horses have been purchased on my account, and are being driven in via The Dalles, Oregon. I am anxious to know whether I can arrange for the payment of the duties here, in lieu of at the Boundary. I cannot say to a month or two when they will be at the line, but would like to forward instructions to my agent, by the Steamer, so that he would not be detained by Mr. Haynes. I presume the Government will have no objections to my paying the duties in the way proposed, as they have the necessary protection in their own hands.[13]

On the back of the letter was a notation from the colonial secretary. "This has been done before, and is advisable as the cash is collected here instead of at the Boundary." A few days later, Barnard was sent a reply, telling him that "the matter has been referred to Mr. Hamley, with instructions to receive the duties on the horses you are about to import here instead of at the S. Boundary."[14] Barnard followed this up in late April, stating, "I have the honor to inform you that the horses will be in, in June, and beg that you will send me a letter to the Customs House Officer at Southern Boundary, stating that the duties on the horses will be paid at New West, so that I can forward it to the party in charge of the band, for presentation at the Custom[s] House."[15] Little did Barnard know that the horses would not reach the border until August 1.

The herd proceeded up the trail that had, by 1868, seen 22,000 head of cattle driven over it. In some places the trail was in very poor condition, but the end was in sight. Reaching the head of Okanagan Lake, Tingley noted men cutting hay, possibly Cornelius O'Keefe and his partners, Thomas Wood and Thomas Greenhow, who had pre-empted land there the previous year.

They did not stay at the head of the lake but pushed north to Round Lake, where on August 9 Tingley left the drive in charge of three men and headed north with two others. The three of them rode to Cache Creek and then Clinton, where they caught the stagecoach to Yale. Once there, Tingley paid off the men, a total of $346, and headed back to the horses on his own. After staying a night at Lewis Campbell's ranch east of Kamloops, he rode to Henry Ingram's ranch at Grande Prairie (today's Westwold). The next day, he rode west through the narrow valley along the Salmon River and rejoined the horses at the "Stump Lake horse camp" that his men had established there. Stump Lake, or Lac des Chicots (Lake of Snags), was located on the former brigade trail through the Nicola Valley to Fort Kamloops, and could have been reached by driving the horses to Grande Prairie and then west to Stump Lake, where extensive grazing was available and a short horse drive north through Kamloops would get to the main route to the Cariboo.

Arriving at Stump Lake on August 24, Tingley found "Stump Lake Horse Camp all well. Indian Teabask [probably Terbasket, a local Indigenous name] cutting [castrating male] colts at $1 [each]."[16] Leaving the men in charge of the horse herd, Tingley made a quick trip to Cherry Creek, east of Priest's Valley (later Vernon), to look at a silver mine he and Barnard had invested in. Then, on August 29, he returned to the "Horse camp Stump Lake." The next day he "left horse camp with 32 horses" and drove them to Clinton, where they would be trained to pull stagecoaches.

Many interesting details can be gleaned from Tingley's diary about this epic cattle drive. Inside the front cover of his diary, Tingley kept an account of "Lost Stock" so we can see how many horses died or strayed on the trail and how many were traded or sold. According to this tally, twelve horses died. One was bitten by a rattlesnake, two colts died of distemper, two were drowned crossing the Klamath River and one crossing the Columbia, one fell over a bluff on the Upper Columbia, and the rest "gave out," as Tingley termed it, from exhaustion. Besides these, two horses strayed and were not found, two were given away as payment of some sort, two were lame and left behind in the Kitittas Valley, and nine were sold or traded, meaning there was some return for them. In some cases, the daily notations in the body of the diary give additional information. In one case, Tingley records trading "one little mare for three saddle horses and $135 to boot." In all, out of the 300 horses that Tingley started out with, twelve died, two were lost by straying, seven were traded and two sold, two were left behind, and two were given as payment. In return, Tingley received seven horses in trade and he purchased a saddle horse early on. By all calculations, 281 horses crossed at the Customs House into British Columbia, an excellent return considering the 1,270 miles (2,044 kilometres) they had come by then, with another 178 miles (287 kilometres) to go.

Tingley's diary also chronicles the significant assistance provided by Indigenous people along the way. Close to the Oregon border, an Indigenous man helped Tingley to find a way through the mountains and was paid $6 for his work. A little further on, in an area that the US Army still considered dangerous, the party was assisted in crossing the Klamath River by an Indigenous man who once again was paid for his efforts. In Washington Territory on the Okanogan River they purchased milk and corn from an Okanagan man. At various points along the way, Tingley recorded trade transactions with the local Indigenous people. He sold a mule and a mule colt to an Indigenous chief in the Klamath Lake area and, near the Wenatchee River, he traded five lame colts for two good ones with an Indigenous man. To put this interaction in context, the entire area of Washington Territory that they passed through had been the scene of open warfare between the US Army and the various Indigenous Peoples less than ten years earlier.

Tingley's diary departs from the story that has persisted for the past hundred years. Historians have maintained that Tingley brought the horses to the area near Priest's Valley where the BX Ranch had been established. The earliest version of the story of the BX Ranch appears to have been in F.W. Howay's 1914 foundational history, *British Columbia from the Earliest Times to the Present*. Howay wrote, "[in] 1864 Forbes G. Vernon and his brother Charles... took up about 1000 acres—the celebrated Coldstream Ranch... About the same time Mr. F.J. Barnard and associates in Barnard's Express obtained the B.X. Ranch, some four miles from Vernon for the purpose of raising horses for their express business. In 1868, Mr. Stephen Tingley, the practical man of the company, went to New Mexico and brought up overland about 400 head of horses to stock the ranch."[17] But Tingley's diary clearly states that the horses were driven further north to be held at Stump Lake. This would have made much more sense, as the Stump Lake area had excellent grazing and was at the time unsettled. It was also a short distance from the Cariboo Road and would allow the easy incorporation of the horses into the stagecoach line.

Considering that Barnard owned a pre-emption and lots at the 134-mile post by this time, it is unlikely he would have been allowed to pre-empt additional lands until he received his crown grant. In fact, it was not until May 10, 1873, that Barnard applied for a pre-emption of 320 acres "situated near Swan Lake, on a flat having rising hills to the north... Swan Lake lies to the West."[18] This is the first reference to Barnard pre-empting land in the Okanagan, designated Lot 51, and it is undoubtedly the first land taken out for the establishment of the BX Ranch. Barnard was a shrewd businessman, so it is unlikely he would have squatted on land for any length of time before filing a pre-emption claim. The establishment of the horse ranch at this time makes additional sense in light of the fact that Barnard's Express had established a branch line from Cache

Creek to the "Okanagon" (as it was spelled at the time) post office at the O'Keefe Ranch in August of 1872, which would provide the company with an opportunity to change horses from their nearby ranch.

The BX Ranch, most probably established around 1872, was to play an important part in Barnard's dream to develop a horse ranch that would support a stagecoach route to Lake Superior. In the meantime, it would have provided for the training and breeding of horses for the BC Express stage line.

THE STRUGGLE FOR YET ANOTHER MAIL CONTRACT

As the year 1867 drew to a close, the contract for delivery of mail from Victoria to Barkerville and all points between lapsed. With the purchase of Dietz and Nelson's company, Barnard controlled the transportation on the mainland of the colony but, without the mail contract, the financial viability of his business was in question. The major rush to the Cariboo goldfields had dwindled to a trickle and the mining had transitioned to deep diggings, requiring capital and large labour crews. Fortunately for Barnard, these diggings were generating a large amount of gold and Barnard's British Columbia Express, the newest name for Barnard's Cariboo Express, was the only means of shipping treasure to Victoria.

Hoping not to alienate the colonial authorities, who held the power to grant a new contract, Barnard refused to carry the mail as of January 1, when his previous contract expired. After a few weeks of no mail, the inhabitants of Barkerville began to express their outrage. A letter appeared in the *British Colonist* in early March asking, "Can you tell us anything as to the whereabouts of the Royal mail, which is said to have left Victoria some two months ago? . . . In fact, why was the mail not sent with the Express, or since Mr. Barnard pushes the Express through, why is the mail left on the road? Four fifths of the population receive nothing by Express, but rely entirely upon the mail for their letters and papers." In another section of the newspaper, the answer was given:

After the express had waited fifteen days in Yale for our up mails, the New Westminster political economists refuse to pay Mr. Barnard for carrying them, though it is now 48 days since we had a foreign mail on Williams Creek—the mainstay of the colony, without whose gold the colony would collapse in a week, and all the hungry officials who are fighting for spoils in the capital would be turned adrift to seek a living somewhere else, where, perhaps, they might be better appreciated. Yes! Here we are, fifteen hundred souls for seven weeks without communication with the outer world... because [of] the imbecile Government we are cursed with, and which neglects everything but taxation.[19]

Two days later, another letter was published in the *Colonist*:

Barnard stands almost alone, as one of the sole surviving representatives of a hundred public undertakings that have languished through the passing stupidity of a wooden headed Government. Barnard is and ever has been a sort of balm to Cariboo—no matter how many crosses and disappointments assailed us... Now alas! Even Barnard's Express seems about to be taken away, an enterprise which should have received the most diligent fostering care at the hands of our Solons, an enterprise that is above all others, the greatest monument of individual pluck and perseverance in British Columbia, and certainly one of the greatest utility.[20]

Alongside this public outcry, Barnard was proposing a solution to the colonial officials. In February he wrote to Charles Good, the acting colonial secretary:

I beg to inform you that an Express will be dispatched from New Westminster on or about the 25th Inst. when I shall be prepared to carry a mail to Barkerville and return to this place about the 4th or 5th of April. Should the Government desire to send a mail by this Express I will leave the matter of remuneration to them. I beg also to state that since the termination of the contract on the 31st December last I have continued to carry the mails, and Government dispatches, downwards the same as if the contract was still in existence and trust I may be liberally dealt with in the matter.[21]

Barnard was playing cagey. He had been bringing the mail down from Barkerville but not up, leaving the denizens of that small city without news from home in the dead of winter. Their outcry was more powerful than anything he could say or write. And what's more, by leaving "the matter of remuneration" to the colonial officials, he was putting the ball firmly in their court. The notes by these officials on the back of the correspondence are significant. Governor Seymour noted on February 4, "Mr. Barnard makes no definite offer. He is prepared to take anything the Govt offers. I think if he got $600 for the next up trip and $300 each for 3 down trips for Jan Feb March, $1600 in all he would not be overpaid. Probably a regular contract would be entered into in March." The acting colonial secretary referred the matter to the acting postmaster general, Arthur Busby, who went even further, noting on March 11 that a three-year contract had been entered into with Barnard. Clearly, the colonial government did not want to repeat this situation every year.[22]

The *Colonist* announced the new mail contract, pointing out that it was at an "annual rate of $16,000 or $48,000 for the three years. The price previously paid for the service was $24,000 a year. The Colony, by the new arrangement, gets three year's work for two year's pay."[23] This reflects the general poverty the combined colonies of Vancouver Island and British Columbia were experiencing in the post–gold rush era. Paying the interest on the debt incurred from the construction of two competing roads to the Cariboo was costing the colony one-third of its annual income. At the time of the union of the two colonies, British Columbia had a debt of $1,002,983 and Vancouver Island of $293,698. A request for approval of a new loan for the colony was turned down by the Parliament in London and citizens called for a drastic reduction in expenditures and in the number of colonial officials. Governor Seymour threw up his hands and declared, "I am not answerable for the debt. It was not incurred by me, yet it devolves upon me to pay and I believe that the doing so, is the principal cause of the outcry of 'miserable government.'

Reductions in salaries to the extent of upwards of $80,000 have been made in my tenure at office. I have never appointed anyone higher than a constable and have no hope in doing so during my incumbency of office."[24]

In the mining industry, the Big Bend had proven to be a short-lived excitement instead of a major new find, and the Kootenay mines had dwindled as well. Judge Begbie wrote to Henry Crease that gold mining on Williams Creek "does not turn out in a week more than half of what many an individual claim turned out in a day."[25]

Feelings of discouragement and distrust toward the government in Victoria, most prevalent on the mainland, reached a new level when Victoria was chosen over New Westminster as the capital of the colony. Governor Seymour, who had the right to choose the capital, left it up to the new executive council, most of whom were mainlanders. But when the vote was taken on March 29, 1867, the surprising choice of Victoria as capital was passed by thirteen votes to eight. Barnard, recently elected as a member of the council, voted against it.[26]

The feelings of helplessness and the need for change came to a head the following summer, on July 1, 1867, when the colonies of New Brunswick, Nova Scotia, and Upper and Lower Canada were united as the Dominion of Canada. Many on the mainland felt that uniting with the new Dominion was the answer to the financial difficulties of the colony.

Barnard was to find himself in the middle of a battle for power and control, in the midst of which a major disaster disrupted life in the colony and Barnard's business. In Barkerville, on September 16, 1868, a fire that started in Adler & Barry's Saloon around 2:30 in the afternoon, by 4:00 had burned the entire town to the ground. The Barnard's Express Office was totally destroyed but the safe in his office remained intact and he managed to salvage a few hundred dollars in cash and gold. Scott's Saloon was saved by cutting the water flume that ran over it, and the Barnard's Express stable on the edge of town was also saved. Losses were estimated at close to a million dollars but, with the indomitable pioneer spirit of the frontier colony, work in rebuilding began immediately and, by the following year, Barkerville was back to being the bustling city it had been before the fire.

BARNARD'S ROLE IN CONFEDERATION

Barnard became a member of the Legislative Council for the Colony of British Columbia just in time for the first session, in early in 1867. The Council consisted of five former colonial officials called the "Executive Council," nine magistrates from the colony, and nine members elected by the people of the colony, four from Vancouver Island and five from the mainland. British Columbia stood at a crossroads with three possible courses of action. It could remain an isolated British colony on the Pacific Coast, join the United States, or enter into the Canadian Confederation that was being formed.[27] When the Legislative Council met in March, Amor De Cosmos moved an initial course of action and, after much debate, on March 18, Joseph Pemberton made the following amended resolution, which was, surprisingly, passed unanimously by the council:

> Resolved that this Council is of the opinion that at this juncture of affairs in British North America, East of the Rocky Mountains, it is very desirable that His Excellency be respectfully requested to take such steps, without delay, as may be deemed by him best adapted to insure the admission of British Columbia into Confederation, on fair and equitable terms, this council being confident that in advising this step they are expressing the views of the Colonists generally.[28]

The unanimous support for this resolution was surprising since members of council represented different factions in the colony. While the colonial officials who formed the establishment in Victoria established friendships with prosperous Canadians like Barnard and others, behind their backs they would refer to them as "North American Chinamen" and members of the "colonial class" because of their tight-fisted attitude to money.[29]

At the same time, a group of disheartened businessmen in Victoria pointed to the United States' purchase of Alaska from Russia in October of 1867 as a justification for the colony's withdrawal from Britain and political union with the US. This group calling for annexation had strong financial motives. Since the beginning of the Colony of British Columbia, San Francisco had been the economic headquarters, with the State of Oregon and Washington Territory the main suppliers of goods and merchandise. The nearest British settlement was at Red River, some two thousand miles to the east, and the next British neighbour to the west was Hong Kong. One historian has remarked, "it is not surprising that an annexationist movement took shape in British Columbia. The wonder is that it was not stronger and that it did not make more progress. It was, in the main, limited to Victoria and secured no foothold on the mainland. The annexation group was composed of Americans and those British subjects who despaired of the maintenance of the British connection."[30]

A letter from Barnard, written in December of 1867 to a friend in the east, reveals his position on the question:

> Well things generally have been gradually getting worse and worse... Some of us think we can see "land ahead" in Confederation and we are endeavoring to direct the minds of others hitherward and I flatter myself that a very strong Confederation feeling has been engendered of late. We are so utterly poor as a community... or we could have sent out a delegate to Ottawa this session to labor in convincing the Dominion that our country is worth having, for the impression seems to obtain in Canada that we are not worth the paper requisite to write the deed of confederation upon. You know, of course, what a stupendous mistake this is; our resources are gradually being developed and every year teaches us that we know nothing, really nothing of the country in which we live... You are aware that the Legislative Council last winter passed unanimously a resolution in favor of confederation. Even the Governor yielded and assured a deputation of the Council that he had no personal interest to come and would further the

scheme to the extent of his power. Since then we have heard nothing from him. We are now only waiting to hear from Ottawa to know what this disposition towards us is & we will again act in accord. I am in hopes that the leading men will come to our rescue or we are done for years.

I presume you are not yet American enough to suppose there is any chance of annexation. If you are, set the notion aside. The great majority of the people would fight against any such move, while Confederation is looked upon as our only salvation.[31]

This letter casts light on Barnard's wholehearted commitment to the confederation movement. He continued to advocate for its acceptance by the colony. Those who supported confederation formed a Confederation League in Victoria and, within weeks, the organization was supported by branches in New Westminster, Yale, Lytton, Clinton, and Barkerville. Barnard also travelled with De Cosmos in June to the Okanagan Valley to solicit support.[32] The movement then organized the Yale Convention, which assembled on September 14, with twenty-six delegates, including three members of the Legislative Council, De Cosmos, Robson, and Barnard. Under their leadership, the convention adopted resolutions advocating immediate union with Canada, the establishment of representative government, the reduction of colonial officials, and the halving of the governor's salary.[33]

In spite of vigorous opposition, this convention and the ensuing movement for confederation would eventually win the day. Barnard never wavered from his belief. When, in July of 1871, British Columbia became a province of Canada, he and his fellow leaders could truly be termed "Fathers of Confederation" in their own province.

BARNARD ATTEMPTS TO STEAM INTO THE FUTURE

In June of 1870, Barnard travelled on the steamer *California* to San Francisco with his fourteen-year-old son, Frank Junior, journeying

The Thomson Road Steamer.
PACIFIC RURAL PRESS, JANUARY 14, 1871

from there by train across the US and into Canada. This was the quickest way to cross the continent to enroll his son in Helmuth Boys' College in London, Ontario. En route, he would also visit his brother, James, and his sister, Margaret, who had married George Sargison. He encouraged the Sargisons to move to British Columbia, which they would do three years later. While he was in the east he read an interesting account of steam-driven road vehicles and the idea caught fire in his imagination.

As we have seen, Barnard was a visionary. In 1868, he had sent Steve Tingley to purchase horses for running a coach from Yale to Lake Superior, but as negotiations to unite British Columbia to the new Dominion of Canada progressed, he saw that a railway would likely be the best means of spanning the distance. Undeterred, he moved on to the next scheme.

He began to read about the Thomson Patent India Rubber Tire Road Steamers. Although the potential for steam-driven road vehicles had been studied and experimented with for some time, R.W. Thomson of Edinburgh, Scotland, came up with an innovation in 1869 that prevented the solid iron wheels from destroying the roads and jarring the vehicle's machinery. The three broad wheels were covered with five-inch-thick (125-mm) India rubber that adhered to the iron wheel through friction, to allow a certain amount of slippage that saved the surface of the tire. The London *Times* reported that artillery officers were impressed with the vehicle's ability in snow and mud. In early 1871, San Francisco's *Pacific Rural Press* reported that "two sizes are made, of 8 and of 12 horse power, which draw loads of 20 and of 30 tons, respectively, on an ordinary level road, and 12 and 17 tons up inclines of 1 in 12. The speed is 2 ½ to 6 miles per hour for freight steamers, and 10 miles for passenger service. The consumption of coal is about ½ ton daily. The prices are $5,000 and $6,500."[34]

Barnard was fascinated by the idea and, despite having invested in 300 head of horses to pull his stagecoaches, he envisioned a fleet of road steamers carrying the mail and passengers of Barnard's Express. His idea was enthusiastically adopted by Josiah Beedy, a successful miner, merchant, and packer at Van Winkle on Lightning Creek. Beedy had been successful in mining and, like Barnard, he had some money to invest. So the two entrepreneurs agreed to import not just one but six Thomson Road Steamers in hopes that they would revolutionize transportation in British Columbia.

In the fall of 1870, when the three-year mail contract was coming up for renewal, Barnard wrote to Governor Anthony Musgrave pointing out that the call for tenders for the conveyance of mail allowed for "any means of conveyance suitable to contractor, due regard being had to the security of mail matter" and proposed "the introduction of steam power on the common roads of the mainland and perhaps importing six (6) of RW Thompsons [*sic*] Patent India rubber tire Road Steamers, two (2) of which will be especially constructed with a new 2-speed to be used in the transportation of Mails, Express and Passengers." To introduce this new form of transportation in the colony, Barnard requested "a mail subsidy [to] render them such protection for a term of years as will justify them in investing their capital in the enterprise. In consideration of a subsidy for conveyance of mail of thirty two thousand dollars ($32,000) per annum," the company would agree:

To carry a mail weekly as per advertisement by means of coaches drawn by Road Steamers, the coaches will afford accommodation for 24 passengers, and the train will travel at an average speed of seven (7) miles per hour. At this rate after allowing 6 hours for rest at Clinton, mail matter and passengers will be conveyed from Yale to Soda Creek in 48 hours and to Barkerville in 72 hours. The cost of passage from Yale to Soda Creek to be not over thirty dollars and from Yale to Barkerville exclusive of steamboat fare, Forty Dollars... The company would also be willing to undertake to deliver on behalf of the post office authorities all letters and newspapers being mail matter intended for parties living between post offices on the travelled road without any additional charge thus virtually bringing the post office to every man's door.[35]

Barnard went on to assure the governor that his company would "expend a liberal sum in advertising and in diffusing information respecting the colony to mines etc. in California," and concluded:

In addition to the subsidy before mentioned that [the company] be allowed to import the requisite Engines not exceeding twelve in number with machinery carriages and wagons and all tools requisite for their repair free of duty and also that they be protected in the exclusive right to use such steamers on the public roads of the mainland for the term of three years and in that event they undertake to have the machines above referred to landed in Victoria in time for the early spring business of 1871.[36]

The government took little time in responding, the colonial secretary writing to Barnard on October 18: "In reply I am directed to acquaint you that the Government is not prepared to recommend to the Legislature the expenditure of so large a sum as the acceptance of your proposal would entail & that Hs Ex. is therefore obliged to decline your proposal." To add insult to injury, even though Barnard had written that he would "agree to continue the service as at present," the government decided to award the mail contract to a new company, Gerow & Johnson's, for the coming year.[37]

In January of 1871, Dr. Carrall, a member of the Legislative Council, introduced a bill that would provide the granting of three years, exclusive privilege to run the steamers in British Columbia. This was enthusiastically endorsed by the *British Colonist*, which referred to the idea as "one of the greatest and most important scientific improvements of the age."[38]

In response to those in opposition, large petitions were signed and submitted to the governor from the communities of "Wagon Road—Richfield to Clinton" (162 signatures), "Williams Creek and Vicinity" (202 signatures), "Lightning Creek and Tributaries" (170 signatures), "Lilloet—Clinton District" (58 signatures), and the "Yale—Lytton District" (42 signatures). The petitions indicated that, having learned "that a company has been formed for the purpose of applying to Your Excellency for powers to enable them to put Road Steamers on the roads of British Columbia ... being convinced of their utility for this country as a cheap and more expeditious mode of transit ... your petitioners hope your Excellency will give the subject your most serious consideration." The *British Colonist* listed every name and concluded, "the Mainland would appear to be very earnest in its desire for their introduction. Who opposes?"[39] Though support for road steamers was not supported by all and there was great debate, the bill passed ten votes to three.

Barnard and Beedy were undeterred that they had lost the mail contract, and went ahead with their scheme. The six road steamers, along with six engineers to operate them, arrived in early April and one of them, accompanied by four of the engineers, was shipped to Yale for a trial run. All eyes in the colony were directed to Yale and the inaugural run in what was being called the "new age in transportation." As the steamers were wood burners, large stacks of wood had to be cut and piled at various points along the road from Yale to Soda Creek.

The *British Colonist* reported on April 22 that their "Exclusive Dispatch from Yale will show our readers the astonishing performance of the Road Steamer yesterday. Finding 20,000 pounds of freight too light a load the steamer returned for additional wagons and will leave again today for Cariboo. Slow-coaches like the organ of bull-teams had better 'clear the track' when the road steamers whistle, or they will be run down."[40] The next day, the *British Colonist* reported that the steamer "moved off at the rate of four miles an hour, dragging two wagons with 18,000 pounds of freight. The result of the test proved in every respect satisfactory. The steamer makes very little noise, and the bull and mule teams regarded the great innovator, as it glided almost noiselessly by, with a look of sleepy indifference."[41]

Before long, optimism began to wane. The Fraser Canyon road tested the steamers and exposed serious flaws. Stoppages were frequent as more wood had to be taken on and, as the steamers were fitted with vertical boilers, going up and downhill affected the level of water, resulting in leakages and overheating of the tubes. What's more, despite the "Patented India Rubber" tires, much damage to the roadbed had to be repaired. It took three days to cover the forty-two miles to Jackass Mountain and the steamer stopped there . . . for good.

Many reports described the main obstacle that stopped the steamer as the steep climb up Jackass Mountain, but the steamer was actually very efficient climbing hills. The *British Colonist* reported the real and fatal flaw:

> We regret to have to announce that there will be a temporary interruption to the road steamer enterprise in the upper country. It is found that the links holding the steel shoes which form the flexible or outer tires, being made of malleable cast iron, will not answer on the rocky roads of this colony, as they are constantly snapping, causing much delay. In every other respect the steamers appear to answer very well. They are singularly tractable, being most completely under the control of the driver, while they climb the severest grade with the utmost ease. This single difficulty can of course be easily overcome, but not, it is feared, in time to enable them to accomplish much this season. The difficulty will be properly represented to the manufacturer and patentees, and there can be little doubt that with the substitution of good wrought iron links the machine will be found to be well adapted to the carrying trade of the country.[42]

Barnard and Beedy decided to cut their losses. They returned four of the road steamers to the manufacturers and kept two at Yale in hopes that some use might be made of them. Between the cost of purchasing the steamers and having them shipped to and from British Columbia, they were out a considerable amount of money. In 1872, the City of Victoria considered purchasing one of them for road work but, as a letter to the editor stated, "When we consider engineer's and fireman's salary, the liability to break (which was made painfully evident when the machines were tried on the Mainland) I think the ratepayers will agree with me when I advise the Corporation to let the machines alone."[43]

Despite this setback, the story has a happy ending. In 1874, it was reported, under the heading "Logging By Steam," that "one of F.J. Barnard's road steamers (Thomson's Patent) has been purchased by Mr. J. Rogers of Burrard Inlet, to be employed in moving spars and saw logs to the sea shore, in other words, to take the place of oxen in the logging business. Sundry experiments were tried with the machine at Yale, with a view to testing its fitness for the work intended, and we are told that the results were highly satisfactory." The experiment turned out to be quite successful. It was reported early the next year that "the road steamer employed by Mr. Rogers is a splendid success as a logger." The following year, Jeremiah "Jerry" Rogers purchased the second steamer, declaring that "Mr. Rogers finds them cheaper than oxen for hauling out heavy timber."[44]

In an interesting side note, Jerry Rogers had his logging camp on English Bay at a place named after him, "Jerry's Cove." The name was eventually shortened to "Jericho" and applied to the beach. So the fine people of Vancouver can thank Jerry Rogers and the Thomson Road Steamers for clearing the timber in Kitsilano long before it was considered fit for habitation. In the meantime, British Columbia had to wait another thirty-five years before motorized transportation would come to the province.

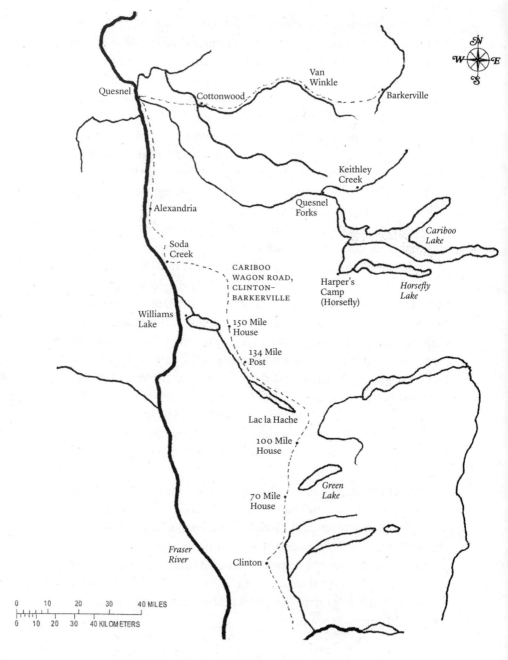

The Cariboo Wagon Road eventually stretched deeper into
the heart of the Cariboo, from Clinton to Quesnel
(formerly Quesnelle Mouth), and onward to Barkerville.

6

F.J. BARNARD
& COMPANY

I T WAS STAGECOACH etiquette that, if there was a woman travelling, she would be offered the seat of honour up on "the box next to the driver and the most comfortable room in a stopping house. This applied whether she was rich or poor, a "woman of the creeks" or a pillar of society. So when a woman arrived at the stagecoach stop in Clinton and booked passage down to Yale, the driver, Steve Tingley, extended the offer to her, despite the fact that she was dressed in men's clothing and, from her demeanor, was hardened to frontier life. As the trip would involve a long stretch through the Fraser Canyon during the night, she allowed that she would prefer riding inside where she could catch a few winks and, besides, pointing to a newly acquired bottle of whisky, she had some "tonic" that might help her sleep.

When night arrived, it proved to be a dark one and Tingley had to trust his horses to find their way. In the darkest part of the night, the horses shied at something only they could see, and over went the coach. Though the coach was easily righted, the accident was somewhat traumatic for the passengers. From the midst of the struggling horses and the overturned coach the woman arose, her bottle of whisky in one hand and pistol in the other. Her avowed intention was then and there to shoot Steve for throwing her out of the coach. Steve looked at her in silence, and then, with the proverbial courtesy he extended to all of his passengers, he begged her pardon and assured her it should not happen again. Somewhat taken aback, the woman acknowledged his apology; the coach was righted, and the journey resumed.[1]

GEROW AND JOHNSON'S BRITISH COLUMBIA EXPRESS

Tenders for the mail contract for the year 1871 were submitted in early October and, despite Barnard's complicated offer involving a subsidy for the importation of road steamers, a decision was made quickly and an announcement came ten days later. "The contract for carrying the mails on the Mainland over the routes now travelled by Barnard's Express, has been awarded to Messrs. Gerow & Johnson for one year at $13,000. The coaches are to be drawn by four horses. The service to be once a week for seven months in the year and twice a week for the remaining five months."[2]

With the awarding of the mail contract to Gerow & Johnson, Barnard was without an interest in conveying the mail for the first time in eight years. Gideon Gerow was a wagon builder and city councillor in Victoria. Johnson had been part owner of the Cariboo Stage Company, known as Humphrey, Poole & Johnson, that provided transportation from Quesnelle Mouth to Williams Creek in 1865 and 1866, driving the stagecoach from Quesnelle Mouth to Cottonwood House. Gerow, with his responsibilities as a Victoria city councillor, was the major financial backer and looked after the Victoria office. Offices were set up in New Westminster, where H.R. Scott was the agent and at Yale, where C.G. Sawyers was the agent. For the first three months, the mail alone was carried but, in March, regular stagecoach service was available to passengers "at greatly reduced rates."[3] To facilitate this, Gerow put his company to work constructing "a fine new stagecoach, built at Gerow's carriage shop and trimmed and furnished at Dalby, Watson & Co.'s ... for Gerow & Johnson, Mail contractors."[4]

Barnard had encountered opposition before and knew how to deal with it. He had the advantage, as his was the preferred carrier for treasure going down from the Cariboo. The situation is clear from a May report from Yale, which said that "both stages arrived here last night. Barnard's bringing an Express of $45,000 in treasure; Gerow & Johnson's bringing the Cariboo mail and an express. Both stage companies are preparing for a vigorous opposition."[5] At Barnard's usual rate of 2.5 per cent, he would have realized $1,125 even if he had no passengers. And so began a price war that saw the fare from Yale to Soda Creek get as low at $15 per person. By the time the year's contract ran out, Gerow & Johnson were struggling to keep up. Their final mail trip of the year left Barkerville on December 25 and did not make it to New Westminster in time, while Barnard's express left a day later with $30,000 in treasure and arrived on time.[6]

British Columbia had joined the Canadian Confederation on July 20, 1871, so Gerow & Johnson had the distinction of having the last Interior mail contract in the colony.

CONFEDERATION BRINGS CHANGE TO BRITISH COLUMBIA

When the delegates from the Colony of British Columbia went to Ottawa in 1870, one of their demands was for the construction of a wagon road from Fort Garry across the prairies and through the mountains to British Columbia. They were surprised when the Canadian representatives, without urging, offered to build a railway to the Pacific instead of a coach road. In fact, commencement of the line within two years and completion within ten years was promised. A million dollars a year would be spent on the British Columbia construction of the line, in return for which, BC would provide a twenty-mile-wide belt on each side of the promised railway for an annual payment of $100,000. These offers, much more generous than the BC delegates were prepared to demand, were taken back to the Legislative Council and, after a brief debate, approved on January 18, 1871.

The only one who might have been disappointed by the terms was Barnard, who had for years envisioned a stage line from Yale to Lake Superior. But even he had to agree that the confederation he had long envisioned was going to become a reality. Barnard was happy to see that one of the first actions of the new provincial government under Premier John McCreight was to abolish all the road taxes.

A much more negative reaction was prevalent among the British colonial officials who, in many cases, were offered jobs in the new provincial government. But, as one official put it, "It is very awkward as a Dominion officer having to apply to Canada for orders."[7] Another official lamented, "We are a conquered country & the Canucks take possession tomorrow."[8] Two years later, this attitude had not disappeared. W.J. Macdonald, who had been connected to Vancouver Island since 1851, wrote to Henry P.P. Crease, the son of a Royal Navy Captain who came to BC in 1858: "Many changes have taken place certainly and a good many of the old landmarks removed by death—and many of the social distinctions removed by the revolution in political affairs. The present administration must be very distasteful to you and all your former associates, as you remark not one of them that you would care to have for a friend, or ask to your house."[9]

The new BC Members of Parliament, among whom was Amor De Cosmos, who had wanted to be the new premier, all supported Prime Minister John A. Macdonald. For this, they expected favours for their friends and allies. Unfortunately, there were few appointments Macdonald could dole out, though one of his areas of jurisdiction was the postal service. This would prove beneficial to Barnard, who had watched Gerow & Johnson carry Her Majesty's Mail through 1871.

On January 20, 1872, the *British Colonist* pointed out with dismay, "Eight days ago today Barnard's Express, bringing letters, draft and treasure, which left Barkerville on the 26th December, arrived at Victoria. The snail mail, which left Barkerville one day before . . . has not yet reached Victoria." The *British Colonist* went on to point out that the mail carried by Gerow & Johnson "was at Yale when Barnard's Express left that point. The contractor's agent tried to get a passenger by Barnard's Express to bring it on, but he declined to perform work gratuitously that others *are paid for not doing*, and the result is that our merchants—except those who had the foresight to direct their letters be sent by Barnard—are unable to close their accounts for 1871." The *British Columbian* wrote in support of the current contractors. In response, the editor of the *British Colonist* wrote in an editorial "Royal Snail-Mail and its Apologists" that there was general dissatisfaction throughout the mainland about the mail being so often late, and suggested "taking immediate and very decided steps to remedy an evil which is unquestionably occasioning much discontent and entailing serious inconveniences in an important section of the Province. Such a course is equally due to the Federal Government and the local interests. We sincerely trust it will be unnecessary to revert to this subject." In early February, the *British Colonist* again wrote, "THE MAILS AGAIN—No Cariboo mail arrived last evening, although two mails are overdue. The telegraph announces that the first January mail only left Soda Creek on the 1st inst. bound down."[10]

Gerow & Johnson had struggled to succeed but, in late February, withdrew from the contract. The Dominion government under John A. Macdonald, moved quickly. On February 20, the new Victoria postmaster, Henry Wooton, posted a call for tenders for the New Westminster and Cariboo Postal Service.[11] Within a few days, the contract was awarded to Barnard's Express and, on March 21, the *British Colonist* announced that "Barnard's Express with the first Cariboo Mail under the new contract arrived yesterday, having been only ten days from Barkerville. The roads were in a deplorable state."[12]

Barnard was proud to announce, in the March 26, 1872, issue of the *British Colonist*, that "Barnard's Express Line Stages carrying Her Majesty's Mails will commence on April 1st to make weekly trips to Cariboo. Connecing at Yale with the Steamer 'Onward,' Capt. W.M. Irving, and at Soda Creek with the Steamer 'Victoria,' Capt. G.B. Wright. Stages leave Yale on arrival of Onward on Mondays, and arrive at Barkerville on Fridays. Leave Barkerville on Saturdays and arrive at Yale on Thursdays in time to connect with the steamer for New Westminster. Fares: To Barkerville—$60. To

Soda Creek—$45." The very reasonable fares, even though they were not close to those set the previous year when Gerow & Johnson had threatened business, reflected Barnard's growing optimism that Confederation and the promised railway across Canada, would bring more and more settlers to the new province.

But Barnard had not escaped unscathed from the failed road steamers experiment or the year-long loss of the mail contract. In May, he announced that he had "admitted Stephen Tingley and James Hamilton into Partnership in the ... business from and after first day of April instant. This business will be continued henceforth under the name of F.J. Barnard & Co. Yale, April 13th, 1872."[13] The *Cariboo Sentinel* expressed its approval of the new partnership:

> Mr. Barnard has taken Mr. James Hamilton and Mr. Stephen Tingley, two of his oldest employees, into partnership in the business. Both of these gentlemen are long and favorably known not only for the efficient manner in which they have handled the "ribbons," but more especially for the uniform courtesy and kindness which every one who has patronized the line has experienced at their hands. We are satisfied that Mr. Barnard has added both to the efficiency and popularity of the Express by joining with him in the business two men so thoroughly acquainted with the country and so deservedly popular with the whole community.[14]

Both Tingley and Hamilton had been with Barnard since his first attempt at running a stage line and each purchased one-quarter of the business. Not only did this relieve some of the financial strain, it also freed Barnard up to undertake new ventures.

NEW BRANCH LINES TO THE OKANAGAN AND CASSIAR

One of these new ventures was in response to a request for mail service to the Okanagan Valley, where settlers were arriving in greater numbers and extolling the agricultural prospects of the region. In March, a resolution had been passed by the settlers in the valley "that a humble address be presented to His Excellency the Lieutenant Governor praying that he will recommend to the Dominion Government the immediate necessity of regular Mail Service through the Kamloops, Okanagan, Spallumcheen and Nicola Lake sections of the Yale–Lytton District, such Mail Service to connect with the different Post Offices on the general route between New Westminster and Cariboo."[15]

The petition brought quick results, the Dominion wanting to appear concerned and helpful to its new province and her citizens. In June, the chief commissioner of lands and works and the surveyor general headed for the Okanagan "to lay out the wagon-road. They will superintend other public improvements en route."[16] By August, Barnard advertised:

Barnard's Express Stages for Okanagan. Under temporary arrangement for conveyance of the Mails from Cache Creek to Okanagan the undersigned has placed a line of Passenger Stages on the New Wagon Road to Okanagan. Running to close connection with the Stage from Yale to Barkerville. Persons visiting the Okanagan District will find this stage by far the most convenient mode of travel. Stages leave Cache Creek on Wednesday mornings at 10 o'clock, and will return the following week in time to connect with the Stages going North and South.[17]

The stage, most likely a two-horse thorough braced wagon, would leave Cache Creek, change horses at Savona's Ferry, then change horses and overnight in Kamloops. The next day, the stagecoach would change horses at Duck & Pringle's (Monte Creek) and at Grand Prairie (Westwold) before reaching Okanagan late on Thursday. The stagecoach would return the following week to connect with stages going north and south along the Cariboo Road.

The name "Okanagan" referred to the O'Keefe Ranch, which at that time was the end of the wagon road. Settled in 1867 by Cornelius O'Keefe and his partners, Thomas Greenhow and Thomas

Smaller Jerky stagecoaches were most often used on the branch lines.

IMAGE I-33597 COURTESY OF THE ROYAL BC MUSEUM AND ARCHIVES

Wood, the ranch was where the Okanagon (apparently misspelled by the authorities in Ottawa) post office was established on August 14, with O'Keefe as postmaster.

As had been Barnard's practice in the past, he had one of his employees, Alexander Vance, bid on and be awarded the mail contract. Vance had been a hosteller for Butterfield's Overland Mail Company at Warner's Ranch, near Temecula, California, in 1860, but by the mid-1860s was working for Barnard. By 1871, he was listed as an agent for Barnard's Express at the Bonaparte River stopping house.[18] Vance took charge of the day-to-day operations of the branch line, called Vance's Express.

Vance would also be instrumental in the development of the famous BX Ranch, which raised the horses for the stagecoaches. The horses driven up from Southern California by Steve Tingley in 1868 were kept at a horse camp near Stump Lake, on the old fur-trade brigade trail from Fort Hope to Fort Kamloops. The Fort Kamloops journal noted that on March 17, 1870, "Barnard's man Vance drove down stage horses on route to Cache Creek."[19] This suggests that the BX Ranch had been established by then, but this is unlikely, given that no pre-emption was filed for the original BX land until 1873. It is more likely that, in 1870, the horses were still being held at Stump Lake or some other place in the Nicola Valley, where they would be at least partially broken.

By 1872, when the branch line to the Okanagan had been established, it made a great deal more sense to have a ranch in the valley. This is suggested by an account in the *British Colonist* that mentions "WINTERING STOCK—Mr. Barnard has, we understand, undertaken the wintering of five hundred mules belonging to the Railway Survey. We believe they will be wintered at Okanagan, where Mr. Barnard has already a drove of some five hundred horses of his own."[20] Barnard's pre-emption in the north Okanagan consisted of 320 acres "situated near Swan Lake, on a flat having rising hills to the north... Swan Lake lies to the West."[21] Designated Lot 51, this was the beginning of the BX Ranch.

The road from Fort Kamloops to the Okanagan Valley was not always smooth sailing. In the spring of 1873, the agent for Vance's Okanagan Express in Kamloops wrote to Robert Beaven, chief commissioner of lands and works, that his driver "was so completely worn out and thoroughly disgusted with the state of the Road that he has given notice to quit... The wear and tear on our Driver, Horses and Stage is so great that unless the road is placed in a state of repair Mr. Vance will be compelled to notify the Postmaster General of his inability to carry out the terms of his contract. Not only has the contractor to suffer from horses giving out in mud holes and stages breaking down, but he has been compelled to refuse Express freight." The driver, John Irving, added that the road was in a "dangerous and almost impassible state" with "several mud holes in which the stage sinks to the axles." He went on to declare that he "had to cut alone in the last two trips sixteen fallen trees." He made "this solemn declaration" before Andrew Mara, Justice of the Peace in Kamloops.[22]

In 1881, the mail contract was extended to Okanagan Mission (later Kelowna), with J.B. Leighton holding the contract on behalf of the BC Express (as it was called by then). Since Priest's Valley (later Vernon) and Okanagan Mission were small settlements at the time, mail and express were carried on horseback beyond the O'Keefe Ranch.

Another branch line was started by R.J. Lamont in 1870 to connect Barnard's Express with the Omineca mining area in northern British Columbia, where gold was discovered in late 1869, with a rush the following year. Lamont's express connected with Barnard's at Quesnelle Mouth, operating no doubt with Barnard's blessing, extending his reach into northern British Columbia. Lamont's Express left Quesnelle Mouth on the fifteenth of every month and used the Barnard's Express office in Quesnelle Mouth as its main depot. By the end of summer, Lamont had gone back to full-time mining in the Omineca and Rufus Sylvester started Sylvester's Omineca Express for the region. He carried express and gold between Omineca and Quesnel through the winter of 1870–71 by dogsled and continued through the following summer.

By 1873, the Omineca gold rush had declined and, two years later, there were only eighty miners in the district. But the mining frontier continued to expand to the north and, in 1874, gold was discovered to the south of the Omineca in the Cassiar country, at McDame Creek and at Thibert Creek, a tributary of Dease Creek. In 1874, more than a million dollars' worth of gold was taken from the region, and Barnard ran a "Cassiar Express" from January to November of that year. Mining continued on a smaller scale in the following years without the Cassiar Express. The Cassiar region had the distinction of yielding the largest nugget ever recorded in British Columbia: a 72-ounce gold nugget, mined from McDame Creek.

F.J. Barnard & Company's infrastructure and proven integrity in carrying gold made it almost unassailable by competitors. In the spring of 1872, Abraham Barlow, a prosperous merchant in Quesnel, started up Barlow's Fast Freight Line of Stages, running from Yale to Barkerville. At the same time, Harry Wilmot of Lightning Creek advertised himself as "The Pioneer Expressman" and ran an express from Barkerville and Richfield to Van Winkle and Stanley on Lightning Creek. By the end of summer, Barlow had been reduced to running a service from Quesnelle Mouth (by then referred to simply as "Quesnel" as opposed to "Quesnel Forks" upriver) to Barkerville and Wilmot had disappeared. But Barnard's competitors were not gone yet.

During the construction of the CPR in the early 1880s, another branch run of the BC Express, as the company was renamed by then, was set up to travel from Spences Bridge to Kamloops via the Nicola Valley. The postmaster and telegraph agent at the time was Lawson Coates, Steve Tingley's nephew. For a time, another contract was established to carry mail from Kamloops eastward to Eagle Pass, where the railway was being constructed through the Monashee Mountains. The driver of the jerky coach on this route was W.J. Church, who had earlier carried mail and express for the CPR survey party. But, once the railway was completed, only the line through the Nicola Valley was kept in service.

WEATHERING THE STORM OF JANUARY 1874

Barnard was no stranger to bitter winters. His first recorded trip as an expressman involved travelling on foot through the Fraser Canyon with a full pack of express matter in the winter of 1861–62, one of the coldest on record. He left Lytton on December 28 and arrived at Yale five days later, on January 2, where the temperature measured –4 Fahrenheit (–20 Celsius). The next day, he left Yale and travelled another four days over the river ice to New Westminster. On January 13, he left New Westminster by canoe with five other travellers. The river was frozen in many places, so they made the journey mostly on foot over river ice, dragging the canoe for fifteen miles before hitting open water. On the first day they reached Plumper's Pass, now called Active Pass, between Maine and Gabriola Islands, where they camped. The cold was intense and they all suffered through the night. The next night was spent at Orcas Island in the San Juan Islands. The party finally straggled into Victoria on January 15.[23] A month later, on the next trip, "Mr. Barnard of the

Express Company, had one foot frozen while making the trip from New Westminster to Yale. He has continued the trip from Sumas on a sledge drawn by Indians."[24]

While those early trips taught Barnard a lesson in handling the cold, his experience with snow during the deadly storm of January 1874 took the prize for "worst ever." An unprecedented storm that closed the Fraser Canyon was followed by a political storm that dealt a devastating blow to Barnard's good reputation. Fortunately, Barnard compiled a scrapbook record of the entire storm which his family preserved, with telegraphs and newspaper clippings that chronicle the storm and its aftermath.

The storm unleashed all its fury in the middle of January and, by the seventeenth of that month, stagecoach driver and partner James Hamilton telegraphed from Lytton that the snow was "30 inches on level, drifts 6 feet, impossible to travel."[25] By the twenty-third, the *Victoria Daily Standard* reported from Yale that "Road Super-intendent Black came from Chapman's Bar this morning, two days making thirteen miles. He reports snow on road six to twenty feet deep in some places. Nothing can be seen of the telegraph line, and says the road could not be shovelled out to permit the passage of teams in less than six weeks. He will at once proceed to shovel a path to permit travel on snow shoes, which is now almost impossible, so as to permit of the mail being packed in from Lytton."[26] The report went on to record from Clinton, "Barnard's down stage is five hours overdue. It is supposed the snow drifts are the cause of detention." A further update from Yale on the twenty-first stated:

> The storm is still raging as fierce as ever. Reports from Alexandra Bridge say the road is completely blocked up and the general opinion is that it will be impossible for teams to come through for six weeks yet, the snow being four feet on a level at least, and drifted up to the depth of sixteen feet in some places . . . No news from the down mail, due here on Saturday last. The up mail reached Cheam [near Chilliwack] last night where they were stopped by the ice. The river from that point to Hope is supposed to be completely closed; from Hope to Yale it is jammed in many places.[27]

As the storm continued, the telegraph lines, still intact, allowed Barnard and his agent in Victoria, George Sargison, to connect with his agents J.W. Morrison in New Westminster, William Dodd in Yale, John McIntyre in Lytton, and George Byrnes in Barkerville. Between January 20 and February 4, no fewer than thirty telegraphs were sent to and from these six individuals. In just one day, January 28, the following were sent (I have added punctuation):

Jan 28 – FJB to Dodd – When did down mail reach? When despatch below?

Jan 28 – FJB to Dodd – What is reason of detention above Yale? Telegraph me particulars.

Jan 28 – FJB to Dodd – Where is Hamilton? Where were down mails when you heard last?

Jan 28 – Dodd to FJB – Not yet. Arrival uncertain. Will advise when it does.

Jan 28 – Dodd to FJB – Immense drifts, dangerous slides, impossible to travel ten miles a day on snowshoes. Black only traveler since storm took two days from Bridge.

Jan 28 – Dodd to FJB – Lytton advised me Hamilton at Salters [42 Mile House at the foot of Jackass Mountain] Sunday night. Think they are safe.[28]

The people living in the canyon, mainly Nlaka'pamux, were always the "go to" people when the roads got snowed in. Barnard had depended on them in the Fraser Canyon many times over the years. John McIntyre telegraphed from Lytton on January 23 that a "Sleigh and ten Indians breaking road. Snow four foot level." The next day, Barnard telegraphed William Dodd at Yale, "Send Indian with bags. Letters only [excluding parcels] if mail not started." On the twenty-ninth, he telegraphed George Byrnes in Barkerville that, "Not an Indian has reached Yale since sixteenth." It turned out that this storm was a challenge for even the most experienced

Indigenous person. The *Victoria Daily Standard* wrote on February 4 that "the road between Yale and Lytton was completely blocked, the snow in many places lying to the depth of 25 feet, rendering travel even on foot all but impossible. An Indian attempting the perilous journey went over the bank under a snow slide and was suffocated and drowned. The up mails were met at Boston Bar on the evening of the 27th January. They experienced great difficulty and incurred no little danger in making their way through the Canyons, scrambling along the face of frightful snow slides at imminent risk of being precipitated into the Fraser hundreds of feet below."[29]

By the end of January, mail was beginning to move and, within the next few days, was getting through. Despite the unprecedented weather and the incredibly hard work on the part of the agents, drivers, and Indigenous helpers, some of Barnard's detractors in Barkerville saw an opportunity to discredit him. On January 27, while the storm was still raging and mail not moving at all, a petition was circulated by teamster Edward Pearson and others at Williams and Lightning Creeks. There is little doubt that much of the anti-Barnard sentiment originated with Pearson, who appears to have been an unsuccessful bidder on an earlier mail contract. He was active in Barkerville social life during the early Confederation era and had political aspirations, having run for the Legislative Assembly in 1872, losing to John Barnston.

The petition was telegraphed to Prime Minister John A. Macdonald bearing 139 signatures. Published in the *Victoria Daily Standard* on January 31 under the heading "The Postal Service Question," the petition made the following accusations:

- That the contractors for carrying mails between New Westminster and Cariboo have made no effort to carry out the terms of the contract, no mail having been delivered here since January 17th;

- That the ostensible reason for the non-delivery of the mails is, that the road in one place is blocked with snow; that the distance wherein such blockage occurs is not more than forty miles ... Such a thing as the non-delivery of the mail for such a length of time, is unparalleled in the history of the country;

- That the advertisements calling for tenders were departed from in making the contract; our "Parcel Post" has been taken away, thereby causing a fall in the price of gold dust, of fifteen cents an ounce,—a very serious loss to a mining community.

The petition concluded with the "request that you will issue such orders to the Department here, that the terms of the contract be strictly enforced, and that such instructions be forwarded by telegraph." In telegraphing this petition to the *Daily Standard*, Pearson was careful to state that, "being an opposition stage man, I think it necessary to inform you that I had no hand in originating it,— I merely signed it, when requested to do so."[30]

Within a day, one of the petitioners, William Rennie, a merchant in Barkerville, began to have grave second thoughts and sent a letter to the *British Colonist* stating that " a more untruthful petition was never got up in this or any other country," and that "this deceiving document was begotten in a place called the 'Barkerville Star Chamber' where a certain number of persons congregate, and over a glass of hot punch, arrogate to themselves the prerogative of being the exponents of public opinion. It was deftly circulated among unsuspecting miners and others who signed it without taking the opportunity, as is often the case, of reading it for themselves." Rennie went on to refute each of the allegations with the indisputable facts. He concluded, "This shameful and uncalled for petition is a disgrace to all lovers of truth and fair play; a dishonor to the people who sent it to Ottawa, and enough to make the people of Cariboo hold down their heads with shame, should its representation be investigated. Its untruth will only recoil upon our own heads."[31]

A few days later, Barnard himself wrote a very lengthy reply and addressed it to Judge Henry Maynard Ball who, as the chief civil servant in Barkerville, was named because "your name appears first on the list of signers; occupying as you do, a high official position in the Cariboo District." The reply covered six columns of print and had been a half-sheet addition to the *British Colonist*. Barnard dealt with each of the accusations in turn, first of all providing statements from A. Stevenson, road superintendent between Boston and Clinton, and Neil Black, road superintendent between Yale and Boston Bar, along with a short statement from driver James Hamilton, who said, "I met the storm at Nicomen; it exceeded anything I have ever experienced anywhere. We were all day working our way to Lytton; I pitied the stock; they suffered badly. I was four hours or more within view of the lights of that town breaking my way downhill. On reaching Lytton, I found that to attempt to go further was useless . . . An Indian was offered $10 to take [medicine to Mr. McPhillips] 11 miles which he refused." Barnard then presented the statement of J.G. Bristol on the condition of the river between New Westminster and Yale. He detailed the trip they made, which covered a mere three to nine miles a day and took ten days to cover the distance.

Barnard then quoted the petition: "The ostensible reason for the non-delivery of the mails is, that the road in one place is blocked with snow; that the distance wherein such blockage occurs is not more than forty miles." Barnard pointed out that, "in point of fact [the distance is] no less than 128 miles between New Westminster and Cariboo,—60 miles of which is without semblance of a road of any description." He went on to deal with the terms of the contract, stating that "my contract calls for nothing more than a two-horse sleigh service during the winter months and I strictly adhere to the letter," clarifying that his contract did not require him to employ Indigenous labour in any form. He pointed out that the contract had been altered by the postal authorities at his request to eliminate the conveyance of parcel post in the winter. This was because merchants were breaking down their delivery of goods from the Lower Mainland into four-pound parcels to get their goods carried to Barkerville by mail. It would appear that the two last items, the use of two- instead of four-horse teams and the suspension of parcel post in the winter, were recommended by Barnard and accepted by the authorities.

In conclusion, Barnard emphasized that he hoped "that my vindication... is now complete. I think it will prove so to a generous public, when they shall have reviewed this, my defence against the attacks that you have seen fit so unreasonably to hurl against me... in your entire procedure aiming so unmistakably at blasting my well known business reputation, which... has been honorably and fairly earned after years of personal hardship, endurance and unflagging industry, coupled with some degree of energy and enterprise, and which to the present hour stands before the world untarnished by any act of which an honest man need to be ashamed."[32]

The issue did not die there. In the *Mainland Guardian* of March 7, there appeared a further diatribe against the postal authorities who accepted Barnard's suggestions regarding the two-horse sleighs and the suspension of parcel delivery in the winter. This letter, which was printed unsigned, pointed out, not unreasonably, that if the postal authorities saw fit to amend the terms stipulated in the call for tenders, "they should certainly allow the other tenders to avail themselves of any departure from the published terms." The letter expressed hope that this debate would "have the effect of inducing a full and complete enquiry, just what the unsuccessful tenderers desire."[33]

Finally, Edward Pearson's real issue with Barnard becomes clear. Pearson, an unsuccessful bidder on an earlier mail contract, was now charging favouritism toward Barnard in allowing him to amend the contract without any reduction in price. The complaints about mail delay and not fulfilling the contract were to point out that Barnard had received special favour by postal officials. In response, the following resolution was passed at a meeting in Barkerville on February 17 with Mr. Joshua S. Thompson, who was campaigning to be re-elected to Parliament: "The Dominion Postal authorities, in departure from the advertisement calling for tenders for carrying the Cariboo mail, committed a great act of injustice to the farmers, and others of this District, said advertisements having called for a four horse service all the year round. Whereas, in winter a two horse service is used, and that the latter service is most inadequate to the requirements of the country. We hereby instruct our representative to take the necessary steps in Parliament, or otherwise, to secure for us a four horse service, as was promised for us, advertised, and tendered for."[34]

It had not taken long for national politics to enter into the new Province of British Columbia. Clearly, certain newspapers were supportive of men like Barnard, who played a significant role in Confederation, while others were more likely to support and recommend members of the opposition party and publish articles that were antagonistic to the governing party and its supporters. While some argued that Barnard may have benefitted from advocating for Confederation, his extensive infrastructure and long record of delivering the mail justified his being awarded the mail contract.

In 1874, Pearson nominated Joshua Spenser Thompson, who was elected by acclamation to Parliament[35] and, in 1875, set up Pearson's Cariboo Express in opposition to Barnard. He advertised, "No Monopoly! Passage to Yale! Cheap Fares!... We make a trip every three weeks... No night travelling—Time guaranteed."[36] Though he had agents in Barkerville and Stanley, Pearson's stage line appears not to have lasted through 1875. That same year, he ran for Parliament for the "Government Party" and finished fourth. This seems to have put an end to his political aspirations.

BARNARD WINS THE TELEGRAPH CONTRACT

In 1871, Sanford Fleming, Scottish born but living in Canada since 1845, was offered the position of chief engineer of the proposed Pacific railway. The following year, he travelled to British Columbia to explore the proposed routes. After travelling on foot through the Yellowhead Pass, he concluded that it had a sufficiently gentle grade to be adopted for the railway route. At the end of his summer of exploration, he was looking for a place to winter the five hundred mules he had used for packing supplies. In November, the *British Colonist* reported that "Mr. Barnard has, we understand, undertaken the wintering of five hundred mules belonging to the Railway Survey. We believe they will be wintered at Okanagan, where Mr. Barnard has already a drove of some five hundred horses of his own."[37] The BX Ranch was proving to be a valuable asset, though Barnard did not actually file a preemption on it until May 1873.

But 1873 was to be a year of great upheaval in Ottawa, with Prime Minister Macdonald and his associates, Cartier and Langevin, revealed to have accepted $360,000 before the election the previous year from Hugh Allen, a financier who was negotiating the transcontinental railway contract. The Pacific Scandal, as it came to be known, clearly implicated the Conservatives in political corruption and bribery. On November 5, after numerous defections from the ranks of MPs, Macdonald and his government resigned and Alexander Mackenzie and his Liberal Party took over control of the government.

Mackenzie was on record that he considered the "bargain" made with British Columbia as "the insane act of the administration," adding that it was "made to be broken."[38] His relations with the members from British Columbia, who had all supported Macdonald, were less than cordial and he considered the railway outrageously expensive for a new and struggling country. He proposed to British Columbians that, instead of a railway, he was prepared to start work on a wagon road and a telegraph line, and to continue railway surveys. His proposal met with outrage in British Columbia, but he was determined to avoid national bankruptcy and ruin.

In 1874, he put out requests for tenders to construct the telegraph line across the country. Construction was tendered in sections and Barnard sent in a tender for the stretch from Fort Edmonton to Cache Creek, where it could tie in to the existing line. In September, it was announced that Barnard had been awarded that section. The *British Colonist* asked, "Is British Columbia so fortunate as to have among her old pioneers a man of sufficient enterprise and pluck to come to the front on occasion and successfully compete with the older Provinces for a great telegraph contract?"[39] The answer was clearly, "yes, Frank Barnard is your man."

The intention of the federal government was to have the telegraph constructed along the same route as the future railway. The *British Colonist* was quick to point out that "the Canadian Pacific Telegraph... might be regarded as clearing a path for the iron horse... The intention is to build the Telegraph on the exact line of the Railway when it is located, and as fast as it is located; and the clearing out of the timber to the width of 132 feet will, in fact, be part of the work of the construction of the railway."[40]

Barnard immediately began gathering materials, equipment, and labourers. Steamboats, pack trains, supplies, wire, and material were purchased. But before long, this potentially lucrative government contract was to backfire badly.

THE BARNARD FAMILY

Ellen Stillman and Francis J. Barnard were married on July 6, 1853, in Quebec City, Canada East. Two years later, the couple moved to Toronto, Canada West, where a son, Francis, was born in 1856 and a daughter, Alice, in 1858. In Toronto, Barnard tried unsuccessfully to establish himself in business. Hearing about the gold excitement in the Colony of British Columbia, he left Ellen and the children behind in 1859 and headed to the west coast to find his fortune. As soon as he got himself established, with a job as purser of the *Fort Yale* steamer, he sent for his family and they arrived in Yale in late 1860. They settled into life in the booming town, but things did not go all that well the first year. In April, the *Fort Yale* boiler exploded and Barnard was lucky to escape with his life, and his brief career as a constable also almost ended in death. But, when Barnard bought out Jeffray's Express in November, things began to change.

With Barnard driven to make this express company a success, the job of raising the children and looking after the household fell to Ellen. The winters in Yale were long and severe. Barnard remarked in a letter to his brother, James, that "Ellen is well & so are Frank & Allice [*sic*]... If my business prospers this summer I will fetch them to Victoria to winter as the climate is not so severe here as at Yale."[41]

Ellen Barnard was FJ Barnard's faithful helpmate and partner in life.

As his express business prospered and Barnard launched his stagecoach line, he was eager to show his family the spectacular scenery through the Fraser Canyon and insisted they come along on a trip. He even provided Ellen with the seat of honour next to him, as he drove the stagecoach. Ellen was not so enthusiastic, having heard stories of the precipitous drops through the canyon, so she agreed to travel "up top" only if she could be blindfolded, assuming there was truth in the old adage, "What you don't see won't hurt you." Barnard could see no benefit in her riding in the seat of honour if she could not see the view, but agreed to his wife's desire. It seemed that Ellen's premonition was founded when the six horses reared up and plunged down the road on being let loose. She hung on to her seat, not daring to hang on to her husband, who held the reins. After a short time, the horses settled in and made their way along the Cariboo Road through the canyon. As they neared the high point, Barnard could not contain himself any longer. He had to show his wife the beautiful view. So he whipped off her blindfold and cried out, "Look at that!" With one shriek, muffled so as not to disturb the passengers that included her children, and after a brief bout of hysterics, Ellen fainted. It was her first and only trip up the Cariboo Road and her husband remained in the doghouse for a long time afterward.[42]

As Barnard's Express became more successful, the family was able to enjoy their prosperity. In June of 1866, Ellen Barnard and the children could afford to take a trip back east to visit family and friends. They left in early June of 1866 and travelled to New York. The *British Columbia Tribune*, published in Yale, reported that "Mrs. Barnard and family arrived in New York yesterday. It is only 23 days since they left Yale. This is, indeed, quick time."[43] Apparently, Ellen and daughter Alice were not well and went to New York for medical treatment, though no specifics are known. Barnard later wrote to a Mr. Crawford, in December of 1867: "First of all thank you & Mrs. C. for your kind attention to her on the voyage out and while in NY City." Later in the letter, Barnard wrote, "and now about the wife and young ones. Ellen is much stronger than before her trip to NY. Alice is improving steadily and we are in great hopes of her ultimate recovery. Frank is still going to Mr. Elberts [?] & is making rapid progress in his studies. He is spoken of to me as a very smart boy. I get this from parents of other children whose excuse for not getting to the head of the class is that Frank Barnard always beats them."[44]

In 1868, with Barnard's ongoing involvement in the Colonial Legislative Council, he decided to move his home base to Victoria, much to the delight of his wife, who admitted struggling with the winters in Yale. Two years later, the Barnards purchased "Duvals Cottage" in Victoria on Belcher Street (later named Rockland Avenue). The original Gothic-style cottage was one-and-one-half stories with a railed "widow's walk" on the roof. It had been constructed for John and Elizabeth Miles in 1861, but John Miles died two days after their marriage and, in 1865, the house was sold to Vancouver Island Chief Justice Joseph Needham. In 1870, when Needham became Chief Justice of Trinidad and Tobago, it was sold to the Barnards, who would occupy it for the next fifty years. The house is still standing today and is considered the oldest house in the Rockland area.

In 1873, Francis Stillman (F.S.) Barnard returned to British Columbia from Helmuth Boys' College in Ontario and was given various clerking positions in his father's Victoria office. The younger Barnard proved to be an adept man of business and, in 1874, when his father obtained the contract for the construction of the transcontinental telegraph line between Fort Edmonton and Kamloops, Frank S. took a lead role in the company with Steve Tingley and James Hamilton.

Unfortunately, the telegraph contract turned out to be a nightmare. After work had begun, in early 1875, the government changed the route on two occasions and suspended the contract for four years, leaving Barnard without any payment for his expenditures. Further damage was done in 1878, when the Conservative Party was re-elected and John A. Macdonald again became prime minister. Having decided that the railway would cross the Rocky Mountains through the Kicking Horse Pass, the telegraph contract was cancelled, leaving Barnard out of pocket. He launched a claim of $225,000 against the government to cover his losses but could see that, even if the claim ended well, it would take years for it to play out in the courts.[45] Bankruptcy seemed the only option, but first he had the BC Express Company incorporated as a separate entity with him holding less than 50 per cent of the stock.

ESTABLISHING THE BRITISH
COLUMBIA EXPRESS COMPANY

In March of 1878, Francis Jones Barnard, his son Francis Stillman Barnard, and his associates, George A. Sargison, Stephen Tingley, and James Hamilton were incorporated as the British Columbia Express Company by special Act of the British Columbia Legislature, and were empowered, among other privileges,

> To construct, hire, purchase and acquire horses, coaches, waggons, boats, steam vessels, and other conveyances for the conveyance and transport of any passengers, goods, chattels, merchandise, money, gold dust, bullion, packages, letters, mail matter, or parcels that may be entrusted to them for conveyance from one place to another within the Province of British Columbia.[46]

The Bill incorporated the group with a capital stock of $200,000 divided into 1,000 shares of $200 each, distributed as follows: F.J. Barnard, 332 shares and Sargison, Tingley, Hamilton, and F.S. Barnard with 167 shares each. This distribution gave the two Barnards a total of 499 shares out of 1,000. For the time being, Sargison, Tingley, and Hamilton were appointed directors of the company. On December 2, 1878, the first meeting of the directors was held in the City of Victoria and a resolution was passed authorizing the take-over of the assets previously held by F.J. Barnard & Company.[47]

Shortly after that, the elder Barnard declared insolvency under the Insolvent Act of 1875 and Amending Acts.[48] Unlike bankruptcy, insolvency is the inability to pay debts when they are due. Insolvency allows the individual to negotiate a debt payment or settlement plan with creditors, to avoid bankruptcy. In most cases, this involves agreeing to pay a portion of the debt, for example fifty cents on the dollar, getting the creditors to agree to the settlement. Barnard, with the assistance of his son, went the whole way. By April of 1880, he had reached an agreement with his creditors, as outlined in the *British Colonist*:

At a meeting of creditors in this estate held at the office of the
assignee on the 23rd inst. an offer of composition was submitted
securing the payment of 100 cents to the dollar with 7 per cent
interest payable in 12 months from June 1st next. The offer was
unanimously accepted. The feeling of the creditors, as indicated
by the proceedings at the meeting, was that of great confidence in
and sympathy with Mr. Barnard.[49]

Barnard had managed to protect his beloved express company, but his own situation was not ideal. Fortunately, his son was
every bit as good a businessman and, thanks to his father, socially
connected to the leaders of the new province. Before long, the
insolvency issue was behind them, even as the claim against the
Canadian government dragged on.

The new BC Express Company, no longer under the control of
Barnard, was in the capable hands of the men Barnard had chosen.
Steven Tingley was born at Point de Bute, Westmorland County,
New Brunswick, on September 13, 1839, the son of Caleb and
Deborah Tingley. His great-grandfather Josiah Tingley had left
Attleboro, Massachusetts, and come to New Brunswick in 1763. He
received a basic-but-good education in public schools and remained
at home until he was eighteen years old, travelling via the Isthmus
of Panama to California in 1858.[50] In 1861, he went to the Colony
of British Columbia and arrived at Yale, then travelled on foot to
the Cariboo mines carrying one hundred pounds of provisions. He
mined for two seasons and drove ox teams from Cook's Ferry (later
Spences Bridge) for the Hudson's Bay Company, before starting
a harness shop in Yale. Tingley was hired by Barnard in 1863 and
remained connected to the express business until 1897.

After successfully overseeing the drive of 300 head of horses
from Southern California to British Columbia in 1868, he returned
to New Brunswick and married Elizabeth Harper, bringing her back
to settle in Yale.

In September of 1873, Tingley was driving his two-horse carriage just outside of Yale, with Elizabeth and their five-month-old

son, Fred, when the horses shied at the sight of a wheelbarrow at
the side of the road. The horses went over the embankment, dragging the buggy and occupants along with them. Steve and his son
escaped with some cuts on the head, but Elizabeth was badly hurt.
One of the horses was killed and the buggy was shattered, but the
surviving horse saved them from plunging into the Fraser. The next
day, Elizabeth died.[51] The *British Colonist*, in an editorial, lamented
her death and called for an improvement to the roadsides along
the Cariboo Road. "The late sad accident to Mr. Tingley's family,
resulting in the death of Mrs. Tingley, brings prominently forward
the crying necessity for having a strong stone parapet built along
the first three miles out of Yale, the most precipitous section of an
unusually dangerous road."[52]

Tingley took his wife's body back to New Brunswick for burial
and left his two sons, Clarence and Frederick, in New Brunswick to
be raised by relatives. He returned to British Columbia immediately
after the funeral and immersed himself in the business. But, like
most men who are widowed and left with children, he remarried.
He met and courted Pauline Laumeister and they were married in
Lytton in 1877. Tingley's two sons returned to BC in the late 1970s.
Frederick became a stagecoach driver like his dad and Clarence
managed managed the horse ranch at the 108-mile post. Tingley's
younger brother, Alexander, arrived in 1878 and also drove stagecoach for the BC Express.

Tingley drove stagecoach for twenty years, most commonly
taking the run from Yale to Clinton, with Hamilton taking the next
run from Clinton to Soda Creek. They were both considered "crack
whips," and the most courteous and well-mannered drivers in the
province.

Like Tingley, James Hamilton was born in New Brunswick, in
Woodstock, Carlton County. His father, Major Hamilton, came
from Ireland in 1823 and started a farm, and his mother was Olivia
"Olive" Kerr Hamilton. At the time of the 1861 census, James was
driving a stagecoach in New Brunswick, but, shortly after, he and
his four brothers, George, Robert, Samuel, and John, hearing of the

gold discoveries in British Columbia, travelled around the Horn to San Francisco and headed north from there. The five brothers spread out in British Columbia, looking for opportunities. James, with experience driving stagecoach, was hired in 1864 by Barnard to drive the leg from Clinton to Lac la Hache. By the autumn of 1866, as traffic on the road diminished, he was given the entire stretch from Clinton to Soda Creek, proving himself over and over to be a conscientious and hard-working driver.

In the early 1870s, the other Hamilton brothers were all involved in ranches in the Nicola Valley, with James having an interest in them. Robert Hamilton pre-empted land just south of Nicola Lake near Quilchena Creek, and John took up land about six miles farther south at what was called the "Horse Carralls," which he renamed the "Mountain Ranch." Both of them raised horses and cattle, and all indications are that the other three brothers were involved. In an article written by Hugh Walkem, son of the British Columbia lawyer, George A. Walkem, published in the *Ottawa Citizen* in 1881, Robert Hamilton was listed as one of "the largest stock owners in Nicola," with 1,000 head of cattle. He is also included, along with the Guichons, John Gilmore, the Moore brothers, and the Mickles, as an importer of stock. "These gentlemen deserve a great credit for their endeavors to introduce a superior class of animal."[53] Many of these horses would have found their way into the ranks of the BC Express and to the BX Ranch, where stage horses were being raised. As part owner of the company, James Hamilton would have been involved in purchasing and training these horses in the Nicola Valley.

In the early 1880s, George, Robert, and Samuel Hamilton moved to southern Alberta, but John stayed on with his brother James and became a stagecoach driver as well. When Governor General Dufferin came in 1876, John drove the stagecoach that transported the rest of the Dufferin party, who had not gotten seats in the Dufferin Coach.

By 1872, James was a one-quarter owner of Barnard & Company Express and, in 1878, he had a one-sixth share of the British Columbia Express Company. In 1876, at age thirty-seven, James married twenty-five-year-old Christine Lindhard, and they had three daughters. In May of 1883, he became manager and partner of the Victoria Transfer Company, with F.S. Barnard. Unfortunately, his time there was short, as he died the following October. The *British Colonist* wrote that "Mr. Hamilton was a sterling man and highly esteemed by all. His widow and children have the deep sympathy of the public."[54]

George Andrew Sargison was born in Yorkshire, England, and lived in Montreal and Toronto in the 1840s and 1850s. He married Barnard's sister Margaret in 1854, and their family included ten children. Sargison came out to British Columbia in 1871 in search of opportunities and, in December of that year, he travelled up the Cariboo Road to Barkerville, experiencing the challenges of winter travel. The Sargison family relocated to British Columbia in 1873 and Sargison worked for his brother-in-law as a clerk in the Victoria office of Barnard's BC Express. He proved to be an excellent accountant and, in 1878, when the BC Express Company was founded, he became a one-sixth shareholder. Given the cost per share of $20 at the time, it is likely that Sargison was helped by Barnard in obtaining these shares. This is even more likely given the fact that Barnard was trying to divest himself of controlling interest in the company, prior to filing for insolvency. Sargison sold his shares in the BC Express in 1881 and became secretary of the BC Mining & Milling Company and was chief census officer, Victoria District, in 1891. He was also an accountant and a notary public and was involved in a number of temperance organizations in Victoria. He died in 1900 and was buried in Ross Bay Cemetery in Victoria.

At the time of the formation of the BC Express Company, Frank S. Barnard was already showing his entrepreneurial skills. He had been serving for five years as a clerk in his father's Victoria office when, in early 1878, he became a commission stock broker and was appointed a member of the British Columbia Mining Stock board. At the same time, he became the Victoria agent for the Globe Mutual Life Insurance Company of New York.[55] When his father was faced with insolvency, Frank S. worked with him to sell off assets and keep his honour by paying back every cent to his creditors.

After helping to secure the Barnard reputation, Frank S. went on to become one of the most successful businessmen in the province. But, in 1878, that was yet to come.

7

THE BC EXPRESS COMPANY CARRIES ON THE TRADITION

ARIOT GEORGINA BLACKWOOD, Lady Dufferin, was thoroughly enjoying her trip to British Columbia, but the highlight was her journey through the Fraser Canyon, riding beside "crack whip" Steve Tingley. Her husband, Frederick Hamilton-Temple-Blackwood, First Marquess of Dufferin and Ava, commonly known as Lord Dufferin, was the Governor General of Canada. In 1876, as the unfulfilled promise of a railway had British Columbians raging against the Ottawa government, the Dufferins were sent to "pour oil on troubled waters" in the new province. The couple arrived in Victoria on August 14 and, despite the chilly attitude of British Columbians toward the politicians in Ottawa, they were enthusiastically received by the people. After a lengthy stay in Victoria, they proceeded across the Strait of Juan de Fuca to the mainland and were feted in New Westminster and then at Yale. There they were picked up in a special coach manufactured by H.M. Black & Company of San Francisco and driven by Steve Tingley, acknowledged by the *British Colonist* as "the most experienced driver on the road." After spending the night in Yale, the party set off up the canyon. Lady Dufferin recorded in her diary, "We set off in a large carriage, which held six inside and three on the box ... We had forty-four miles to drive and the road is a wonderful piece of engineering: a wall of rock on one side, and a great precipice upon the other, almost the whole way, with every now and then a sharp turn round some fearful bluff, where, looking forward, the road seemed to end, and there was nothing but the river to be seen, a hundred feet below." The entourage met with numerous delegations along the road, most of them Indigenous people.

The coach stopped at Savona's Ferry and the party took a steamer to Kamloops, where they spent two nights receiving delegations and having a "pow-wow" with the Secwépemc people. Then the party returned to Savona's Ferry and climbed back onto the coach. At the start of the journey, when offered a seat next to Tingley "up top," Lady Dufferin had declined, obviously quite nervous about the precarious perch. But she proudly recorded in her diary that now, departing from Savona's Ferry, she "got on the box (or 'fore-top' as we call it ...) to see Mr. Tingley drive; this was an easy part of the road, so I thought it a good place to take a front seat."

The next day, Lady Dufferin "again got on the box, and drove over the worst piece of road—such awful turns, and such a precipice at the edge of the narrow road! It certainly requires good driving, and the coachman has to work hard all the time." There was no stopping the lady then. She climbed up to the box for the final leg to Yale, remarking, "We had a successful journey back to Yale, and D. [Lord Dufferin] and I sat on the box for the last hour of the way. The driver and Yaleites were delighted that we had enjoyed the trip, and were not frightened; and the coachman's testimony to my courage during the perilous drive to Kamloops was 'that I hadn't a scare in me.'"[1] Lady Dufferin's day, and trip, was made.

CHANGES IN BC EXPRESS MANAGEMENT

Barnard decided to run for the District of Yale in a by-election in 1879 to support John A. Macdonald, who had been returned as

Prime Minister the preceding year. The *British Colonist*, noting his nomination, wrote, "To show you how popular Mr. Barnard is in this district it was the candid opinion of nine-tenths of the voters that there was no necessity of giving the district a personal canvas and he could have stayed in Victoria and returned a good majority." His opponent was John Trapp, whom the *British Colonist*, informed by voters, described as "a very nice man; but... he knows nothing of Dominion politics whatever, and... at such a critical period as the present men are wanted who are thoroughly informed in politics."[2] Sure enough, Barnard won by 200 votes to 99 and was off to Ottawa. This absence from the province meant that, for the first time, Barnard was not in British Columbia to guide his beloved express company. His involvement in running the company would gradually diminish.

At the first meeting of directors of the newly formed company, on December 2, 1878, George Sargison was appointed as president and managing director and a motion was approved and noted in the company minute book that the "business of the company come into operation on the first day of January next, by taking over on that date the assets and liabilities, and the good will of the firm of F.J. Barnard & Co."[3] Though an excellent accountant, with the advice of Barnard when he was in town, Sargison was in over his head as manager of a large company. He resigned these positions in January of 1881 and, shortly thereafter, sold his shares to Frank S. Barnard, who was also elected as the new president and managing director.

Young, energetic, and eager to uphold his father's reputation, Frank S. Barnard was the best man for the job. He had already received his father's 332 shares in 1879, to which he added another 167 shares from George Sargison in February of 1881. This gave him 666 shares and controlling interest in the BC Express Company. For the next seven years Frank S. steered the company, showing a significant profit at the end of every year.

In the meantime, the senior Barnard remained active in Parliament, even as his claim against the government on the Canadian Pacific Telegraph debacle ground on in the courts. The pressure of this claim on his financial situation was manageable but extremely

Francis Stillman Barnard was an astute businessman and became lieutenant governor of British Columbia. IMAGE G-08024 COURTESY OF THE ROYAL BC MUSEUM AND ARCHIVES

debilitating to his health. On April 12, 1881, the *British Colonist* reported, under the heading "Illness of Mr. Barnard, M.P.," that "a dispatch from Ottawa of the 28th March says: Mr. Barnard, M.P. for Yale, BC had a stroke of paralysis this morning before rising. Dr. Grant was summoned to his assistance. The unfortunate gentleman was for a time speechless, and deprived of the use of his limbs on the right side, but at a late hour tonight was so much improved that his early recovery is expected."[4] Further reports indicated that his health was improving and he was resuming his work as a member of parliament. Though the following year he would run successfully for the Conservative Party, his failing health was becoming an issue.

In the meantime, the younger Barnard was spreading his wings in business in British Columbia, and not just with the BC Express. In May of 1883, along with several others, he was granted an Act of Incorporation for the Victoria Transfer Company Limited "for the purpose of constructing and operating street railways in the City of Victoria and Esquimalt and Victoria Districts adjacent thereto, and carrying on a general transfer, delivery, hack and livery business in the Province of British Columbia."[5] This company was to prove very successful during the 1880s. One of the partners was former BC Express driver James Hamilton, who was manager at the time of his death in the fall of 1883.

Despite his various business ventures, Frank S. Barnard did not neglect the BC Express Company. One of his areas of focus was the BX Ranch in the Okanagan.

THE BX RANCH SELLS HORSES IN THE NORTH-WEST TERRITORIES

Barnard had established the BX Ranch in the north Okanagan in 1872 to raise horses for use with the stagecoaches of F.J. Barnard & Company. While Barnard's dream of a trans-continental stage line ended when the Canadian government promised to construct a rail line connecting BC with the eastern provinces, the BX Ranch continued to be a valued company asset. Barnard placed Alexander Vance, who was operating Vance's Express between Cache Creek and the O'Keefe Ranch in the North Okanagan, in charge of the horse ranch. Under Vance's management, the ranch went on to grow fields of wheat on its ranges. In 1877, Vance went to California and purchased an eight horsepower portable steam engine, a stacker, a threshing machine, and sawmill machinery, all to provide extra income for the ranch, though raising horses continued to be the major activity.[6]

For the next forty years, the BX Ranch supplied stagecoach horses and sold as many surplus horses as it could to the ranchers in the BC Interior. The BX horse herds flourished in the lush bunch

grass ranges of the Okanagan and, before long, there was a significant surplus of horses.

The company continued to improve the stock of horses at BX
Ranch. In 1875, Chief Factor John Tait at Fort Kamloops wrote to
William Charles in Victoria that he had "made a sale of 20 Head of
Horses to F.J. Barnard & Co for $880.00 the voucher accompanying
this which you will please cause to be presented at Barnards Express
Office for payment. Mr. Hamilton & Tingley were here and would
have purchased more had we succeeded in getting them in. It is very
difficult doing so at present as they are in small bands and scattered
all over the range."[7]

In 1876, the *British Colonist* reported that "Mr. S. Tingley arrived
here yesterday from Oregon bringing over three fine stallions for
Messrs. F.J Barnard & Co. The horses will be shipped to the mainland—Nicola and Okanagan—where their owners already have
large bands of animals. The improvement of stock is a matter of
great importance to a young country and should be more generally
observed."[8] By 1879, in the *District of Okanagan Assessment Roll*,
the BX Ranch was listed as belonging to Barnard and consisted
of 320 acres, the standard pre-emption east of the Cascades. The
ranch contained 449 horses and $10,000 worth of "Personal Prop-
erty," which would have included the machinery for threshing and
cutting lumber.[9]

When Frank S. Barnard took over as manager of the BC Express,
he began to cast his eyes eastward to the wide ranges of the newly
created Alberta District of the North-West Territories, where eastern Canadian entrepreneurs were starting to establish ranches.
Initially, the cattle, mostly longhorn breeds, were driven up from
the United States to stock the ranches. But by the early 1880s, the
ranches were beginning to bring in purebred breeds of cattle such
as British Shorthorns and Herefords. The resulting cattle were particularly heavy and not as agile as the scrawny longhorns, a problem
because the small, wiry cow ponies of the prairies were not up for
roping and controlling the larger cattle. This looked like an opportunity to the British Columbia ranchers, whose horses, thanks to

imported mares like those at the BX Ranch, were heavier and less agile—in short, just what the Alberta ranchers needed.

As early as 1874, Barnard had seen the potential for horse sales on the eastern side of the Rocky Mountains and, in July of that year, the Hudson's Bay Company's fort journal reported that "Mr. Barnard has 100 head of Horses here which he had brought from his Band at Okanagan. They start for the east side tomorrow. A man the name of Adam Furgession [Ferguson] that has been in Barnard's employ for some time is partner in the arrangement and goes with the animals. I am told a change has been made since the Horses came here and that the 'Christie' that wanted to buy from us last spring has bought Barnard's interest and goes across too."[10] These horses, all from the BX Ranch, were driven by Adam Ferguson and James Christie through the Yellowhead Pass and reached Fort Edmonton, where they were sold.[11]

In 1882, the younger Barnard was interested in improving the BX Ranch horse herd and was convinced that the southern Canadian prairies would provide a market that would buy up all his surplus horses. In May, the *British Colonist* wrote, "Mr. [F.S.] Barnard has imported two very fine animals for his own herds, which are said to comprise 600 animals of all ages. It is his intention to move the greater part to the Bow River country."[12]

The first recorded attempt to drive horses through the southern Rocky Mountains was by Oscar Rush, who worked for Johnny Wilson of the JW Ranch in Grande Prairie (now Westwold). In the spring of 1882, he drove 150 horses through the Okanagan Valley and then crossed into the United States at Osoyoos where he was given a temporary permit to cross east through US territory. Normally, a special envoy accompanied the herd through the US, at a cost to the drovers of $4 a day plus expenses, to ensure that the horses were not sold in the US without paying customs duty. Rush and his cowboys drove the herd down the Okanogan River (as it was spelled in the US) to Omak Lake and then across the Colville Reservation. The herd was swum across the Columbia River and then via Spokane Falls to cross back into Canada north of Bonners

Ferry. From there they travelled through the Crowsnest Pass to Fort MacLeod, where the horses were broken. When Rush heard that the Oxley Ranch was looking for horses, he drove them to the Garnett brothers' ranch near Pincher Creek and held them for inspection. John Craig, manager of the Oxley Ranch, was impressed and bought 116 of them. Craig was later to record: "The first purchase of stock for the Oxley Ranch was a band of 116 horses from a Mr. Rush, who had brought them in from British Columbia and was holding them at Garnett's ranch. They were a very good sort, and cost seventy dollars per head."[13]

The ranchers of British Columbia heard about the demand for horses and the excellent prices in Alberta. The following year, Frank S. Barnard, along with John and William Roper Hull, who had settled south of Kamloops in the 1870s, decided to try their luck. The Hulls rounded up a herd of 1,200 horses in the hills south of Kamloops and drove them through the Okanagan Valley. Frank S. was not far behind and sent Alexander Vance with a herd of 200 horses to follow the Hull brothers. Vance assembled a group of men to help him drive the horses, including Thomas Newlands, Joseph Brown, and Michael O'Keefe, brother of Cornelius O'Keefe, who ranched at the head of Okanagan Lake.

Driving horses is quite different than driving cattle, as the cowboys found out. One old-timer remembered:

> It was usually a profitable business but not so straightforward as might be imagined. From 75 to 800 head or more would be brought in at a time, and a number of mares in foal or with colts were usually included, making traveling slow. Mares foaling on the trail always wanted to stay where they were, and the whole bunch would often take sudden spells of homesickness. Naturally this was emphasized at a bad crossing or on stormy nights, causing delay and loss. Old timers agree that a herd of horses on the trail or grazing ground was much more easily stampeded than the jumpy, longhorned cattle. The whiff of a cougar or some slight sound, and they were gone. Their speed and the communicated panic that

rippled through the herd made them lethal to anything in their
way, even to one another.[14]

Vance and the cowboys drove them along the same trail as the
Hull brothers and then, arriving at Rathdrum, Idaho, just east of
Spokane on the Northern Pacific Railway, he arranged to have the
horses shipped ahead to Clark Fork prior to driving them back into
British Columbia and through the Crowsnest Pass. While holding
them along the rail line awaiting an eastbound train to load them
on, another train ploughed through the herd, killing eight head and
injuring four more that had to be put down. Frank S., on getting a
telegram from Vance, immediately launched a claim for the death of
ten "of the best American full-bred mares in the band and two well-
trained stock horses, the former valued at $120 a head, the latter
at $150, making in all $1500."[15] It is uncertain how this claim was
settled, but Vance and the cowboys drove the remaining horses into
Alberta. Like the Hull brothers, Vance was able to sell the whole herd.

The BX horses, mostly older mares, had been driven to and held
at Fort McLeod and then sold to Fred Stimson of the North West
Cattle Company on the Bar-U Ranch for $65 a head. One of the
cowboys from the BX Ranch, Joseph Harrison Brown, agreed to help
Stimson drive the horses to the ranch and, once there, decided to
stay. He would be in charge of the Bar-U horse herd for the next
fifteen years. Eventually, Brown got a ranch of his own and used
the brand "BX" in memory of this start in the horse business. "7U"
(after his cattle brand) Brown became a legend in Southern Alberta
and was chosen as "roundup captain" by the Alberta Stock Growers'
Association from 1894 until 1907.[16]

Frank S. was delighted with the prices he had obtained in Alberta,
as was his father. He spent the fall of 1883 writing to ranchers in
Alberta to see if there was interest in the rest of the horses remaining on the BX Ranch that he and Vance considered expendable. He
also wrote to R. Davies in Victoria, who was an agent for Colonel
Charles P. Hutchins, who had come out with the first North-West
Mounted Police and finished his service in 1880. Hutchins had been

given a land grant upon retirement. Frank S. provided the details of
the horses he could supply:

> In regard to the band of horses at Okanagan which I offer for sale
> next spring, I would say that there will be by Spring about 400
> head of mares & fillies from yearlings up, say about 270 head [of]
> 3-yr old & upwards, but none of them old mares for we drove to the
> North West & sold Mr. Stimpson nearly all the old stock. Added to
> this there will be about 80 head of 2 yr old fillies and 50 or more
> yearlings. Of these I desire to keep 40 head of the best mares, the
> rest are for sale and I am satisfied [they] are as fine a band as can
> be found in America. The 200 head we drove this summer into
> the North West were below the average of the band and were pro-
> nounced to be the finest ever driven to that section of the Country.
> They brought from the Nor. West Cattle Raising Co. $65 a head
> and if they had been a month earlier these could have got $75. If
> Col. Hutchins desires to purchase he can have these at $50 a head
> all found on the range.[17]

Frank S. Barnard also wrote to Frank White, manager of the
Cochrane Ranche west of Calgary; Fred Stimson, manager of the
North West Cattle Company; and Godfrey Levigne, manager of
the Mount Head Ranche Company, providing similar details and
prices.[18] But, as Alexander Vance was not prepared to take on
another long horse drive and Frank S. had no one else to drive them
to the North West, he hoped to sell the horses on the range and have
the buyer drive them to their ranch. He suggested that the horses
could be driven to Rathdrum, Idaho, and shipped by rail to Missoula,
Montana, but this was not acceptable to men trying to run a new
ranching operation. Finally, Frank S. found Arthur Best, who lived in
the Mission Valley, later known as Kelowna, who agreed to drive 350
head to the Mount Head Ranche on the High River in Alberta.[19] The
final price is not known but it was certainly far better than anyone
in British Columbia was willing to pay. By the fall of 1884, the BX
Ranch was left with about forty head of horses on the range, not to

mention the approximately 800 head kept in the twenty odd road-houses along the Cariboo Road.

The demand in southern Alberta for British Columbia horses continued through the 1880s. It was generally agreed that "these 'BC' horses, as they were locally called, were derived from Morgan and thoroughbred crosses on Spanish foundation stock. Exceptionally active, good looking mounts, they were big and tough as rawhide."[20] But, having disposed of the majority of his horse herd, Frank S. was beginning to see that land was an even better commodity to invest in.

THE CANADIAN PACIFIC RAILWAY
BEGINS CONSTRUCTION IN BC

The Canadian Pacific Railway Bill was approved in Parliament, and the company came into existence in February of 1881, with 25 million dollars in credit and a land grant of 25 million acres. Beginning in 1879, Andrew Onderdonk, an American of Dutch and English descent, was contracted to supervise the construction of the railway between Port Moody and Savona's Ferry on Kamloops Lake. The section extended for 212 miles, running mainly through the Fraser and Thompson River Canyons. Running on the west side of the Fraser Canyon, the proposed line was hoped to have minimal impact on the Cariboo Road, which ran mainly on the east side.

From the beginning of construction, there was a shortage of labourers to work on the line. British Columbia had a population of only two or three thousand Europeans, all of whom together would not have been enough for the job. So Onderdonk contracted labour agents in Kowloon, China, to supply six thousand Chinese. Despite the Chinese labourers being subject to discrimination and racism, paid less than white workers, often given the most dangerous jobs, and given only rice for food, they turned out to be efficient and hard-working employees. It is estimated that about fifteen thousand Chinese workers were employed on the project.

While every attempt was made not to interfere with the Cariboo Road, conflicts were inevitable. In June of 1880, Joseph Trutch, who had been the Lieutenant Governor of British Columbia before being appointed a "Dominion agent for British Columbia," wrote to George Walkem, chief commissioner of lands and works:

> In the course of building the portion of the Canadian Pacific Railway between Emory and the Alexandra Bridge now under construction it is found necessary to permanently divert the Waggon Road in many places and in some cases for considerable distances, and in many more places and for greater distances the line of Railway is so near the Waggon Road that it will be most difficult if not altogether impracticable for such portions of the Waggon Road to be kept continuously open for traffic without great risk to the lives of persons, and danger to property passing along the road. Under these circumstances... some Agent of your Department should be specifically appointed to watch on behalf of the Government of the Province, the construction of these necessary Waggon Road diversions so as to give the assurance that the work thereon shall be carried out to the satisfaction of the Provincial Government... There are nearly 1,000 men now at work on this Section of the Railway and the work of diverting the Waggon Road is already being carried into effect. I consider it therefore urgently advisable that an accredited Agent of the Provincial Government should as soon as possible be on the ground.[21]

The provincial government took this warning to heart and, at considerable expense, maintained the road through the canyon during the course of construction. Still, the road was damaged by floods in the spring of 1882, when banks, walls, and cribbing were washed away.[22] It was sixty-four days before heavy freight wagons were able to travel the road, but Frank S. Barnard reported in August that, "although the road is impassible as yet for heavy freight teams, our stages are running on regular time, and passengers travel through without inconvenience or delay."[23]

The people of British Columbia were delighted to see work finally underway on the railway that would connect them to the rest of Canada. In August of 1880, a correspondent of the *British Colonist* wrote a series of articles entitled " 'Through to Yale' and Beyond" that described a trip to "see the sights" of the railway construction. The party stayed in Yale and, during the night, were awakened to a "sound which rends the evening air and leaping from crag to crag in long rolling peals like distant thunder sweeps through the narrow passes and gorges and shakes the ground ... the tunnel men are working on the 'nightshift,' and the rapidity with which the shots were fired is evidence that as good progress is being made as the contractors could hope for. The next morning behold our party seated in a substantial wagon behind two spirited bays driven by the great Jehu, Steve Tingley, on our way up-river." Travelling up the canyon, the correspondent noted that "at several points the mountains have to be pierced by tunnels ... Less than a mile out of Yale, the first bluff is being tunneled ... In many cases the railway line adopts the line of wagon road, in which case a new piece of road is made ... On we speed, faster and faster, reposing the utmost confidence in the skill of our famous driver. No fear is now expressed." Even at this earliest stage of construction, the Chinese workers were prominent. The writer notes, "As the wagon ascends a hill, a distinguished looking Chinaman, well-mounted on a powerful horse with a large umbrella protecting his head from the rays of the sun, and followed at a respectful distance by a Chinese servant, is passed. He is described to us as the 'chief' of all the Chinese working on the river—a sort of commissioner, who passes up and down the line to ascertain their grievances and settle disputes between them and their employers."

Just a few miles further up the canyon, the wagon reached Rombrot's 16 Mile House, established in 1861 by Claude Rombrot and, in 1880, still being run by his brother, Vincent. There the party had a hearty lunch and observed that "nearly opposite Rombrot's the advance guard of the railway parties is at work." Having seen the first evidence of the long-awaited Canadian Pacific Railway, the party headed back, "sweeping around curves and skirting precipices." [24]

Frank S. Barnard saw this fascination with the railway construction as an opportunity and advertised excursions to the construction site. "After this date, the British Columbia Express Comp'y will dispatch from Yale on Thursdays after the arrival of steamers from Victoria, AN EXTRA STAGE for Spences Bridge, Savona's Ferry & way points. Parties desirous of Visiting the scene of railway construction may leave Victoria by Tuesday's or Wednesday's steamer and return the following Monday without incurring unnecessary loss of time."[25]

After completing the construction through the Fraser and Thompson Canyons to Savona in 1883, Onderdonk was awarded the contract for the construction from Savona to Craigellachie, in Eagle Pass. The first passenger trains began to make their way along the completed section of the railway and Frank S. negotiated with the CPR to lease an "express car" to carry express matter along the line. He advertised:

> A convenient arrangement has been perfected by the BC Express company, by which every passenger train on the British Columbia section of the Canadian Pacific Railway will be provided with an express car and messenger; so that those wishing to forward parcels safely and expeditiously, can do so by this means, a most popular one, as has been proved by success with which this method has been practiced in the States. As the line of the Canadian Pacific Railway extends, so will the system which has been adopted, accompany it, until the time arrives when this immense railway line having been completed, the public will be enabled to send packages and parcels direct to Canada with the greatest certainty and security offered by their transmission under the auspices of the BC Express company.[26]

As the railway line progressed, the BC Express Company offices were moved from Yale to Boston Bar, and then to Lytton to connect with the terminus of the rail line. In 1885, they were moved from there to Spences Bridge, and to Savona the following year. Once the bridge was completed across the Thompson River at Ashcroft, the company moved there, where it remained for the next thirty years.

Dr. Mark Wade, a visitor to Ashcroft before it became a main depot on the CPR, gave his initial impressions: "When I first visited the site of the present town of Ashcroft, there was no road and no bridge. I alighted from the stage at Cornwall's hotel, walked down to the Thompson as best I could, following an Indian trail, and crossed the river in a canoe. Ashcroft was then, in June 1884, very much in embryo, consisting of two buildings, a hotel and a log cabin." Wade went on to describe how the town changed with the coming of the CPR. "Ashcroft began to grow. First a store opened for business then a competitor came along but when the bridge was built and the road to the Cariboo Road completed, business increased by leaps and bounds. Forwarding agents erected large warehouses, teamsters came and went with their loaded wagons, and the little town thrived apace. It had become the gateway to the Cariboo country; the head-quarters of the British Columbia Express Company."[27]

Also, the BC Express made an arrangement with the Canadian Pacific Railway and the Canadian Pacific Navigation Company, which ran steamboats from Victoria to Vancouver, New Westminster, Yale, and various locations up the coast, to sell "Through Tickets, which can be purchased at the office of the B.C. Express Co., Yates Street."[28] This allowed the BC Express to form a link in the transportation network for the short time that overland travel was still required to reach the Interior.

THE BX RANCH GROWS AND PROSPERS

In 1881, when construction of the Canadian Pacific Railway began in British Columbia, there was a rush for land in the Okanagan. The following year, Frank S. Barnard sent word to Alexander Vance: "Enclose find cheque for $500. Purchase at once 160 acres NW corner of Section 36, and 320 acres Eastern half of Section 35, making in all 480 acres. Please lose no time as others may be on the same day." In 1884, he applied to purchase and was given Crown Grants on lots 52, 53, and 54, amounting to 320 acres and adjoining the original pre-emption. He also applied for Crown Grants on lots 339, 340, 341, and 342, located to the northeast and east of the above lots and containing a total of 960 acres, which were crown granted in 1891. Also in 1891, he acquired lots 239 and 240 west of Lumby, each containing 480 acres. Rights to these two lots were obtained from James Smyth and William Mitchell, who claimed the lots and had them surveyed before selling them to Frank S.

Although legal, this process was a way of preventing anyone else from applying for the land. Barnard had obtained land in this way in 1886, as revealed in a letter dated May 20, 1886, to E.H. Wood: "I enclose your form of application to sign, also a declaration and cheque for $160 to purchase the NE quarter of Section 36. Make the application and get your certificate of purchase at once for next mail ... I find that we can make Walker, Girouard and Lyons pay their proportion of fencing at once and if you will send me the exact cost that each is liable for, I will serve them proper notice serving to protect ourselves. Don't lose any time about securing the land."[29]

Clearly, there was a scramble for good agricultural land in the North Okanagan, and Frank S. was not going to lose out. By the early 1890s, the BX Ranch comprised 2,240 acres of contiguous land and an additional 960 acres east of the other holdings, near Lumby. Frank S. also owned 320 acres on Equesis Creek on the west side of Okanagan Lake. He continued to see a bright future for the Okanagan Valley and, having expanded the BX Ranch by as much land as was available, he set out to get seriously involved in land acquisition.

In 1883, when land was opened up in the North Okanagan and much of British Columbia for purchase, Frank S. saw an opportunity to expand the BX Ranch even further and acquire the land between his present holdings and Swan Lake. But he was slow off the mark and Thomas Greenhow applied to purchase the same land. Outraged, Frank S. wrote to the chief commissioner of lands and works:

I learn that Thos. Greenhow of Okanagan has applied for a large tract of grazing land ... adjoining my father's ranch at Okanagan, and on which his large band of horses have been grazing for 19 [?] years. If this application is granted it will shut us off completely from the range and remove the ranch of 500 acres of arable land valuable to us for a horse ranch. We have at present about 500 head of horses and desire to purchase grazing land adjoining our ranch sufficient to pasture this number.[30]

The younger Barnard must be forgiven for a few exaggerations. First of all, it is quite clear that his father had used this piece of land for more like twelve years, not nineteen. Second, he was in the process of selling off the majority of the BX Ranch's herd of horses, with his intention stated in a letter written a month earlier to "keep forty head of the best mares. The rest are for sale."[31]

Still, there is no doubt Frank S. saw the incredible potential in the Okanagan Valley once the railway was completed and settlers began to arrive. Having lost land to Thomas Greenhow, he applied to purchase "four thousand one hundred and twenty acres of land situated in a valley running from Back Creek to Shuswap Lake, beginning at a post near Deep Creek running north eight miles thence west one mile, thence south eight miles thence west one mile to point of commencement."[32]

Over the years, Frank S. would continue to cash in on this land rush. In 1889, he became a shareholder in the Shuswap & Okanagan Railway that was constructed to Okanagan Lake and the following year, he was part of a syndicate that purchased Amos Delorier's land in the North Okanagan and laid out the town of Vernon. Not surprisingly, the main street of the new town was called Barnard Avenue. Also in that year, he also became a shareholder in the Canadian Western Central Railway.

THE END OF THE BARNARD FAMILY'S INVOLVEMENT

Frank S. Barnard was becoming involved in many other business interests in addition to his role as manager of the BC Express. Aside from his land speculations and related interests, Barnard was president and majority shareholder of the Victoria Transfer Company Ltd. and its counterpart, the Vancouver Transfer Company Ltd. He was director and secretary of the Vancouver Improvement Company, and a director of the Hastings Sawmill Company, the British Columbia Milling and Mining Company, and the Selkirk Mining and Smelting Company. He served as a Victoria city councillor in 1886 and 1887. It became clear that these many activities were compromising his position as president and managing director of the Express.

In 1884, Frank S. had sold 333 of his shares in the company to Steve Tingley. This left Frank S. with 333 shares and gave Tingley 500 shares, half interest in the company. With the death of James Hamilton that year, the only other shareholder was E. Garvin, who purchased Hamilton's 167 shares. Despite holding only one-third interest in the company, Frank S. continued on as president and managing director until 1888. That year, Tingley acquired Garvin's 167 shares, giving Tingley 667 shares in the company. At the July 1888 annual board meeting, Frank S. resigned his roles and, in September, sold Steve Tingley 166 shares and Tingley's wife, Pauline, another 167 shares. J.J. McKay, who had been a stagecoach driver, purchased 50 shares, leaving Steve Tingley a controlling 834 shares and his wife, Pauline, with 116 shares.

Before the younger Barnard left the company for good, he wanted to provide some legacy to his father for the assets he had brought to the company he founded and carried on for twenty-six years. At the July 7 meeting, at which he had resigned,

> [He] informed the shareholders that he had disposed of his stock in the Company in part consideration for which it was necessary that the Company should authorize him as Manager and President of the Company to execute a bill of sale of the chattels of the Company to Francis Jones Barnard to secure the said F.J. Barnard in the payment to him of $19,200.00 in monthly installments of $400 each payable by the said company out of this postal subsidy for the carriage of the mails between Ashcroft and Barkerville and Ashcroft and Clinton.[33]

To that end, Frank S. made a motion to pay above "four hundred dollars each on the 15th of every month commencing on the 10th day of August 1888 and continuing until the 15th day of August, 1892 ... to come out of the subsidy for the carriage of mails between Ashcroft and Barkerville."[34] What exactly was going on here? It appears that unspecified chattels of F.J. Barnard were being purchased by the company for $19,200 and that monthly amounts were to be made to him in payment. This seems to represent a "pension" paid to Barnard in recognition of the assets he had brought to the company.

One of the assets that Barnard had brought to the company had been the BX Ranch, which had supplied horses to pull the stagecoaches. But, with the end of the Barnard family's controlling interest in the company, the BX Ranch remained a family asset and was treated as one from then on. Perhaps part of the arrangement to pay Barnard a pension was a recognition that the over 200 horses that were distributed along the Cariboo Road were part of what the company was purchasing from Barnard. From then on, the company raised its stagecoach horses at ranches along the Cariboo Road.

Whatever the understanding reached by the company directors, the meeting spelled the end of the Barnard family's involvement in the BC Express Company that had variously been Barnard's Express, Barnard's Cariboo Express, and F.J. Barnard & Company Express before becoming the BC Express. F.J. Barnard did not seek re-election to Parliament in 1887 and declined a position as a Canadian Senator in 1888. He passed away on July 10, 1889 in Victoria and his wife and partner for the previous thirty-six years, Ellen Stillman Barnard, passed away one month later. Barnard's estate amounted to less than $30,000, a pittance considering his contribution to the Colony and Province of British Columbia.

Frank S. went on to amass a fortune in mining, lumbering, real estate, and transportation. He was elected Conservative member of parliament in 1888 and sat until 1896. He was the lieutenant governor of British Columbia from 1914 to 1919 and was knighted in 1918. His younger brother, a "chip off the old block," was Conservative MP for Victoria from 1908 to 1917 and a Canadian senator from 1917 to 1945.

STEVE TINGLEY TAKES THE
REINS AS OWNER AND MANAGER

At the meeting on July 7, 1888, in which Frank S. Barnard resigned as president and managing director, a motion was made to resolve that "Mr. S. Tingley be and is hereby appointed President, Manager and Managing Director with full authority to deal with the Company's bank accounts."[35] At a meeting on August 23, it was approved "that the head office of the company be removed from Victoria to Ashcroft, and that all necessary steps be taken to effect this change."[36]

While Barnard had been the owner and driving force of the company that had become the BC Express, Steve Tingley had, for many years, been the face of the company. When Barnard had taken on Tingley and James Hamilton as partners in 1872, the *British Colonist* enthused about the province-wide reputations of these men for their outstanding courtesy and skill at handling the "ribbons."[37]

Unlike Barnard, Tingley was a "hands-on" manager of the BC Express. Over and over, he demonstrated the practical skills and adaptability that remained a model to all the drivers. Tingley knew every inch of the Cariboo Road and proceeded to improve the infrastructure of the company and adjust the schedule now that the stagecoach run started from Ashcroft and not Yale. The result was a much more efficient stage line and, for the first time, a letter could reach Barkerville from Ashcroft in four days.

Tingley continued to drive the first thirty miles (48 kilometres) of the road from Ashcroft to Clinton. One of his passengers in 1875, "Russian" Jack, who owned the Black Jack claim at Lightning Creek, later wrote, "Up above Hat Creek the water was running down the [Cariboo] Road and was not passable by the stagecoach, but these drivers were men of resource. Mr. Tingley had provided plenty of rope and drove the coach up the hill and went along till the road was clear. Then the rope was tied to the coach and all the passengers held on to the rope while Tingley drove down the steep hill . . .

Later Tingley told me he had sent a man on horseback to find out if he could drive along the flooded road."[38] This foresight and ingenuity was typical of Tingley both as a driver and as the owner of the BC Express.

Tingley also began to acquire and expand the holdings of the BC Express along the Cariboo Road. In 1887, he bought the Hat Creek House and Ranch from William Cargile to use as a stage stop and horse ranch.[39] He then proceeded to build a barn large enough to accommodate 200 horses. In 1889, Tingley bought the 108 Mile House for $2,500 and installed his son, Clarence, as the BC Express agent and storekeeper. He also built a large horse barn there and expanded the size of the ranch to 1,000 acres. In 1896, he purchased land at the 158-mile post, where he kept horses on what came to be known as the Mountain House Ranch. The following year, he purchased the 83 Mile House and Ranch, originally called the Loch Lomond House, and totally renovated and enlarged the house. He also had a local builder, Alexander "Sandy" Innis, an excellent axe-man, construct a large horse barn there with room for fifty horses. The intent was to make the 83 Mile an important depot on the Cariboo Road.[40] At the 134 Mile House and Ranch, acquired by Barnard in 1867, where many of the BX horses were raised, Tingley built extensive shops for constructing stagecoaches from scratch.

The branch lines to the Okanagan and Lillooet continued to be serviced by the BC Express or companies it set up. For instance, J.B. Leighton, an employee of the company, held the mail contract for the Okanagan in his name from 1881 until the completion of the Canadian Pacific Railway eliminated the route in 1885. Tingley also established a branch line from the 108 Mile House to Harper's Camp, now called Horsefly, in 1895. At first, Harry Walters carried the mail and, for a time, gold, on horseback from J.B. Hobson's Horsefly Hydraulic Mine to the 108 Mile, where he connected with the regular stagecoach. The following year, William Parker, who had been a BC Express driver between Quesnel and the 83 Mile

House for many years, set up Parker's Stage Line to carry mail and express material along the same route.

Tingley emphasized the transportation of freight as well as express and passengers, purchasing a number of freight wagons to deliver the necessities and equipment to points in the Cariboo. When the Cariboo Gold Fields Ltd. was established in 1895, A.D. Whittier, manager and promoter of the company, intended to use a hydraulic lift method to work the bed of Whittier Creek, which runs into Williams Creek, in the Cariboo. At that time, a tender was let for the transportation of 341 tons of freight, consisting of steel hydraulic pipe, cast iron collars, lead, and steel bars, over the 240 miles (386 kilometres) from Ashcroft to Barkerville. Under Tingley's guidance, the BC Express secured the contract. There was no way Tingley could supply the necessary freight wagons, oxen, and horses to fulfill this contract, but he knew every teamster on the Cariboo Road and made a handshake agreement with them: he would pay them full value to carry this freight if they agreed to stay at his stopping houses and purchase his oats for their livestock. The freight arrived in Ashcroft and over the period of a year it was hauled bit by bit up the road to Barkerville. Such was Tingley's reputation for fair dealing that every teamster in the Cariboo stepped up and helped him move this mountain of freight, making themselves a good profit in the process.

Under Tingley's management, the BC Express continued to show a profit for its shareholders. Each year, after the company's year end, a meeting was held of the shareholders: Steve Tingley, with 834 shares; Pauline Tingley, with 116 shares; and J.J. Mackay, with 50 shares. At the end of Tingley's first year as manager, 1888 to 1889, the company made a profit of $16,967.47, which it carried over to the next year, granting a dividend of $14,000 to shareholders. Over the next seven years, profits continued as follows:[41]

YEAR	INCOME	EXPENSES	PROFIT	DIVIDEND
1888–89	$80,181.58	$63,214.11	$16,967.47	$14,000
1889–90	$43,428.98	$33,829.30	$9,599.68	$7,000
1890–91	$42,870.47	$39,400.45	$3,470.02	$3,000
1891–92	$43,794.29	$37,454.59	$6,339.70	$6,000
1892–93	$43,038.88	$39,634.14	$3,404.74	$2,500
1893–94	$42,605.49	$37,458.26	$5,147.23	
1894–95	$53,438.61	$41,820.98	$11,617.63	
1895–96	$56,369.22	$47,433.18	$8,936.04	

The annual income in this period included the federal mail subsidy of $24,000, with the profits carried forward and accumulated after 1893. This table makes clear that, without the mail subsidy, the BC Express Company could not have operated.

Tingley's family figured significantly in the BC Express. In 1878, Steve's youngest brother, Alex, came to British Columbia at age eighteen. Twenty-five years younger than Steve, he was carefully trained by his brother and became a stagecoach driver on the Cariboo Road. Sadly, only five years later, Alex was struck by typhoid fever and, while convalescing at his brother's house in Yale, died from the disease. He was fondly remembered in the *Inland Sentinel*, which wrote: "Few young men could be more regretted, for his mild manner, and unblemished character, together with strict attention to duty, made him a favourite along the line."[42] Steve Tingley's two sons from his first wife, Elizabeth Harper, also worked for the BC Express. Clarence was the BC Express agent and storekeeper at the 108 Mile House, purchased in 1889 by Steve Tingley to raise horses once the BX Ranch near Vernon was no longer connected with the BC Express. Tingley's son, Fred, also became a driver for the BC Express in the 1890s.

TRAVELLING UP THE ROAD IN 1894

In the Vancouver *Weekly World* on December 27, 1894, a reporter described a trip up the Cariboo Road he had taken the previous August. His description of his journey is an interesting glimpse of the changes that had taken place during the tenure of Steve Tingley. "On the 24th of August I left Ashcroft on the main line of the CPR for a thorough trip to the old historic town of Barkerville." Shortly before the coach left Ashcroft, a flood of the Thompson River had destroyed the bridge that connected the town to the Cariboo Road. "The flood having carried the bridge away, our stagecoach and team were ferried across the river by a scow built for the purpose, 38 feet long by 12 wide. It was not large enough, and there was some risk in driving horses and load on it. Still the article appearing in one of the Provincial weeklies, a sentence reading, 'not one single teamster is rash enough to risk putting freight on the scow' was somewhat exaggerated. Stephen Tingley, the energetic and capable manager of the British Columbia Express Co., on this occasion was our driver, and he had no hesitation in driving on and never left his seat while we were crossing."[43]

"Mr. Tingley," the reporter continued, "is the sole survivor of the original company, and although he is manager of the concern he is not above relieving a driver at any time. He can handle the reins as skillfully today as he could 25 years ago. He is and always will be plain 'Steve' Tingley, and owing to his executive ability they have now a splendidly equipped stage line. He is very popular along the stage line and with all the employees." The reporter acknowledged J.J. Mackay as the chief agent of the company at Ashcroft and praised him as "highly esteemed by all who know him, painstaking in all that he does, and to him also belongs praise for the success of the company."

Tingley drove the stagecoach as far as Clinton, where the passengers were greeted and fed by Joseph Smith, the proprietor of the Clinton Hotel. From there, Steve's son, Fred Tingley, took over driving and shared the driver's seat with the reporter, who remarked that "the stagecoach was filled with mining men on their way to Cariboo to look after their interests there or to prospect." The Cariboo was no longer a place where a single miner could get rich, as was indicated by the traffic on the road, largely comprising those who owned or worked for the large, highly capitalized mines that had taken over the industry. The stagecoach stopped at the 70-mile post, where William Boyd, an Irishman, operated a dairy farm and the passengers were able to get a "drink of good, fresh mountain milk" before proceeding to the 83 Mile House, then leased by the BC Express. This was the point where the southbound stage met the northbound one and passengers stayed the night.

The next day, with fresh horses and a new driver, Ed Owens, the stagecoach made good time through the Cariboo country, arriving at the 134-mile post, where the horses were changed. The ranch, referred to as the "big stables," was a key link in the BC Express network. The reporter described the post and the vicinity: "Wm. Morrison, the manager of the farm, and a man well posted on the country, informed me that he could locate 40 settlers on good land in that vicinity. He considers the Horsefly a wonderfully rich country, and is of the opinion that there will yet be big strikes made... A very handsome and substantial new coach was just finished at the 134 shops. It was of as fine workmanship as can be turned out of any carriage shop in the Province." Proceeding onward, the reporter pointed out that "the stage does not stay for the night at the 150-Mile house, as has usually been the custom, but we had our tea there and drove some eight miles further to Carpenter mountain for the night. The 150-Mile House, however, was all alive with mining men. Messrs. Veith & Borland own nearly everything at this place. They carry on an extensive merchandise and hotel business, besides working several farms in the vicinity." The shift from the popular 150 Mile House to Carpenter's House at the 158-mile post was part of Tingley's reorganization of the BC Express route and schedule. Also known as the "Mountain House," it was situated on top of the "eight mile hill" and became the preferred stop for overnighting. The reporter was impressed with the location, remarking,

Quesnel was originally called Quesnelle Mouth to distinguish it from Quesnelle Forks. UL_1019_0022, UNO LANGMANN FAMILY COLLECTION OF BRITISH COLUMBIA PHOTOGRAPHS, RARE BOOKS AND SPECIAL COLLECTIONS, UBC LIBRARY

"The 158 station at Carpenter mountain, is managed by H.P. Lewis and wife. It is a place neatly kept and very like home. Passengers are usually well pleased with the treatment accorded them. Mrs. Lewis had been fishing in the creek close by on the day of our arrival and succeeded in hooking 230 fine trout in four and a half hours." In 1896, Tingley purchased the stopping house and land for the BC Express and raised horses there. As can be seen, his strategy was to have smaller horse ranches along the route for greater efficiency and economy.

After an early breakfast at Carpenter's, the stage was on its way, arriving in Soda Creek "in time for a second breakfast" while the mail for the Chilcotin and other offices was sorted. The place was a beehive of activity with many of the old-timers still present. "'Bob' McLeese, the old land mark of the country, is still there ... P.T. Reed is still conducting the business of P.C. Dunlevy, and has charge of the express office. Mrs. Reed takes a pardonable pride in her flower garden, which she keeps in order herself. It is, so far as I am aware, the finest in Cariboo."

The horses were changed at Soda Creek and, after changing again at Moffat's Ranch at Alexandria, the site of the old Hudson's Bay Company post, the stagecoach arrived at Quesnel before dark, having made fifty-two miles that day. The reporter, once again, gave a description of the local bright lights. "The Occidental hotel, formerly conducted by J. McLean, is now run by Messrs. Perkins & Bowron. They are clever young men, full of business and they enjoy what they justly deserve—a big trade. Hon. Jas. Reid was as usual busy in his store. The Senator's business is one of the most extensive in Cariboo. He is an old timer, a resident of British Columbia for the past 32 years... He has been a resident of Quesnelle since the year 1871; was one year a guard on the stage. He informed me that he has guarded $20,000 to $100,000 of gold dust on a trip and was never molested."

The next morning at five o'clock the stagecoach was off again. This stretch was usually driven by Alexander "Sandy" Locke but on this occasion, Ed Owens drove right through to Barkerville. The reporter concluded, "Thundering along our way from Stanley we soon reach Williams' creek and follow its historic banks until we reach the end of the wagon road, nearly 300 miles long, and which is considered to be as good a through road as any in the world. The journey occupies four long days, and good, fast travelling it is. A trip to Cariboo costs money. The distance is so great that miners are kept from going into the country. Freight from Ashcroft to Barkerville is carried by wagons at a cost of about $125 per ton. Very few miners can afford to land machinery there at such a cost... Residents of Barkerville are not discouraged. They are looking for the stirring days of the early sixties."[44]

TINGLEY'S LONG RUN COMES TO AN END

Tingley saw the potential for a transportation network that ran into Northern British Columbia, the first leg of which was the then-abandoned steamboat run from Soda Creek, first used in 1863. In the spring of 1896, he joined with Senator James Reid of Quesnel and Captain John Irving to form the North British Columbia Navigation Company. The partners planned to construct a steamboat to run between Soda Creek and Quesnel and possibly upriver. The keel was laid in June and, on August 3, 1896, the *Charlotte* was launched.[45]

Just when it seemed that the BC Express was entering a new era of development, the company lost the mail contract. In the spring of 1897, it was announced that the contract had been awarded to a group of Toronto businessmen. In July, the *British Colonist* reported that "yesterday saw the completion of a deal which marks another mile post in the history of the development of the Interior. The exchange of papers took place in this city by which Mr. S. Tingley, the proprietor of the British Columbia Express Company transferred to Messrs. Charles Millar and James Kilgour of Toronto, his interest in that well known forwarding business in the Cariboo District . . . The present transfer includes all the coaches, sleighs, harness, etc. and 50 head of horses and it is understood to be the intention of the new proprietors to lease the old stables and most of the business premises of the former owners."[46]

8

HOLDUPS AND ACCIDENTS

ARNARD'S BRITISH COLUMBIA Express Company ordered the Dufferin Coach to be built by the Black & Miller Carriage Company of San Francisco for the 1876 visit of Lord and Lady Dufferin. Constructed as a "convertible," its canvas top could be either open or closed. The carriage could accommodate six passengers inside and one up on the box. After its initial use, the coach was used whenever dignitaries came to the province. In 1882, the Marquis of Lorne, Governor General of Canada and Queen Victoria's son-in-law, having married Princess Louise, travelled in it when he toured the BC Interior. But, from time to time, the coach was rented by those who had pretentions of nobility and it could occasionally be seen on the Cariboo Road, pulled by four horses.

On one such occasion, the coach was rented by a well-to-do mining promoter on a trip to a prospective mine in the Cariboo. The promoter brought along with him two potential investors, who had arrived in Ashcroft by train. The coach made good time and, whenever it stopped for meals or to stay the night, the passengers were treated like royalty and provided with the best food and accommodation, the men assuming that the Dufferin Coach made them special. When the potential backers arrived at Barkerville, they carefully examined the mining property and decided they would forgo the investment.

The Dufferin coach, summer of 1901. J.B. Leighton is driving, with
Judge Galliher beside him, Charles Millar leaning forward in the coach,
and James Cran, a banker of Ashcroft, next to him.   IMAGE A-03072
COURTESY OF THE ROYAL BC MUSEUM AND ARCHIVES

On the trip back down the Cariboo Road, the would-be investors
found that the food and accommodation fell short of the previous
standard. Arriving at Ashcroft, they tipped the driver generously
and inquired why on the trip back down, except for one or two stopping houses, they had not been so well treated. The driver grinned.
"Well, it's this a-way. When you turned down that mining prospect,
the owner telegraphed ahead and cancelled all them chicken sup-
pers. The places where you still got special treatment were those
that didn't have a telegraph. He'd a sent you back down in a wagon,
if he hadn't already paid for the Dufferin anyways."[1]

STAGECOACH HOLDUPS

From the earliest days, carrying mail had been a function of the
expressmen of British Columbia. Miners found nothing better than
receiving a letter from home, no matter how mundane its news. But

an even more significant aspect of the express business was carrying the "treasure," often consisting of tens of thousands of dollars in gold, to the Wells Fargo or Freeman's Express offices. Each miner's gold was most often placed in a leather "poke" that was sealed with wax, stamped with the agency seal along all its seams to ensure that none of the gold could be removed, and carefully labelled as the sender watched.

Despite the colonial government's attempt to establish a gold escort to carry the treasure to Victoria or New Westminster, the miners preferred the express companies and trusted them to deliver without complications. The expressmen did not disappoint. Millions of dollars in gold was carried down from the Cariboo and other gold regions over the years without incident. In their first year alone, the combined Barnard's and Dietz and Nelson expresses carried an incredible $4,619,000 in gold to the coast.

For some years, the colonial or provincial police provided a special guard to travel on the stage when the value of the treasure was significant. When this service was discontinued for economic reasons, the company notified stagecoach drivers that, since the treasure was always insured, they should not carry any firearms or resist an armed holdup. Despite the absence of guards, not one serious holdup took place on the Cariboo Road until 1885. There were two good reasons for this.

First, the isolated nature of the Cariboo meant that there was really only one way out and that was the Cariboo Wagon Road. Second, the British justice system in British Columbia involved the presence of the BC Provincial Police and swift and sure punishment for offenders.

A police force had been established in colonial times, when Chartres Brew, a former member of the Royal Irish Constabulary, was appointed chief inspector of police. Qualified individuals being scarce, one person often filled a wide variety of roles in their community, such as magistrate, constable, gold commissioner, tax collector, and meteorologist. Eventually, these positions separated out and individuals were given more specialized roles. The colonial police force became the British Columbia Constabulary in 1871, when BC joined the Canadian Confederation. Constables were under the direction of the government agent in a district and covered a wide geographic area, where they were expected to uphold the law with their gun, horse, and plenty of courage and common sense. The duties of the force included patrolling the land, enforcing laws, maintaining peace, controlling smuggling, and generally enforcing provincial statutes. Special constables were also deployed as required. These men were held in great respect by their communities and, in the event of a serious robbery, they could telegraph down the line to their fellow officers to watch for the robber. Their presence in the community and their quick response acted as a deterrent to those seeking a quick fortune.

THE FIRST STAGECOACH HOLDUPS

The first recorded holdup of a stagecoach on the Cariboo Road took place in 1885 at the 82-mile post, about thirty-five miles above Clinton and a short distance from the 83 Mile House operated by Murdoch Ross. Ned Tate, of Irish stock but born in Ontario, was driving the stagecoach with only one passenger, a Chinese miner, when two robbers stepped out of the woods and levelled their firearms at the driver. Tate threw down the strongbox and was ordered to drive on. The highwaymen escaped with about $4,000 in gold and were never tracked down. The BC Express did not provide any more details, not wanting other desperados to get ideas.

A few years later, the second recorded holdup took place on a lonely stretch of road just south of Harry Moffat's Landsdowne Farm near Alexandria, twenty-six miles below Quesnel. This time, it was Jack Tate, Ned Tate's brother, who was driving an empty stagecoach with only mail and freight on board. A single robber stopped the stage and carried off between two and three thousand dollars in cash and small quantities of gold from the express bags. Once again, the highwayman escaped and, once again, few details of the holdup are known. There was speculation, however, that Jack Tate staged the robbery and escaped with the proceeds, since he left the province soon after the holdup.

THE BIGGEST HAUL FROM A STAGECOACH HOLDUP

The biggest haul from a robbery of the BC Express occurred on July 14, 1890. The British *Colonist* provided dramatic details:

> The most daring stage robbery chronicled in the history of British Columbia was perpetrated on the B.C. Express Co.'s stage which runs from Cariboo to Ashcroft on Monday evening at about 5 o'clock, involving a loss of about $4000. On the road at the 97-mile post a masked man met the stage and, at the muzzle of a Winchester, called a halt, demanding the treasure. The driver offered a bag with $2,000 in it, but the robber refused to take it. He said he wanted the safe and didn't intend to make a third request, so he was allowed to take the iron safe. After throwing it from the stage and saluting the driver and the single passenger with mock politeness, followed with a volley of the most profane language, the robber ordered the stage to drive on. Usually the stage is not worth much. But as it was washing up time now [collecting the gold accumulated through the summer and sending to the banks] the man knew his game and took a good time to make his attack, indicating a thorough acquaintance with the neighborhood and the arrangements of the express company. A posse of Indians and a white leader are on the hunt, and Constable Barr, of Ashcroft, has joined in the chase. There is no news of the robber yet. Mr. Soues, the Government agent here, is working hard to run the villain down.[2]

Further details were provided the following day. William Parker, the driver of the stagecoach, and the only passenger, a Minneapolis fur buyer by the name of Baldwin, described the robber as being crouched behind a stump on the steep hill just out of the 100 Mile

House and wearing a black mask. He spoke with a hoarse voice with a slight Scottish accent and implied the presence of additional gang members in the bushes behind him.

Steve Tingley was quick to report that "not the slightest fault can be found with Parker ... He is a man enjoying the fullest confidence of the company, having proven his worth, and not one who would allow his stage to be robbed if he had the slightest chance to successfully resist. No matter how much courage a man has, however, he could not expect to resist the argument contained in the shining barrel of a Winchester."[3]

The actual amount in the safe was $4,122 and the provincial government immediately offered a $2,000 reward for the capture of the highwayman. In the meantime, the loss was covered by the insurer, the Guarantee Company. The *Colonist* commented that the "the robbery suggests the advisability of, or more properly the necessity, in future of providing an armed guard to accompany or follow the treasure laden coaches."

The robbery prompted one of the most extensive manhunts of the era. The *Colonist* reported that "news from the man hunters already scouring the country is looked for hourly. McKinley has gone out with Ogden's Indians from Lac la Hache; Brown from the 150 Mile House has gone down the Fraser after Constable Allen, who is wanted to join in the search, and also to inform the people all along the river of the robbery, and obtain their assistance in running down the outlaw. Barr, of Ashcroft, is at work on the case, and men from Hussey's, Savona, Copper Creek, and Kamloops are also engaged upon it."[4]

Despite the widespread search and the reward offered, no trace of the robber was found. As time passed, it was feared that, once again, the culprit would escape undetected. The concern of the BC Express shareholders was recorded in the company minute book at the annual meeting the following September: "Regarding the robbery of the stage on the 14th July last, near the 99 Mile Post, the shareholders present regret to be unable to report any substantial clue to the identity of the perpetrator."[5]

Shortly after the holdup, an old man named Martin Van Buren Rowland showed up near Clinton from the Fraser River. He told the locals that he had been prospecting in the Barkerville area and headed down the road, eventually staking a claim on Scottie Creek about nineteen miles north of Ashcroft on the Bonaparte River. He built several sluices and employed some Indigenous and Chinese men to help him work the claim. His regular clean-ups were quite rewarding and he claimed to be making from one to two hundred dollars a day. Years before, there had been several rich strikes on Scottie Creek when a little coarse gold had been found, but the creek was generally thought to be mined out. Rowland's success prompted another small rush and soon the entire creek was staked. But Rowland seemed to be the only one making any money, sending regular shipments of gold dust via the BC Express to F.W. Foster's store in Ashcroft, where Rowland would occasionally go to spend his gold in the town's saloons.

It was noticed that Rowland made his clean-ups only when there was no one else around. This aroused the suspicion of two old-timers, Benjamin F. "Doc" English and Johnny Wilson of Savona. They asked the bartenders in Ashcroft to set aside the gold Rowland spent so they could take a look at it. Miners of the Cariboo knew that gold nuggets vary greatly in colour, feel, and size, depending upon which creek they came from. But Rowland did not return to Ashcroft that fall.

In the winter of 1890, Rowland sent a large amount of gold to Barkerville to be melted down to bullion by the gold commissioner. After close examination, it was clear that Rowland's gold came from the Upper Fraser and Cottonwood mining areas. Shortly after this discovery, Rowland headed to Ashcroft planning to catch a train back east as soon as his bullion arrived. But acting on a tip from English and Wilson, Chief Constable Burr apprehended him and sent him to Kamloops, where Justice of the Peace Isaac Lehman placed him in custody.[6]

At the ensuing trial, a great number of witnesses were called, but none could confirm Rowland's identity. The evidence was circumstantial, but what clinched his conviction was the testimony of various experts that "the gold found in his possession, and which he claimed he had washed out from a claim on Scotty Creek, was declared ... to be of the character of gold found on the Fraser, Cottonwood and other camps and entirely dissimilar to the gold obtained on Scotty Creek. Miners testified that Rowland's sluices were so poorly constructed that it was impossible for him to have saved the gold that the prisoner claimed he had panned out." On the basis of this testimony, and since there was not enough evidence to convict him of robbery, Rowland was found guilty of receiving stolen property and sentenced to five years in prison.[7] English and Wilson were paid their reward.

Rowland later revealed that, before the holdup, he had been prospecting unsuccessfully around Barkerville and was heading south with a saddle and a pack horse when he conceived of the robbery. He waited for the stage near the 99-mile post, where stages usually stopped on the four-mile-long hill to rest their horses. After the robbery, he rode some distance up Bridge Creek before he chopped open the safe with his axe and took out the gold. He then backtracked sixty miles to the Horsefly mines, where he waited for the dust to settle. After a few weeks, he headed to Alkali Lake, south of Williams Lake, from where he took the river trail to Clinton.[8]

At the meeting of the BC Express shareholders that September, the following entry was made in the minute book: "Satisfaction was expressed at the result of the trial of M.V.B. Rowland for the robbery of the stage near Bridge Creek in July 1890, who was convicted and sentenced by Judge Walkem at the June Assize at Clinton to a term in the Provincial penitentiary in New Westminster."[9]

TWO HOLDUPS IN ONE MONTH

The month of June 1894 saw holdups of two BC Express stagecoaches. The first occurred on June 7 on the branch road that ran from the 150 Mile House to Quesnel Forks and Keithley Creek.

Angus MacRae held the mail contract for that line and Colin Sinclair was driving the stagecoach, when a masked man stepped into the road and levelled a rifle at him. He had little recourse but to throw down the mail bags as ordered. The robber grabbed the bags and told Sinclair to drive on, which he did. He wasted no time in telegraphing the BC Provincial Police and, within a day, the mail bags were found a few hundred yards from the road, torn open with letters scattered. The police began interviewing people in the vicinity and talked to two Chinese miners who told of how, a few days, they were robbed at gunpoint of the gold in their sluices and all their provisions by a man with a Winchester rifle.

On June 25, another holdup occurred on the main Cariboo Road, just two-and-a-half miles below the 150 Mile House. As this robbery took place so soon after the previous one and the first bandit had not yet been captured, it was assumed to be the same robber, but this turned out not to be the case. This time, Ed Owens was the driver and the southbound stage had five passengers on board. The stage had stopped for the night at the 150 Mile House where the passengers, including a man named Samuel Bankley, slept in the stopping house. In the morning, Bankley said he would go ahead on foot and board the stage when it caught up to him. He must have been a little nervous, as he mistook another passenger's hat for his own. The stagecoach had hardly got out of sight of the 150 Mile House when he stepped out from behind a tree and confronted the driver with a Winchester rifle.

Owens was not your ordinary stagecoach driver. He was renowned for being the slowest, most careful driver on the road. Passengers would often say that he starved his horses because he took so long to make it to the next stop. The strong, quiet type who, despite his 200 pounds, could outrun anyone in a race, he never talked about his background and always carried a high-calibre pistol in the waistband of his trousers. He slept with that gun and always sat with his back to the wall when indoors. When asked why he was so cautious, he replied, "there's a fellow after me and I want to see him first."

Cariboo resident William Phelps was sitting next to Owens on the box and later gave a first-hand account of the robbery. The stagecoach left the 150 Mile House at daybreak and the lone bandit appeared about half an hour later, wearing a mask made out of a gunny sack. He demanded that Owens throw down the express box. The driver replied that it was in the boot, in the back of the stage, and the bandit could get it himself, but the bandit insisted that Owens climb down and get it for him.[10]

Owens was known to be extremely quick and accurate with his six-shooter and, when the bandit ordered him to climb down from the seat and get the strongbox out of the boot, he had an excellent opportunity to draw his gun and shoot the culprit. But, as he started to reach for his gun, a passenger reached out and restrained him. Owens held back, knowing that the bandit would get very little from the holdup.[11] The bandit told Owens to get back on his seat and drive on and not look back if he didn't want to get shot.

For a change, Owens made record time to the next stagecoach stop, where he telegraphed the alarm. Coming so quickly after the first holdup, the crime created considerable excitement among Cariboo residents. The same day, Superintendent of Provincial Police Fred Hussey issued instructions to the constables at 150 Mile House and other places on the Cariboo Road to make every effort to capture the highwayman. The resident constable at 150 Mile put together a posse and went to the scene of the robbery, where they found a gunny sack with the name "Pinchbeck" stencilled on it. They quickly concluded that the robber was none other than Bankley, who had walked ahead of the stagecoach.

Superintendent Hussey arrived at the 150 Mile House, and immediately organized parties to scour the countryside. As details began to accumulate, it soon became apparent that the two holdups were not connected. Bankley, who gave his name as Sam Slick, was captured four days after the robbery, by a posse from the Esk'etemc People at Alkali Lake, and brought in to Clinton by Basil Eagle, in possession of the gold stolen from the stagecoach. Bankley was tried by Judge Cornwall for highway robbery and sentenced to ten years in prison.[12]

The search for the first robber continued, with Superintendent Hussey involved in the hunt. A man named Sharp was taken into custody near Horsefly by Constable Bain from the 150-mile post. Sharp admitted to taking supplies to Harry Brown, who was hidden in the area. This helped narrow down the search, and Hussey, along with Constables Sutherland of Lytton, and Bain of 150 Mile House, assisted by Thomas Walters, focused their efforts in that region. At five o'clock in the morning on July 5, Bain came upon the bandit asleep in a cabin about sixty miles from Horsefly. Brown awoke to find the muzzle of a revolver pointed at him and three constables in his cabin. He was tried by Judge Cornwall and sentenced to fifteen years in prison, the extra years because he had taken Her Majesty's Mail in the robbery. James Sharp was charged with aiding Brown to evade capture and was sentenced to five years.

Superintendent Hussey began to achieve the status of a hero of law and order. The *British Colonist* extolled his abilities when he arrested Bankley: "Superintendent Hussey has added another to his long list of cases successfully brought to an issue, according to advices received by wire from the Cariboo country last night. He left here early in the week... upon the receipt of news of the second robbery of the stage between the 150 Mile House and Quesnelle Forks on Monday. His object was to capture the robber, and he evidently has succeeded as he usually does."[13]

BILL MINER ATTEMPTS A STAGECOACH ROBBERY

Few robbers have achieved the status of legend. South of the border, Butch Cassidy and the Sundance Kid and Jesse James reached this level of recognition bordering on myth. But in Canada, only Bill Miner has entered into the legends of the frontier as a folk hero. His two train robberies in British Columbia, one successful and the other not, have been portrayed in print and on the big screen, capturing the imagination of the public for the past century. Missing from his story, though, is the role played by the BC Express in his first, successful train holdup. The story is told by Willis J. West,

general manager of the company at the time and, if not totally ver-
ifiable, it at least adds to Miner's legend.

After a long and, at times, noteworthy career in robbing stagecoaches and an even longer time in prison, Ezra Allen "Bill" Miner
emerged from San Quentin California State Prison in 1902. He
wasted no time in returning to the career he knew so well. But, as
stagecoaches were disappearing from the American West, Miner
decided to diversify. In September 1903, Miner and two other bandits bungled an attempt to rob a train in Oregon. One bandit was
killed, and another wounded and later arrested. Miner escaped and
headed to British Columbia, where he assumed the name George
Edwards. Settling in Kamloops, he posed as a semi-retired rancher.

According to the story, in the summer of 1904 Miner entered
the main office of the BC Express in Ashcroft, identifying himself
as a gold miner specializing in reworking dry ground. He inquired
about stage transport along the Cariboo Road and was given a folder
showing the stagecoach schedule. Miner had a long talk with the
agent and spent some time describing his technique of mining,
which involved the use of a firehose and pump in a modified hydraulic mining process. Ironically, while he was chatting to the agent,
there was a wanted poster on the wall from the Pinkerton's Detec-
tive Agency offering a reward for his capture. The photograph on the
poster showed a grizzled and unkempt individual, not at all like the
well-dressed older gentleman who was in the office.

Miner left the office and went over to one of Ashcroft's three
saloons, where there was always a poker game in progress. He lost
a couple of hundred dollars, indicating that he was far from broke
at the time, no doubt still living off the proceeds of his previous robbery. Later, one of the men in the poker game would identify him as
being in Ashcroft at the time.

On September 7, 1904, the BC Express stagecoach arrived
in Ashcroft from the Cariboo, carrying a large number of miners
who had just been laid off from the famous Bullion Pit mine near
Quesnel Forks. They boasted that the season had been particularly
productive and the mine was sending down a big gold shipment

on the next stage. Miner, or one of his accomplices, was on hand to note the fact and planned to intercept the gold shipment on the train once it left Ashcroft. The next stage was due to arrive from Barkerville on Friday, September 9, and the train was scheduled to leave shortly after the arrival of the stage. What Miner did not realize was that the stage from Quesnel Forks that connected with the Barkerville stage in Williams Lake ran only once a week and the Bullion Pit shipment would not arrive until Tuesday, September 13.

On September 10, 1904, the Miner gang held up the CPR's Transcontinental Express a few kilometres west of Mission in the Fraser Valley. They got away with $6,000 worth of gold dust, more than $900 in currency and $50,000 in US bonds. But, if they had held up the train on Wednesday, September 14, they would have intercepted a $60,000 gold shipment from the Bullion Pit mine. As it was, the holdup would be considered a success and Miner, in his new alias of George Edwards, lived comfortably for two more years before the urge overcame him again and he robbed the train east of Kamloops.

A FAILED ATTEMPT AND THE LAST HOLDUP

Not every attempt at robbing the BC Express ended in success. Despite the fact that the company advised all drivers to not resist robbers and assured them that all thefts were covered by Lloyd's of London insurance, some drivers considered it an insult to have their stage held up. In 1899, Charles Westaby had long been a driver for the company when he was confronted by a highwayman just a few miles south of the 150 Mile House. Westaby was not about to have a robbery "on his watch" and whipped the horses to rear up and speed away, leaving the potential robber staring slack-jawed at his dust.[14]

The last robbery of a BC Express stagecoach on the Cariboo Road occurred on November 1, 1909, on a stretch of road between the 141 and 144 mile houses. Ironically, Charles Westaby was the driver again and this time he had no opportunity to escape. He was driving the regular mail stagecoach full of passengers that had left the 150 Mile House that morning. It was still dark when he reached a stretch of road with a large tree on one side and a big boulder on the other. A man and a woman stepped out and levelled their rifles at him. The man demanded that he throw down all the registered mail bags. Westaby knew exactly what was happening, but he was quite deaf and stalled for time pretending he could not understand the instructions. He succeeded in keeping back some of the registered mail bags and threw down some empty sacks that were being returned to the Ashcroft station. The robbers made no attempt to rob the passengers and ordered Westaby to drive on. This he did in quick time until he reached the 134 Mile House, where the first telegraph office was located. From there, word was sent to telegraph stations up and down the road and the police were immediately alerted.

As usual, a posse was formed, this time consisting of local BC Express employees and ranchers, who proceeded to the scene of the robbery. There they were joined by the BC Provincial Police who, a short distance into the woods, found the stolen mail bags cut open, with currency removed from the letters but cheques and money orders left behind. The posse followed the unshod horse tracks of the bandits for a few miles until they joined with the tracks of a band of wild horses, making it impossible to continue following them.

Most of the passengers took the incident as a small but exciting addition to the trip to Ashcroft, but a newspaper reporter from the coast stormed into the BC Express office in Ashcroft demanding to be told what efforts were being made to apprehend "the dastardly scoundrels who had robbed Her Majesty's mail."[15] Willis J. West, superintendent of the BC Express, was in the office at the time, and he remarked, "We of the B.X. were somewhat taken aback. Secretly we had felt rather pleased, since the Company was not responsible for the loss of the mails in the event of an armed holdup, no-one had been hurt, and we had made the front pages of the newspapers across Canada."[16]

The BC Provincial Police, on the other hand, was not at all pleased with this daring robbery in its territory. An extensive search was begun around the 150 Mile House, with all inhabitants in the sparsely populated area visited and interviewed. Locals told of seeing a man with a woman who called him her brother-in-law. A couple matching this description were arrested in a cabin, outside of which were two newly shod horses. While the evidence was circumstantial at best, the pair was arrested and taken to Ashcroft for questioning. Although nothing could be proven, they were generally assumed to be the guilty party and were put on the train in Ashcroft and told to stay out of Canada. They probably received this "sentence" with delight, having stolen some $2,000, though they had missed a package of about $5,000 in currency, thanks to Westaby's apparent hardness of hearing.[17]

The scene of the robbery became a regular stagecoach stop, drivers having to pull over and provide details of the holdup while passengers climbed out and took photos with the popular Brownie box cameras. The regular driver on that run, Al Young, was often asked to pose with his arms raised and a look of terror on his face alongside the very stagecoach and horses used in the last stagecoach robbery on the Cariboo Road.

A STAGECOACH ROBBERY OF ANOTHER SORT

Aschel Sumner Bates was one of the first American miners on the Upper Fraser River in 1858. With the gold dust he accumulated in the early 1860s, he began cattle ranching near Savona on the Thompson River and later invested in a number of business enterprises in the Cariboo. These included the Colonial Hotel in Soda Creek, the sternwheeler *Victoria,* and ranches at Sugarcane, near Williams Lake and Deep Creek. In 1871, he purchased the 150 Mile House where he had 2,000 acres of land, several hundred head of cattle, a store, a roadhouse, and a blacksmith shop.

In 1875, the stopping house was operated by a former Cariboo miner, Jim Griffin, who also served as postmaster. In those days, there was no bank in the Cariboo, and cash was often sent through the mail in a registered letter carried in special mail bags by the BC Express that were kept in a locked strongbox on the stagecoach. Only the postmasters along the road had keys to the box, and at each post office the box was opened, the registered letters for that post office removed and safely stored, and the box relocked and put back on the stagecoach.

On one occasion, the well-known cattleman Thaddeus Harper, who had made a fortune in bringing in cattle during the gold rush years, sent a registered letter containing $1,800 in cash to Cornelius O'Keefe, a rancher in the Okanagan Valley. But the letter never reached its destination. It was traced to the 150 Mile House where it appeared to have gone missing. Fortunately, Harper, a shrewd businessman, had made a note of the serial numbers on the currency in his letter and these numbers were circulated to all the postmasters along the road.

A young Englishman, Fred Harrison, was living in the area, a true "remittance man" who, every six months received his $500 allowance from his parents in England. He would go to the 150 Mile where everyone was welcome to join in his celebrations, which included a big poker game. It was during one of these games that the letter from Harper to O'Keefe had gone missing. As the evening progressed, Harrison, well into his cups, became less aware of his surroundings. It is believed that the thief of the letter slipped several hundred dollars of the stolen money into Harrison's pocket, hoping to frame him for the theft. In the course of the game, these notes were won from Harrison and kept by the winners.

It was only a matter of time before the postal authorities found the numbered bills in circulation around the 150 Mile and traced them back to Harrison. He was arrested and committed to trial before Judge Begbie. Although the evidence was circumstantial, Harrison was found guilty and sentenced to five years in the New Westminster penitentiary. It is believed that his relatives soon got Harrison out of prison and brought him back to England.

At the close of the trial, Judge Begbie remarked that "those parties who were in that poker game and won that money had better make restitution to the post office department." That was done somewhat sheepishly by the men who had taken advantage of the young Englishman. Even though Harrison paid the price for his foolishness, it was generally agreed that he had not had access to the letters at any time and was undoubtedly innocent of the crime. Jim Griffin, who had been in the poker game, was considered the most likely culprit. Described by J.B. Leighton, "he had only one arm, the other was taken off close to the shoulder. He was a very slick poker player, especially with a confederate. I hardly know what he would have done with two arms."[18]

STAGECOACH ACCIDENTS WILL HAPPEN

Stagecoach drivers took great pride in never having accidents in their hundreds of trips up and down the Cariboo Road. Though occasionally, through circumstances or driver negligence, an accident would happen, fatalities were avoided thanks to the quick wits of the drivers. In the fifty-year history of stagecoaches to the Cariboo, there is no record of a fatal accident, a true tribute to the drivers who navigated the hills and cliffs of the canyons and curves in darkness and daylight.

The first recorded stagecoach accident is reported in the *British Colonist* of September 12, 1864. Though the driver is not named, it is certain he did not remain a driver for long. The stagecoach was leaving Robertson's Ranch at the 90-mile post and heading south when it became apparent that the driver was quite intoxicated. He began whipping the horses and kept them at a full gallop for about two miles, causing the passengers to fear for their lives. At that point one of the wagon wheels hit a rock and the tongue of the stagecoach broke in two, with the jagged end contacting the horses' flanks. They became entirely uncontrollable and dashed on at top speed, causing the stagecoach to sway from side to side as it bounced over the stony road.

After this went on for some time, with the passengers hanging on for dear life, the road climbed up and ran along a narrow stretch with a long drop on one side. The passengers, one by one, jumped from the stage, led by a woman who had her leg severely sprained. The only remaining passenger was an invalid who could not make the jump. All that would have been required was for the driver to apply the brake, but the stage careened on over the road before coming to a stop.

Fortunately, no one was seriously injured, but the passengers reported insult to injury in enduring a second harrowing experience on that same trip, though with a more competent driver. The *British Colonist* explained:

> The same party had a very narrow escape coming over that very dangerous portion of the road known as China Bluff, about twenty miles above Yale. The road at that point is a narrow track blasted out from the cliff, the turbulent stream of the Fraser roiling several hundred feet below. The stage was passing this point at night, it being very dark, when suddenly one of the four horses began to rear and plunge so frightfully that the travellers momentarily expected to be hurled into the abyss below. The driver, however, who on this occasion was a careful and steady man, managed to unhitch the fractious animal, and the remainder of the way to Yale was safely accomplished with three horses.[19]

It is likely that the second driver, who exhibited such coolness in handling the frightened horse, was Steve Tingley, who had driven that stretch of road all that summer. It is fortunate that neither incident resulted in serious injury, especially in this first year of Barnard's Express stagecoach service on the Cariboo Road.

A potentially more fatal accident happened in March of 1881, with Steve Tingley's brother Alex driving. He had come from New Brunswick in 1878 to join his brother and had become an excellent stagecoach driver. On a particularly steep stretch of road on the Thompson River, a few miles south of Nicomen at the 64-mile post, the stagecoach reached what appeared to be a snow drift.

Tingley attempted to drive through the drift, but it was actually a snow slide that had wiped away the road. When the weight of the stage went over it, the snow gave way and the stagecoach, horses, and passengers all plummeted down the embankment, falling and rolling about 150 feet (46 metres). The stagecoach, a new one, was smashed to pieces and the two lead horses were killed in the fall. Tingley and most of the passengers escaped with a few bruises, except for Crookes, a railway carpenter, who had a broken leg and split kneecap, and Paul Ercole, who had a sprained ankle.

Alex Tingley clambered up the bank and headed back toward Nicomen as fast as his bruised legs could carry him. Discarding his coat and boots in the climbing, he walked the three miles to Nicomen in his stocking feet to get help. A wagon was dispatched to pick up the passengers and freight and deliver them to Lytton, where Dr. Shelton attended to them.

The heavy spring snowfall that had caused the snow slide also brought down the telegraph lines in the Fraser Canyon, so no word was received for a few days. When Steve Tingley heard of the accident, he took Dr. E.B. Hannington of Yale to Lytton to have a look at Crookes and Ercole, who were found to be doing as well as could be expected. The cost to Barnard's Express was almost $1,000. An examination of the road at the place where the stage went over showed that the gravel had been washed away, leaving only a sheet of ice, which broke from the weight of the stage.[20]

There were plenty of minor accidents over the fifty years that stagecoaches travelled over the Cariboo Road. During the construction of the Canadian Pacific Railway, as Steve Tingley was navigating through rocks scattered by the extensive blasting in the Fraser Canyon, one of his back wheels struck a large rock, causing the heavily loaded stagecoach to spill passengers and freight onto the ground. No one was hurt, but if the accident had happened a few yards ahead or behind, the stagecoach would have plunged down the bank.[21]

Another near accident happened with Harry Moffat at the reins in the early 1880s. Moffat arrived in British Columbia from Ontario in 1876 and, for a time, ran two light wagons suitable for

Lytton was located at "The Forks," where the Fraser and
Thompson Rivers merged. UL_1001_0031, UNO LANGMANN
FAMILY COLLECTION OF BRITISH COLUMBIA PHOTOGRAPHS,
RARE BOOKS AND SPECIAL COLLECTIONS, UBC LIBRARY

hauling perishable goods. Sometimes as many as sixteen horses
were hitched to pull heavy freight but mostly Moffat carried goods
using two or four fast horses. "Moffat's Fast Freight," as it came to
be known, soon attracted the interest of Steve Tingley, who offered
Moffat good money as a stagecoach driver on the route into Barkerville. Moffat accepted the job on this difficult stretch of the Cariboo
Road, where winter came early and stayed late. On one occasion,
Moffat was driving a six-horse stagecoach from Cottonwood to
Quesnelle Mouth, when his team was spooked by something on
the road and took off at a run down the Eleven-Mile Hill. Moffat
was concerned for the full load of passengers, so he jumped from
the box onto one of the wheel horses and worked his way to the lead
horse. He got a hold on the reins and slid over to one side and, brac-
ing his feet on the ground, he managed to pull the head of the horse

down until it came to a halt. Moffat's feet were badly trampled and his knees injured, but he had saved the stagecoach from overturning on the steep hill. All in a day's work for a BC Express driver.

Perhaps the most bizarre stagecoach accident occurred sometime in the 1880s, when Auguste Gauthier was driving the BC Express stagecoach through Lytton. Gauthier had grown up in Lytton and must have been a new driver, as he was not familiar with carrying "delicate" cargo—this time honey bees destined for the Botanie Valley junction near Lillooet.

Honey bees were brought to the Americas by European settlers and had adapted well to the environment. The first honey bees in the Colony of British Columbia arrived in 1858, when a shipment of two hives arrived in Victoria from W.H. Hoy of San Francisco for J.B.D. Ogilvie. Chinese miners in the Interior soon heard of this other form of gold and began using tea chests as hives. Tea chests were lightweight and sturdy enough and ideal for shipping bees by train.

But when it came to transport by stagecoach (the only way to move them through the British Columbia Interior), the tea chests were a little frail for the bumpy Cariboo roads. Steve Tingley, always up for a challenge, developed a technique for shipping the hives. He put them on the back shelf (in the boot) of the stagecoach with a quick-release rope the driver could pull in case leaks developed in the hives. The frequent use of the release rope meant that honey bees began to populate the areas along the Cariboo Road. Tingley and the other senior drivers soon learned to delegate the transportation of hives to the junior BC Express drivers. Hence the situation in which Auguste Gauthier found himself one fateful day.

As the stagecoach rattled through the town of Lytton, one of the bees escaped. Apparently, the bee was not happy about the bumpy ride and, making its escape, it stung one of the wheel horses on the flank. The horse reared, Gauthier was unable to control it, and the stagecoach tipped over just across from the Globe Hotel. Once the tea-chest hive hit the ground, all of its inhabitants found their freedom and the people of Lytton rushed indoors for protection from the stinging menace, most of them preferring the Globe Hotel where refreshments could be had.

Mr. Loring, to whom the bees were destined, was contacted by telegraph and asked to come as quickly as he could. He assured the telegraph operator, who passed the message on to the people of Lytton, that the bees would return to the hive when darkness arrived. By that time, Mr. Loring had arrived to carefully transfer the bees to a hive and transport them to their new home. The stagecoach was righted and Gauthier left at dawn, chastened by his experience but wiser for it.[22]

9

THE BC EXPRESS UNDER NEW OWNERSHIP

I N MANY WAYS, the roadhouses of 1910 hadn't changed much since the 1860s. Excellent meals could be had at a reasonable price and hospitality was extended to all travellers, from the richest mining magnate to the humblest labourer on the creeks. The downside of this unchanging nature of stopping houses and hotels was the heating system in the winter. The concept of "central heating" consisted of a large box stove in the centre of the downstairs, with the rest of the building heated by the stovepipe that extended through the floor to the roof. Most roadhouse stoves were stoked up in the evening and restoked in the wee hours of the morning only during the coldest nights of winter. The upstairs rooms got colder and colder as the night wore on and most sleepers would wake up in the morning with their face stuck to the hoar frost on their pillow, their breath leaving clouds of condensation. This is why most roadhouse keepers offered their guests the artificial warmth of a late-evening and before-breakfast "hot toddy."

Small-town boy Alvin Johnston, born and raised in Quesnel,[1] made his first trip to the "big city" of Vancouver at the age of eighteen, in 1910. On the way back from Ashcroft to his home, he travelled by the BC Express. He was given the last available room at the 150 Mile House, a tiny chilly closet at the back of the building, far from the warmth-giving stovepipe. There being no legal drinking age, Johnston consumed several hot toddies before retiring to his "room" and buried himself under as many blankets as he could obtain. Early in the morning, after a fitful sleep, he woke up, got dressed, and went down to the lobby to see if he could warm up by the box stove. A few minutes before, an early morning traveller arrived and stumbled up to the heater to try and warm up. When Johnston came down the stairs, he came face to face with the frozen stranger, his wool cap pulled over his ears to meet his mackinaw and his frozen fingers combing the icicles from his moustache. Johnston stared at him and asked, "My God, which room did you have?"[2]

NEW OWNERS LED BY CHARLES MILLAR AND JOSEPH KILGOUR

With the completion of the Canadian Pacific Railway in 1885, British Columbia was officially open for business. Frank S. Barnard, who had seen the potential of the British Columbia Interior early on, was followed by a large number of businessmen and entrepreneurs from Eastern Canada, mainly Toronto. It was obvious that the BC Express, especially under the Barnards, enjoyed a virtual monopoly on the mail contract and that, as long as John A. Macdonald's Conservative Party was in power, things were unlikely to change. This is not to say the mail contract was inflated in any way, as good value was given for service. But, when a federal election was called for 1896, Wilfred Laurier and the Liberal Party made a strong case for a change in government. In the Yale-Cariboo riding, Hewitt Bostock, who had founded the *Province* newspaper, was the Liberal candidate and campaigned for a change in the long-time patronage that had existed in British Columbia since Confederation. Whether well-deserved or fictitious, the Cariboo mail contract was included among the patronage appointments that Bostock vowed to eliminate. And, despite his incredible service and dedication, Steve Tingley was portrayed by Bostock as a Conservative patron.

Wilfred Laurier won the election by a large majority and Bostock rode in on the wave. The new postmaster general, William Mullock, advertised for tenders for the Cariboo mail contract and, not surprisingly, found that no one except Steve Tingley was prepared to invest in a horse-drawn mail service in an era when railways were taking over. The postmaster general, who was vice-chancellor of the University of Toronto and had practised law in Toronto, began to look among his Eastern Canadian friends for someone who might invest in the business.

After unsuccessful negotiations with several prospective contractors, Mullock approached Charles Vance Millar, also a Toronto lawyer and graduate of the University of Toronto. Millar gathered together a group of Toronto businessmen who contracted for the service for four years. They agreed to a price slightly lower than Tingley's with the understanding that, at the completion of the contract, if a profit was not realized, they could obtain a contract price for the next four years that gave them a reasonable return on investment. It was also agreed that the contract would be renewed without going to tender as long as the Liberal government was in power.[3] Millar and another Toronto-based entrepreneur, Joseph Kilgour, travelled to British Columbia to take the lead in negotiating with Steve Tingley for the purchase of the BC Express Company assets.

Millar was the son of a well-to-do farmer who, despite his father's relative wealth, attended the University of Toronto on a meager allowance of $5 a week. This kept him from realizing much of a social life and forced him to concentrate on his studies. He finished with a gold medal and an average of 98 per cent in his undergraduate courses, and he went on to study law. By the 1890s, he had achieved a reputation as a brilliant lawyer who took great satisfaction in representing the underprivileged against the rich. "He hated all forms of deceit and hypocrisy, and acquired an unpopular reputation with a certain class of citizens who did not appreciate his advanced ideas of human rights and privileges."[4]

Kilgour, with his brother Robert, had established the Kilgour Brothers & Company paper box manufacturing company in 1874, which grew into the Canada Paper Company Ltd. It had made them millionaires. In 1894, he came to the booming city of Vancouver to open a branch of his company and saw that the province was ripe for investment.

Tingley realized that, while the company's extensive infrastructure was essential to carrying out the mail contract, the company was unlikely to survive without the contract. He and Millar negotiated a fair price for the stock and assets of the company and for the assets owned by Steve Tingley and used by the company, such as horses and buildings. At the end of June 1897, Tingley parted ways with the company that had occupied his life for thirty-four years.

From the time he helped negotiate the purchase of the BC Express, Millar took a personal interest in its operation. For the next twenty-five years, he remained as the managing director, under the title of manager, and often travelled to the Cariboo. He loved horses and also took great pleasure in travelling by stagecoach up the Cariboo Road and meeting people along the way.

The first meeting of the newly purchased BC Express Company took place on July 2 in the offices of Wilson & Campbell in Vancouver. The five shareholders listed in the minutes were Charles Millar, J.J. Mackay, Major C.C. Bennett, Frank S. Taggart, and (by proxy) Joseph Kilgour. Of course, Mackay had been the chief agent of the company based in Ashcroft during Steve Tingley's time and had held fifty shares of the company. At the time of purchase, he sold forty-nine of those shares and kept one, which allowed him to be retained as the secretary treasurer, no doubt to provide some continuity with the well-run Tingley era. Vancouver resident Major C.C. Bennett was involved in mining companies in the BC Interior and was well connected in the Vancouver business community. Of these shareholders, only Mackay had any experience in the transportation and express business.[5]

According to the BC Express stock register, Taggart had bought 834 shares from Tingley, 116 shares from Pauline Tingley, and 47 shares from Mackay, making a total of 997 shares. On July 2, he sold one share to Joseph Kilgour with Charles Millar, Major Charles Bennett, and Mackay each retaining one share. This allotment of shares indicates that Taggart bankrolled the purchase of the BC Express shares but that Millar and Kilgour retained the assets purchased from Steve Tingley.[6]

At the meeting, Kilgour, Millar, Bennett, and Mackay were elected directors, effective July 1, 1897. Once that meeting was adjourned, a directors' meeting was held and elected Kilgour as president, Millar as managing director under the title of manager, and Mackay as secretary treasurer, indicating that Millar would manage day-to-day operations and Mackay would look after day-to-day administration. Millar was a busy lawyer, so he needed to find someone familiar with the company who could take over operations. At a meeting on September 14 in Ashcroft, James B. Leighton became the superintendent of the company, based on an agreement signed on September 7.[7]

JAMES BUIE LEIGHTON TAKES THE REINS

If anyone could follow in the footsteps of Barnard and Steve Tingley and steer the BC Express into the twentieth century, it was J.B. Leighton. Born on November 8, 1851, in the village of Yarmouth on the River Spey in Moray, Scotland, he travelled with his parents at nine months of age around the Horn to California. After suffering no fewer than three shipwrecks, the family arrived in San Francisco in 1853, where they made their home for the next ten years. In 1863, after the death of his father, Leighton's mother took him to British Columbia, where she had two brothers in business. He spent two years at the Collegiate School, when he saw one of the famous camels brought in to pack supplies to the Cariboo. Leighton would see the camels again in 1865 near the 144 Mile House on his way by stagecoach to Barkerville and, much later, in 1883, he would see three of the surviving camels at Grand Prairie (Westwold).[8]

When James proved to be more active and mischievous than scholarly, he was apprenticed to his uncles, Buie Brothers Merchants, who had stores in Lytton and Barkerville. When he arrived in Lytton on March 14, 1865, at age thirteen, his uncle Thomas began to teach him the fundamentals of business. James proved to be a handful for his uncle, who sent him to Barkerville in early June. His uncle Robert ran the Barnard's Express agency in Barkerville, where James began a long career in connection with the express company. As one of only a few young people in the gold rush town, he was referred to by all as "The boy."

In 1868, Leighton worked on the branch line of the Collins Overland Telegraph to Barkerville and became interested in telegraphy. He was in Barkerville that September to see the great fire burn the booming town to the ground. After the fire, he worked as a telegraph operator in various locations in the Cariboo, including Bridge Creek, Cache Creek, and Spences Bridge, during which time the line had been taken over by the Colony of British Columbia and then the Dominion government. In all those places, he acted as the express agent, purchasing agent, and sometimes "special" driver for Barnard's and later the BC Express. His last posting, in 1882, was at Clinton, where he met and married Elizabeth Jane Uren, whose parents had operated the Clinton Hotel. Elizabeth had been the postmistress and telegraph operator at Savona before their marriage.[9]

On behalf of the BC Express, Leighton obtained the contract to deliver the mail from Savona to the Okanagan until 1886, when the completion of the CPR rendered that service redundant. Upon the expiry of the mail contract, Leighton purchased the Gotan Ranch at Three Mile Creek near Savona, which he renamed the Glenbrook Ranch and owned for the rest of his life. There he raised cattle and indulged his lifelong love of horses, being rated as an expert judge of horse flesh.

In 1897, Leighton served as Indian agent for the Kamloops agency for four months, working with reserves from Spuzzum in the Fraser Canyon to Osoyoos in the Okanagan.[10] With his background and experience, he came highly recommended by J.J. Mackay, who knew him well and noted his long connection with all the points on the BC Express line. After a short interview, Charles Millar offered him a contract and, at a board meeting on September 14 in Ashcroft, the directors approved "the appointment of James B. Leighton as Superintendent upon the terms contained in the agreement with him dated the 7th September, 1897."[11] An interviewer later described Leighton's enthusiasm for the job: "At last he had reached the acme of all his desires—work ever among and for horses. His first job was to stock the line with good animals, about seventy-five [more likely fifty] head, and verily he had the time of his life and he felt as young and gay as when he was 'The Boy' in Barkerville."[12] Leighton's love of horses was shared by Charles Millar and the two of them added fifty head of the finest horses to the stage line.

One of Leighton's duties was to negotiate with the various sub-contractors who carried the mail to outlying districts. These consisted of a line from Clinton to Lillooet via Pavilion Mountain and one from the 150 Mile House westward to Big Bar, Dog Creek, and Alkali Lake in the Chilcotin. Another line went eastward, via Beaver Lake to Quesnelle Forks and Horsefly, where there were several large mining operations. The contract for this run was held by William Parker, who had driven for the BC Express for several years from Quesnelle to the 83 Mile House and back. Parker obtained 343 acres at the north end of Big Lake, east of the 150 Mile, and constructed a large stopping house, barns, and cowsheds. Parker, as a sub-contractor of the BC Express, advertised, "Parker's Stage Line. Leaving Ashcroft every Monday for Clinton, 150 Mile, Quesnelle Forks, Cariboo Mine, and Horsefly. Stage will connect with steamer 'Charlotte' at Soda Creek for Quesnelle, Barkerville and other northern points."[13] In 1898, the sub-contractors were paid $5,260 in total, a significant portion of the overall contract obtained by the BC Express Company.[14]

To oversee these branch lines from the 150 Mile House, Leighton hired John "Jake" McKay Yorston as express agent and assistant superintendent. Eventually, Jake and his brother Robert, a driver for the BC Express, purchased the Australian Ranch, an important roadhouse on the way to Quesnelle.

One of the major developments in the area east of 150 Mile House was the Bullion Pit. In 1894, J.B. Hobson of the Cariboo Hydraulic Mining Company purchased the mining rights to what was called "Dancing Bill" Latham Gulch, which ran into the

Quesnelle River about three miles above Quesnelle Forks. His intention was to use gigantic hydraulic monitors (like large hose nozzles) to remove the gravel overburden from the gulch and reach the gold on the bedrock below. First of all, Hobson had to obtain a vast water source. Over the next four years, he dammed a number of creeks and lakes in the area and dug a system of ditches and canals to move the water quickly over seventeen miles to the awaiting monitors. In 1898, the mine began work and, in the initial season, took $92,000 worth of gold out of a previously mined area. The gold was melted into bullion and carried to the outside by the BC Express branch line that connected to the mainline at 150 Mile House.

The largest shipment of bullion to come out of the mine was in the fall of 1901. To create publicity for the mine, the total cleanup of gold was smelted down into a giant chunk shaped like a naval gun shell. The only way the giant shell could be moved was to place it in a cradle with handles so that four men could lift it and carry it on and off the stage. This "nugget," weighing 650 pounds and estimated to be worth $178,000, was carried by stagecoach to Ashcroft and shipped by rail to the Bank of Montreal in Toronto, where it was put on display. Customers could look at it and touch it, as the bank officials weren't too concerned about someone picking it up and walking away.[15]

Leighton kept in regular correspondence with managing director Charles Millar and, for quick contact, the Great North Western Telegraph could be used from Ashcroft to Toronto. Whenever Millar could take time from his busy law practice, he would come to Ashcroft and head up the Cariboo Road by stagecoach.[16] In 1899, he visited Barkerville and was the talk of the town, appearing in a yachting cap, a type of headwear never before seen by the rough Cariboo miners. He was a guest of Lester Bonner, manager of the British company Cariboo Gold Fields. Bonner described him "as a man with a nonconformist conscience. His appearance was striking and he was excellent company."[17]

During Leighton's tenure, what is considered the fastest trip from Ashcroft to Barkerville and back was taken. Although some historians have claimed the trip was done in thirty hours, that 390-mile (628-kilometre) drive would have required an average speed of 12.66 miles per hour, impossible on the rugged Cariboo Road. The record was actually set during the 1900 British Columbia provincial election campaign. Francis Carter-Cotton, a member of the incumbent party headed by Charles Semlin, had advertised that he would deliver a speech in Barkerville on Friday, May 25, but needed to be back in Ashcroft by Sunday night. Leighton was consulted and made the arrangements for the record-breaking trip. Carter-Cotton left Ashcroft on Wednesday morning and arrived in Barkerville in time to give his speech Friday evening. He then boarded a stagecoach and headed back down the road, arriving in Ashcroft at midnight on Sunday. The round trip with a speech in the middle had taken three days and fifteen hours. Sixteen relays of horses, the usual BC Express stock, were driven by A.C. Minty.[18]

WILLIS J. WEST TAKES OVER AS MANAGER

Little is known about the background and early life of Willis J. West. The first historical record appears in the 1901 Canadian census, when at age twenty-four he was living in Toronto with his mother, Matilda, his work listed as "Clerk Office." Later information reveals the office to have been Charles Millar's law office, where Willis worked as an office boy. West next appeared in the BC Express minute book at a meeting held on November 26, 1902, in Ashcroft. The shareholders included Joseph Kilgour with 50 shares, Charles Millar with 297 shares, W.W. Ferguson with 50 shares, E.A. Carew-Gibson with 400 shares, J.A. Bremner with 1 share, and Willis J. West with 202 shares. As the meeting took place in Ashcroft, it is not surprising that all except Carew-Gibson, who owned and operated the Cariboo Trading Company at 150 Mile House, and Bremner were absent, the rest there "by proxy," having likely given their vote to Bremner, the secretary treasurer. The appearance of West's name as a shareholder seems to have caused some consternation to Carew-Gibson, who had purchased shares the previous year. The minutes recorded an "objection having been taken by Mr. E. A. Carew-Gibson by the proxy by Willis J. West for 202 shares, which Mr. Gibson claimed to be a breach of an alleged pooling agreement between himself and Mr. Charles Millar."

The "Shareholders" book for the BC Express Company showed 202 shares obtained from D.L. Rowlands by Willis J. West on October 23, 1902, noting them to be on "a/c Chas Millar," suggesting that Millar had acquired them on his behalf. It seems Charles Millar took a shine to his office boy and gave him 202 shares of the company.

At the next meeting, meeting on December 18, Millar was recorded as having 499 shares, meaning he had taken back the shares from West. Carew-Gibson's shares were not listed and he was not present. But, at a meeting the following October in Ashcroft, West was not only back with 202 shares, he was the only shareholder present, so it appears he had the proxy votes of Kilgour, Bremner, Millar, and Ferguson. West approved the minutes of the previous meeting and the financial statements, and did the same at the next meeting, on July 25, 1904, at which Carew-Gibson was still listed as a shareholder but was not present in person or by proxy. At the next meeting of the executive, Willis J. West was elected secretary treasurer, a position he held until the company was liquidated in 1925.

Sometime during 1905, Millar purchased enough shares to gain a controlling interest in the company. One of his first actions was to hire West as superintendent of the BC Express, a position he would hold for the next fifteen years. There was no doubt that Millar saw the native intelligence and work ethic of the young man, thirty years old at the time. Seeing West handle the duties of secretary treasurer, Millar must have concluded that he was the person to guide the company into the new era that was dawning. West did not disappoint. Under his control, not only did the stagecoach company flourish; it was his initiative that prompted the new offering of steamboat service on the Upper Fraser River.

PADDLEWHEELS NAVIGATE THE UPPER FRASER

Prior to the BC Express board meeting on December 13, 1909, Willis J. West wrote to the manager, Charles Millar, and the president, Archibald Hutchison, expressing his vision for the future. His proposal, expressed in the minutes of the meeting, was "that owing to the development of Northern British Columbia and the building of the Grand Trunk Pacific Railway... it would be in the interests of this Company to build and operate a steam boat on the Fraser River so as to carry passengers and mail if the contract therefor could be obtained between Soda Creek and Quesnel, and Quesnel and Fort George, the latter being a station on the line of the Grand Trunk Pacific and distant north on the Fraser River about 150 miles." He was instructed to prepare an information package and present it to the board.[19]

At the next meeting, which included Hutchison, Millar, and Ferguson, West presented all the information concerning the proposed investment, including a drawing of the boat that had been prepared by Alexander Watson, an outstanding designer and builder of sternwheeler river boats. The board adjourned to examine the information and reconvened later that same day. They agreed to build a boat for service between Soda Creek and Fort George by the spring of 1910.

The new sternwheeler, *B.X.*, completed and launched on Friday, May 13, 1910, was designed to carry up to one hundred tons of freight and 130 passengers. The builders were opposed to launching her on a Friday, especially Friday the thirteenth, but the river was falling rapidly and Watson felt the launch had to take place. The *B.X.*, with barely enough water to slide into the Fraser, officially launched the BC Express into the riverboat business.

The *B.X.* was not the first steamer on the Upper Fraser. During the construction of the Cariboo Road, a sixty-mile stretch between Soda Creek and Quesnelle Mouth was used for steamer navigation. The steamer *Enterprise* was launched in 1863 and operated until 1871, when she was pulled and navigated through the Cottonwood

and Fort George Canyons, north of Quesnelle Mouth, to the Omineca goldfields. The *Victoria* covered the journey until 1886. Ten
years later, the North British Columbia Navigation Company Limited was organized by Senator James Reid of Quesnel, Captain John
Irving of Victoria, and Steve Tingley, who even at that time saw the
potential for the BC Express to use the Fraser River for transport.
They constructed the steamer *Charlotte* (named after Reid's wife)
to run from Soda Creek to Quesnel and possibly further upriver. For
thirteen years, the *Charlotte* had the Upper Fraser all to herself until,
in 1909, the Fort George Lumber & Navigation Company launched
the *Nechacco* and Quesnel businessmen Telesphore Marion and
John Strand launched the *City of Quesnel* (never successful because
it tended to sit deep in the water).[20]

In direct opposition to the *B.X.*, that same year the Fort George
Lumber & Navigation Company started work on the *Chilcotin*. In
spite of rumours, spread by *Chilcotin* supporters, that the *B.X.* was
too wide to pass through the Fort George Canyon, it was constructed
and launched on time.

One of the finest sternwheelers on the river, the *B.X.* had three
decks and a pilothouse above the third, or "Texas," deck. Officers'
staterooms were on the Texas deck, with quarters for crew and
firemen on the main deck. The *B.X.* boasted a dining room for fifty
people and staterooms with steam heat, reading lights, wash stands,
and fans. The rooms were finished with red velvet carpets and green
curtains. When fully loaded with a cargo of one hundred tons, the
B.X. drew only thirty inches of water.[21]

After a month of plying the waters between Quesnel and Soda
Creek, the *B.X.* headed upstream over the 93 miles to Fort George.
The two potential challenges were at the Cottonwood and Fort
George Canyons. Eighteen miles above Quesnel, the Cottonwood
consisted of a mile of rapids and rocks, with a particularly steep
"hill" at the upper end. In the Fort George Canyon, fifteen miles
below the growing town of that name, the river split into three
channels, each narrow and full of rapids. On June 23, the *B.X.* left
Quesnel with forty passengers and a load of freight at about 1 PM

The sternwheeler *B.X.* navigating the Fort George Canyon.
IMAGE I-57868 COURTESY OF THE ROYAL BC MUSEUM AND ARCHIVES

and arrived at the growing town of South Fort George at about 4:30 the next afternoon. As her license at the time did not permit her to carry passengers all the way through the canyons, they had to disembark and walk on trails around the bluffs before re-embarking. A cable was put out to help the steamer navigate the rapids, which was accomplished without difficulty through both canyons. On the return trip downriver, the *B.X.* needed all her power to navigate the Fort George Canyon but the Cottonwood Canyon presented no difficulties.

Once it was clear that the *B.X.* could navigate the Upper Fraser to Fort George, the BC Express began a twice-a-week service between Soda Creek and Fort George. West also arranged with the post office to carry the mail on those trips as long as the season lasted. The *B.X.* connected at Soda Creek with the BC Express stagecoaches from Ashcroft to transfer mail and express matter quickly and efficiently. The stages left the railway at Ashcroft at four in the morning on Mondays and Fridays and travelled the 167 miles to Soda Creek by Tuesday and Saturday nights at about ten o'clock.

Since it was dangerous to navigate the Upper Fraser in the dark, the
B.X. waited until the break of day before heading upriver. She would
reach Quesnel by noon and, after unloading mail and cargo into a
stagecoach that ran from Quesnel to Barkerville, would continue
on her way. When it became too dark to navigate safely, the schedule was arranged to tie her up at a wood pile and wait for the break
of day. Depending on the time of year, she would reach South Fort
George at about eleven o'clock in the morning. On the return trip,
the B.X. left on Tuesdays and Saturdays at 7:00 AM and arrived at
Soda Creek around 4:30 in the afternoon.[22]

The timing on the launch of the B.X. was excellent. Thanks to
the extensive advertising by land promoters for Fort George and
South Fort George, 1910 was an extremely busy time on the Cariboo Road. Among the rush of honest people looking for land in the
BC Interior were unscrupulous individuals who would take anything
they could get their hands on. In the past, stagecoaches had been
left unattended at stopping houses with the gold safe and mail on
board, but now the driver had to take them into his room overnight.
Even barns had to be locked to keep thieves from taking harness,
feed, and anything else they found. Times had changed since the
days when everyone knew and looked out for their neighbours and
no one would think of stealing unattended merchandise.

The B.X. enjoyed a reputation for providing the most comfortable and reliable service of all the sternwheelers on the Upper
Fraser. Captain Owen F. Browne was not just one of the best pilots
on the river, he was accommodating and helpful to the people who
lived along the way. Settlers or prospectors would put out a white
flag if they wanted him to stop and Browne would turn the B.X. into
the bank and respond to their needs.

When low water came in the fall, navigating the river became
even more difficult and, early in October, the B.X. hit a rock about
five miles above Fort George Canyon. A large hole, about sixty feet
long and three feet wide (eighteen by one metres), was punched in
her hull but her watertight compartments allowed Captain Browne
to reach shore. The hole was repaired in two weeks and the ship

taken to Quesnel for more thorough repairs. She was back in the water on October 20.

With the Fraser closed for navigation during the winter months, mail and express were packed over a 110-mile (177-kilometre) trail that started on the west side of the river at Quesnel and wound its way via the Blackwater River to South Fort George. By 1910, the BC government had constructed a wagon road all the way and contracted the BC Express to deliver mail along this road once river navigation ceased. The company constructed an office building and stable on the west side of the river, across from the town of Quesnel. The challenge was to get the mail across the river. When the river froze over, an ice bridge worked fine, but when the river was still open with floating ice, a boat was needed to bring the passengers, mail, baggage, and express across. The Ashcroft stage reached Quesnel on Wednesday night and passengers would leave for Fort George on Thursday at 4 AM, overnight at Blackwater, and make it to Fort George around 6 PM on Friday, the whole trip from Ashcroft covering 330 miles (530 kilometres).

As construction of the Grand Trunk Pacific Railway continued into British Columbia in 1912, the BC Express Company decided to construct a sister ship to the *B.X.* to ply the Fraser from South Fort George to Mile 53, the head of navigation on the Fraser and the point where the Grand Trunk Pacific Railway dropped off passengers and freight. By that time, another townsite, called Fort George, was being developed by C.J. Hammond, who was advertising all over the world to sell 12,000 lots. This increased the demand for transportation to the area. So the *B.C. Express* was constructed by Alexander Watson, who had built the *B.X.* He built the hull of the *B.C. Express* six feet shorter than its sister ship and about a foot shorter in beam. Captain J.P. Bucey, who had piloted sternwheelers on the treacherous Skeena River for fourteen years and was considered one of the best swiftwater pilots in the business, was given command of the *B.C. Express.*

The *B.C. Express* was launched in June of 1912 at a cost of about $65,000, or 20 per cent more than the *B.X.*, indicating inflation in the booming region. While the surveyed railway route between Fort George and Mile 53, the head of navigation on the Fraser, measured 183 miles (295 kilometres), the distance by river was 315 miles (507 kilometres).[23] The true test of the ship would be the three rapids: the Giscome Rapids, 23 miles (37 kilometres) upstream from Fort George; the Grand Canyon, 104 miles (167 kilometres) upstream; and the Goat River Rapids, 208 miles (335 kilometres) from Fort George. The worst of these was the Grand Canyon, actually two canyons with a basin or lake in between. The narrow upper canyon has the strongest current of any part of the Upper Fraser and the lower canyon has the infamous whirlpool that took so many lives. The *B.C. Express* steamed through these without problems and spent the summer running from Fort George to the Grand Canyon. The weekly round trips carried capacity loads of cargo and passengers downstream from Mile 53 to South Fort George and a full complement of passengers, but little freight, upstream. The fare for passengers was a hefty $35, with meals and staterooms extra, and the rate for freight $80 a ton.

In 1913, the *B.C. Express* was the only sternwheeler providing passenger and freight service on this stretch of river.[24] The year 1912 showed a significant profit, despite the low water in the Fraser stopping service up and down the river regularly until the water level rose. But 1913 was a boom year. Railway construction between South Fort George and the new town of Tete Jaune Cache, just a mile upstream from the *B.C. Express* landing at Mile 53, employed no fewer than 5,000 men and the communities of South Fort George and Fort George each had 1,500 residents. While Fort George was the residential town, South Fort George was a rip-roaring frontier town. At the Northern Hotel there, men stood five or six feet deep at the ninety-foot-long bar, served by twelve bartenders. In one day, serving drinks at twenty-five cents each, the bar grossed $7,000 in sales. On one upstream trip of the *B.C. Express*, the entire cargo of one hundred tons consisted of liquor.[25]

Just as the completion of the Grand Trunk Pacific Railway had stimulated traffic on the Upper Fraser, its completion meant the end of river transportation from Tete Jaune Cache to South Fort George. In 1913, the Grand Trunk directors insisted they needed a bridge across the Fraser at Mile 142 and stretched a cable across the river, making steamer traffic impossible. The BC Express Company issued a writ against the Grand Trunk for damages due to loss of revenue but lost out when the claim was dismissed. Now that passenger and freight services were available at a lower cost on the Grand Trunk Pacific, traffic on the BC Express to the CPR line in Ashcroft dwindled. But the company still operated the South Fort George to Soda Creek section of the Fraser, using the *B.X.* for regular runs and the *B.C. Express* for special trips. While the movement of freight over the Cariboo Road from Ashcroft slowed to a trickle, the passenger service still did an excellent business. But, by the spring of 1915, the sternwheeler days were over. Company owners announced, "This is [the *B.X.'s*] last trip of the year, and probably her last trip on the Fraser River. It is the intention of the B.C. Express Company to ship the machinery of their boats to the north country, where business will be conducted on the Peace."[26]

THE BC MOTORIZED EXPRESS

The coming of the automobile was watched with interest by the BC Express Company. It was only a matter of time before competitors would appear in motorized transport. The downfall of the automobile was seen as its inability to navigate roads during the winter months, whereas stagecoaches and sleighs provided year-round service. Despite this concern and the realization that the Cariboo Road could turn to a sea of mud during spring runoff and summer rains, in the spring of 1910, the directors decided the time had come to purchase automobiles and see how they worked out. Competitors on the Cariboo Road had already purchased a variety of Canadian and American vehicles and a Victoria company had imported an English Simplex for use on Vancouver Island. The trouble with the Simplex was its lack of clearance, which may not have been an issue

The BC Express fleet of Winston Six automobiles, here seen
at Ashcroft, were not successful on the Cariboo roads.

in Victoria, but the deep and rocky mudholes of the Cariboo Road
rendered it useless.

After a thorough investigation of the options, BC Express officials decided on the Winston, the first six-cylinder car on the market.
Company representatives travelled to Seattle to view two seven-
passenger Winstons. Since they had been used for demonstration,
the manager, one of the first "used car salesmen," offered to sell
them for $1,500 each. This appeared to be an excellent buy, until
the representatives were told that glass windshields were an extra
$75, brass headlights with a carbide generator an extra $150, canvas
tops an additional $150, Klaxon horns $50, trunk racks $50, and
seat covers $100. Despite the expanded cost of the cars, both were
purchased with the agreement that the Winston Company provide
two driver-mechanics to drive them to Ashcroft and along the Cariboo Road for the rest of the 1910 season—necessary since, at the
time, few people in British Columbia were able to drive a car, let
alone repair such a complex machine.

The next day, the two cars were shipped by boat to Vancouver
and then by rail to Ashcroft. They were painted the company's
colours, with bright red bodies and yellow wheels, and spent the

season carrying passengers and mail on the route from the railway to Soda Creek. The company was constructing fully equipped machine shops where the cars could be serviced. The summer of 1910 being a relatively dry one, the cars performed without any major difficulties. When the winter snows began to fall and the horse-drawn sleighs went into action, the cars were taken to the new shops where they were stripped to the frames and rebuilt. Since the frames were made of wood, the coach makers of the BC Express were able to fabricate additional bodies. By the spring of 1911, there were six cars in service. The assets of the BC Express Company for that year included:

Stages and sleighs — $14,890
Horses and harness — $31,928
B.X. steamer — $48,788
Six automobiles — $15,499
Garage machinery and tools — $2,254[27]

There were no service stations for motorized vehicles or storage of gasoline along the Cariboo Road. At the time, gasoline was marketed in four-gallon cans, but Imperial Oil agreed to ship gasoline from Vancouver in large reuseable iron drums, along with oil and grease, for the Winstons.

This venture into automobile transportation did not prove profitable for the BC Express. With the rush of freight and people over the Cariboo Road heading for Fort George, more freight was being shipped over the road than at any time in the road's history. The cost of shipping gas, oil, and grease was extremely high and, even worse, the freight wagons loaded with as much as four tons of supplies cut the roads into mud with their heavy wheels. The narrow, high-pressure tires on the automobiles would sink the vehicles up to their running boards and make it impossible to move at more than a crawl. This slowed down the automobiles and required more maintenance. The automobiles were also proving to be more accident prone than stagecoaches.

The BC Express never exhibited any superstition about leaving Yale or Ashcroft on Friday the thirteenth, or carrying thirteen passengers on coach number thirteen, but when motor cars started travelling the road, Car No. 13 earned a reputation as being jinxed. After months of travelling in low gear over terrible roads, perhaps it's not surprising that the car started developing a bad habit of running off the road. This was not often serious on level terrain, but it could be frightening for the driver and passengers.

Car No. 13 gave a rather dramatic display of its tendency to Jim and Sarah Shepherd, who ran the Kersley House stopping place south of Quesnel. They started off in the notorious car to catch a train for a hard-earned extended vacation. "As soon as we stepped into the car," Sarah later reported, "I had a sort of feeling that something was going to happen before we reached Ashcroft. But I did not know that we were riding in No. 13 until we got to Soda Creek, about two hours later. I told Jim then that I didn't like riding in it. Only a few weeks before that the car had run off the road near Lillooet and rolled over a steep embankment . . . We had heard other stories about the 'jinx' car, as it was becoming to be known. But Jim was not in any way superstitious about the number thirteen. Not at that time. He laughed at my fears."[28]

Sure enough, when they rounded a bend along the Bonaparte River near Cache Creek, Car No. 13 swerved, turned upside down, threw three of the seven passengers clear, and hurtled down a ten-foot bank into the river. The rest of the passengers, including the Shepherds, were dumped into the river. Sarah's immediate concern was that the new hat she had bought for the trip was floating downstream. Bishop Adam de Pencier of the Church of England rose to the occasion, saving the hat and dragging two women out of the car before extricating Jim Shepherd, who was pinned under the car with a broken arm. When Sarah then realized she had lost her purse with $600 intended for their trip, the bishop once again dove into the river and rescued the purse. About this time, Willis J. West, superintendent of the BC Express, came along and collected the injured and soggy passengers and took them through to Ashcroft.[29]

When business up the road reached its peak in 1913, it cost the BC Express a total of $67,233 to maintain and operate eight Winston Sixes, which brought in a total revenue of $70,570, leaving a very narrow margin of profit. The significant sum of $15,836 was spent on tires and tubes alone.[30]

THE BC EXPRESS REACHES THE END OF THE LINE

By the time the Great War broke out in August 1914, circumstances were conspiring against the BC Express. The dramatic slowing of traffic on the Cariboo Road and the completion of the Grand Trunk Pacific Railway meant that the two steamers were no longer useful on the Upper Fraser. And on the roads, the Winston Sixes were causing more problems than stagecoaches ever had. Not only were they costly to operate, they were slowed down by the rough and muddy roads, causing the people of the Cariboo to complain about delayed delivery of their precious mail.

In 1913, to combat growing discontent with the BC Express mail delivery, West had reported to the Ashcroft *Journal* that "the B.C. Express is spending $75,000 in equipment with which to handle the mail services during the coming winter." The Canadian Postal Service had announced a new parcel post service that provided for delivery of parcels of up to eleven pounds (five kilograms), to begin in February of 1914. West conducted an extensive survey of the Cariboo region serviced by the company and a thorough examination of stagecoaches, automobiles, and steamboats in anticipation of this new demand. When asked what would be the implications of the new service, he replied, "It will be impossible for any company to contract for the carrying of parcel post matter; it can be handled only at a certain rate per pound." In preparation for this, the company was making a huge investment in the future.

West was also asked about a second challenge that confronted the BC Express: the construction of the Pacific Great Eastern Railway. He admitted, "The P.G.E. will do us out of business, but not for five years to come. We have got before us five years of the most prosperous the company has ever seen. We will move north with our entire equipment and will stage from Fort George north and out beyond the Peace River." The article concluded, "The B.C. Express is like an immortal animal; when it has eaten up all the pasture in one field it moves to another, for it must live on; and what would the northern interior be without the conveniences afforded by the company?"[31]

West's optimism was short lived. The situation came to a head in early 1914, when the president, Archibald Hutchison, "recited the long negotiations which had taken place with the Post Master General in connection with the continuance of the Mail Carrying Contract and said that, on account of not coming to terms, the Company had decided not to reduce their tender and consequently had not obtained the renewal, it having been awarded to a new company who were operating under the name of the 'INLAND EXPRESS CO.' This result, together with the fact that the Grand Trunk Pacific were now operating over their line into Fort George had entirely changed the possibilities of this Company."

Willis J. West advised the board that he thought he could sell the horses, harness, feed, and even the vehicles for a reasonable price to the Inland Express Company. The board authorized him and Charles Millar to proceed, but noted that "Mr. West was cautioned to exercise the greatest possible care in extending credit on the sale of the assets of the Company, and rather to accept a less price for cash than to run any risk of bad debts in any sale which he might make."[32] And so it was that the BC Express disposed of the horses, stagecoaches, and all associated material to the Inland Express Company, ending the stagecoach line that was started by Barnard fifty years before.

Despite having disposed of horses and equipment, Charles Millar and Willis West made one last-ditch effort. Aware that the mail contract was coming up for tender the following year, Millar had West prepare a tender to cover the routes from Clinton to Alkali Lake and from 150 Mile House to Alexis Creek in the Chilcotin,

Keithley Creek, and Harper's Camp. West carefully prepared the estimates and determined that the four routes would cost the company about $60,000. He recommended to Millar that they submit a tender for $64,000 because he felt that carrying passengers and express matter would bring in an additional $15,000. By the next year, when the mail contract was put out for tender, Millar had realized that plans to build the Pacific Great Eastern Railway from Vancouver to Prince George would change the contract significantly. In June of 1920, he sent a letter to the postmaster general, offering to carry the mail from Williams Lake (expected to be the end of the PGE Railway) to 150 Mile House and from there to Quesnel and Prince George to Quesnel, at a total cost of $43,959. Millar concluded, "I think I would reduce the tender to $39,500 for the aggregation." [33] The tender was not accepted and, for all intents and purposes, the BC Express had carried its last letters.

The BC Express Company retained the real estate and buildings in Ashcroft and elsewhere on the Cariboo Road, along with the automobiles, garage machinery, and the two steamboats, the *B.X.*, valued at $48,495, and the *B.C. Express*, valued at $56,122. [34] With these latter two assets, the company made a final attempt at reviving its prospects. Early in 1918, the Quesnel Board of Trade had appealed to the provincial government to grant the BC Express Company a subsidy to keep the *B.X.* active carrying freight from Fort George to Soda Creek, serving the settlers along the way. An arrangement was made for the government to provide an annual subsidy of $10,000 for the service. So, in May of 1918, the *B.X.* resumed its regular in-season trips. Unfortunately, the service only continued until late August of 1919, when the *B.X.* struck a rock about five miles south of Fort George while carrying one hundred tons of sacked cement to Soda Creek, tearing a twenty-foot hole in its hull. The company realized the repair of the *B.X.* would take a long time and tried to activate the *B.C. Express*, which had been out of service for five years. After a thorough recaulking, the *B.C. Express* was refloated and operated until November of 1920. During the following winter, the restored *B.X.* and the *B.C. Express* were dismantled and their machinery, boilers, and furnishings shipped to Waterways in Northern Alberta, where they became part of two sternwheelers built to ply the Mackenzie River. In part payment, an agreement was made between the BC Express Company and the Lamson & Hubbard Canadian Company merging their assets into the Alberta and Arctic Transportation Company Limited with a capital of $750,000, all shareholders receiving shares in the new company.[35]

A final meeting of the BC Express Company board, consisting of Archibald Hutchins, Charles Millar, Justice N.N. Ferguson, and A.W. Hunter, took place in April 1924, when the remaining assets of the company were distributed as follows:

- Charles Millar, 539 shares, $7,633.92
- A. Hutchison, 216 shares, $3,031.21
- W.N. Ferguson, 45 shares, $633.67
- Willis J. West, 100 shares, $1,412.60
- A.W. Hunter (in trust), 50 shares, $706.30
- Willis J. West (in trust), 50 shares, $706.30

In a final ironical twist, when Charles Millar died on October 21, 1926, he left a will that has sparked humour and controversy ever since: "This will is necessarily uncommon and capricious because I have no dependents or near relatives and no duty rests on me to leave any property at my death, and what I do leave is proof of my folly in gathering and retaining more than I required during my lifetime."

After making bequests to his employees and friends, he left to three of the most sworn enemies of horse racing a share each in the Ontario Jockey Club; to three fellow lawyers who hated each other, joint ownership of his summer home near Kingston, Jamaica; one share of O'Keefe Brewing Co. stock (founded by Roman Catholics) to each Protestant minister resident in Toronto; and, among other strange bequests, the bulk of his estate, as summarized in a subsequent article, was to "the woman who, in the ten years following Millar's death, happened to give birth in Toronto to the largest number of children." This "stork derby," as it was called, resulted in four fertile, if not exhausted, women receiving $165,000 each!

Oh yes, and Millar left half of his shares in the BC Express Company, long since liquidated, to Willis J. West.[36]

CONCLUSION

I N CONTRAST TO the colonial officials who were arriving in the new Colony of British Columbia in 1859, F.J. Barnard arrived with no means of supporting himself or returning home.He had no other choice than to roll up his sleeves and set to work, for he had no intention of returning home. But, despite the great wealth in the colony, his first attempt at running an express business struggled for lack of capital.

In his earliest endeavors in the colony, and as his express business grew, Barnard began to connect with like-minded individuals. These included young men who, like Barnard, had arrived from the British North American colonies to the east and who, unlike the mostly "American" mining population, had come to stay. They also brought with them notions of a government based upon talent and hard work, instead of birth and connections. Their ideas, based upon classic British liberalism, included an abhorrence of social, economic, and political privilege and a belief in representative and responsible government rather than an elite ruling class. In these beliefs, they were more like their neighbours to the south.

The "Canadians," as they were called, had settled mostly on the mainland Colony of British Columbia, where the resources and opportunities were to be found. There they were in a minority compared to the thousands of Americans whose allegiance was to the growing nation to the south and, at the same time, they were subject to a small but powerful group of colonial officials based in Victoria, whose authority came from the Queen herself. While the officials in Victoria viewed the Canadians as "colonials" and not of the right class, they had to admit that they were at least loyal to the Queen. For this reason, they were begrudgingly given preference for contracts over which the government had control. This goes a long way to explaining why Barnard was given preference over the much more suitable Ballou for the first mail contract. Awarded in 1862, this contract provided the struggling Barnard's Express with the boost it needed to overcome its competitors.

While many of the "Canadians" were too busy searching for gold or establishing businesses, farms, and ranches to think about government, there was a small group who supported each other and shared the same liberal ideals. Chief among these were the newspaper men, Amor De Cosmos and John Robson, whose newspapers, the *British Colonist* in Victoria and the *British Columbian* in New Westminster, became platforms for social reform. Not surprisingly, when the group of British colonies in the east pushed toward Confederation, the two newspapers strongly advocated for British Columbia joining in. The Yale Convention brought together the supporters of Confederation, which included Barnard, who was there as one of three members of the Legislative Council. His extensive connections along the Cariboo Road and throughout the mainland were crucial, and his advocacy for union with Canada has not been adequately recognized, primarily because his support was largely spoken as opposed to written. But, when the combined Colony of British Columbia voted in favour of joining Canada, it was the support from the mainland that clinched the union. For this reason, Barnard can truly be considered a "Father of Confederation."

Barnard was not an "educated" man, having left school at the age of twelve to run his father's hardware business. But he was intelligent and articulate, with an ability to make a convincing argument. These abilities served him well in his business and political dealings, in which he could be aggressive and, when necessary, ruthless. He was also a visionary and an entrepreneur. His scheme to operate a stagecoach line from Yale to Lake Superior would have gone forward if the Canadian government had not "sweetened the pot" in negotiating Confederation and offering to build a railway instead. Barnard's investment in road steamers was another idea ahead of its time, and their failure to negotiate the Cariboo Road cost him heavily. His loss in this venture prompted him to sell off half of his beloved express company to Steve Tingley and James Hamilton, two fellow Canadians who wholly shared his vision for the company.

The continuing success of Barnard's and later the BC Express had everything to do with the mail contract. To operate an express and transportation business over the 580-kilometre (360-mile) route from Yale to Barkerville required a huge amount of infrastructure. Changes of horses had to be made at least every 32 kilometres (18 miles), requiring a minimum of 120 head of horses and an equal number of sets of harness. In its heyday, the company needed at least twenty-six full-sized stagecoaches and an equal number of two-horse coaches and sleighs. Aside from the drivers, every stop along the way required a hosteller to care for the horses and each of the large depots had a company agent. During the stagecoach era, except perhaps for the palmy days at the height of the Cariboo gold rush, the mail contract was essential to subsidize the costs of the transport and express business.

For the next fifty years, except for a brief interlude in 1870, whoever held the mail contract controlled the express and transportation business in the BC Interior. So, in 1896, when Laurier's Liberal Party won the election and vowed to eliminate the "patronage system" that had awarded contracts to government favourites, the mail contract was taken out of the hands of the BC Express as a political statement. Despite Steve Tingley's excellent management and virtual control of transport in the BC Interior, the contract was given to a Toronto-based consortium, headed by Charles Millar. (Billy Ballou would have sympathized, having himself been passed over in spite of being the company best suited to carry the mail.)

Tingley was left with no recourse other than to sell his company name and assets to the consortium.

The final chapter of the BC Express saw yet another Canadian at the helm. Charles Millar, despite his busy law practice, kept an interest in the company that in many ways became his favourite venture. The transition was relatively seamless, thanks to the able management of J.B. Leighton, and the company continued into the sternwheeler and automobile era. The BC Express carried on for another seventeen years before the political tides turned again and it lost the mail contract to the Inland Express Company. By this time, the transition to motorized transport had left the company weakened and vulnerable. The new mail carrier, even though it continued to operate the branch lines with horse-drawn stagecoaches, would move into the future with automobiles and trucks. The colourful stagecoach era in British Columbia had come to an end.

ACKNOWLEDGEMENTS

MY FRIEND ALAN ARNDT first approached me in 2018 and asked if I could put together a short history of the BX Ranch in Vernon, where he still cuts and sells hay. So I went to the usual historical sources and put together a one-page history telling the story that historians have accepted for the past century. But my curiosity was piqued. My interest in Barnard's Express and its later incarnation the BC Express, both of which were known simple as the BX, went back to when I was working in Barkerville in 1979. Its significant role in the province's history convinced me at that time that someone should tell the story of this crucial connection between remote Barkerville and the seats of power in Victoria and the Lower Mainland. At the time, it appeared that the attempt to chronicle this story would be fruitless, because the original records of the company had been lost to history. But when I revisited the subject in 2018, I was convinced that the story could be cobbled together from existing primary documents. So I started to dig a little deeper and contacted Linda Peterat, who had transcribed the diary that Steve Tingley wrote on that amazing horse drive from southern California to British Columbia. What became immediately apparent was that the story of the founding of the BX Ranch in 1864 and the raising of the horses from Mexico didn't square with the traditional story. The result was this book.

Special thanks to Linda Peterat, who not only shared the research material on the BX that she had accumulated, but also encouraged, advised, and assisted me in the research and writing of this book. She also convinced her sister, Donna Stout, to use her extensive genealogical talents and resources to research the Barnard, Tingley, and Hamilton families. I would also like to thank the staff at the Royal British Columbia Museum and Archives, the Greater Vernon Museum and Archives, the Kamloops Museum and Archives, the University of British Columbia's Rare Books and Special Collections (Vancouver and Okanagan locations), the Hudson's Bay Company Archives, the City of Vancouver Archives, and the Bancroft Library. I also am thankful for the online resources offered by the University of Victoria (the *British Colonist* newspaper and the collections Colonial Despatches, Official Gazettes of the Province of British Columbia, and Early BC Maps), the University of British Columbia (Open Library), Library and Archives Canada, and the Dictionary of Canadian Biography, and by websites such as *Canadiana Online* (canadiana.ca) and *Internet Archive* (archive.org). Since I started researching British Columbia history forty years ago, the work of the researcher has been significantly eased by the availability of such online resources.

I would like to acknowledge the people at Heritage House, notably Nandini Thaker, who made my manuscript into a book, and my copyeditor, Marial Shea, who provided her considerable experience and talents in editing the manuscript of this book.

NOTES

INTRODUCTION

1 The term "New Eldorado" is first found in *Kinahan Cornwallis, The New Eldorado; or British Columbia (London: Thomas Cautley Newberry, 1858)*.
2 Colonial Despatches, Douglas to Labouchère, Secretary of State for the Colonies, May 8, 1858, 6113, CO 60/1.
3 Margaret A. Ormsby, *British Columbia: A History* (Vancouver: Macmillan, 1958), 241.
4 Dorothy Blakey Smith, ed. *The Reminiscences of Doctor John Sebastian Helmcken* (Vancouver: UBC Press, 1973), 247.

1 · BILLY BALLOU, PIONEER EXPRESSMAN

1 This story is based upon the information supplied by Ballou in 1878; based on the recorded fact that McMullen visited Douglas on September 30, 1857, the story is credible.
2 Hubert. H. Bancroft, *History of British Columbia 1792–1887* (San Francisco: The History Company, 1887), 352.
3 Bancroft Library, "Adventures of W.T. Ballou," 21–22.
4 James Moore, "The Discovery of Hill's Bar in 1858," *British Columbia Historical Quarterly* 111 (1938): 220.
5 *Victoria Gazette*, July 3, 1858.
6 Quoted in Philip L. Fradkin, *Stagecoach: Wells Fargo and the American West* (New York: Free Press, 2002), 11.
7 Ibid.

8 *Victoria Gazette*, August 6, 1858.

9 Bancroft Library, "Adventures of W.T. Ballou," 4.

10 A.C. Milliken, "The Forgotten Expressman—Billy Ballou," *Canada West Magazine*, 4, no. 4 (1972): 19–20.

11 Quoted in Alexander Begg, *A History of British Columbia from Its Earliest Discovery to the Present Time* (Toronto: Ryerson Archive Series, 1972; first published in 1894), 267.

12 Quoted in Laura Elaine Scott, "The Imposition of British Culture as Portrayed in the New Westminster Capital Plan of 1859 to 1862" (master's thesis, Simon Fraser University, 1983).

13 Bancroft, *History of British Columbia*, 406.

14 Colonial Despatches, Douglas to Labouchere, May 5, 1858.

15 Matthew Baillie Begbie, "Journey into the Interior of British Columbia," *Journal of the Royal Geographical Society of London* 31 (1861): 237.

16 Colonial Despatches, Douglas to Labouchere, November 9, 1858.

17 Ibid., Douglas to Labouchere, November 30, 1858.

18 *British Colonist*, July 22 and August 8, 1859.

19 Charles Edward Barrett-Lennard, *Travels in British Columbia: With the Narrative of a Yacht Voyage Round Vancouver Island* (London: Hurst & Blackett, 1862), 225.

20 Bancroft Library, "Adventures of W.T. Ballou," 7.

21 *British Colonist*, March 17, 1860.

22 Ibid., April 24, 1860.

23 Ibid.

24 Ibid., May 22, 1860.

25 Colonial Despatches, Douglas to Lytton, September 16, 1861.

26 Richard Mayne, *Four Years in British Columbia and Vancouver Island* (London: John Murray, 1862), 71.

27 *British Colonist*, April 15, 1861.

28 Colonial Despatches, Lytton to Douglas, August 14, 1858.

29 F.W. Howay, "The Early History of the Fraser River Mines," Archives of British Columbia, Memoir No. VI, 1926 (Victoria: Charles F. Banfield), Brew to Lieut. Governor Moody, 20 February 1857.

30 Colonial Correspondence, Anderson to Douglas, April 5, 1859.

31 *Victoria Gazette*, May 5, 1859.

32 Colonial Correspondence, Ballou to Douglas, January 14, 1861.

33 *British Colonist*, February 26, 1861.

34 Bancroft Library, "Adventures of W.T. Ballou," 4–5.

2 · BARNARD'S EXPRESS

1 Vancouver *Sunday Province*, October 5, 1925: "Frank S. Barnard recalls his father's claim location and partner Dennis Murphy, later proprietor of the 141 Mile House on the Cariboo Road."

2   RBCM, Series MS-0060, Mary Susanna Moody, "Letter to Mother," August 4, 18[?], and April 16, 1860.

3   Colonial Correspondence, Barnard to Young, October 10, December 28, 1860 and January 28, 1861.

4   *British Colonist*, May 5, 17, November 22, 30, 1860.

5   Colonial Correspondence, Barnard to Chief Commissioner of Lands & Works, March 30, 1861.

6   Bancroft Library, "Adventures of W.T. Ballou," 5.

7   *British Colonist*, December 9, 1861.

8   Ibid., January 6, 1862.

9   Ibid., January 16, 1862.

10 Ibid., February 17, 1862.

11 J.B. Kerr, *Biographical Dictionary of Well-Known British Columbians* (Vancouver: Kerr & Begg, 1890), 92.

12 Among many others: F.W. Howay, British Columbia from the Earliest Times to the Present (Vancouver: S.J. Clark, 1914), 597; Margaret A. Ormsby, "Barnard, Francis Jones," Dictionary of Canadian Biography, vol. 11 (Toronto: University of Toronto, 1982); and Kerr, "Francis Jones Barnard," 91.

13 Derek Pethick, *Men of British Columbia* (Saanichton, BC: Hancock House, 1975), 125.

14 Colonial Correspondence, Barnard to W.A.G. Young, April 10, 1862.

15 Ibid.

16 *British Colonist*, May 24, 1862.

17 Ibid., May 20, 1862.

18 Ibid., June 5, 1862.

19 Alfred Stanley Deaville, *The Colonial Postal Systems and Postage Stamps of Vancouver Island and British Columbia* (Lawrence, Mass.: Quartermain Publications, 1979), 78.

20 Ibid., 84.

21 *British Columbian*, June 28, 1862.

22 *British Colonist*, June 24, 1862.

23 *British Columbian*, January 21 and March 4, 1863.

24 Colonial Despatches, Douglas to Newcastle, October 24, 1861.

25 Walter Moberly, "History of the Cariboo Road," *Art, Historical and Scientific Association, Session 1907-8,* Historical Papers (Vancouver: Clark & Stewart), 29.

26 Hills, Bishop George, *Columbia Mission Report for 1862* (London: Rivington's, 1862), 47.

27 Moberly, "History of the Cariboo Road," 37.

28 Colonial Despatches, Douglas to Newcastle, October 27, 1862.

29 Bruce Hutchison, *The Fraser* (Toronto: Clark, Irwin, 1950), 74.

30 *British Colonist*, June 24, 1862.

31 Ibid., August 5, 1862.

32 Marie Elliot, *Gold and Grand Dreams: Cariboo East in the Early Years* (Victoria: Horsdal and Schubart, 2000), 49.

33 A.J. Splawn, *Ka-mi-akin, Last Hero of the Yakimas* (Portland: Kilnam, 1917), 178.

34 *British Columbian*, August 13, 1862.

35 *British Colonist*, August 20, 1862.

36 Ibid.

37 *British Columbian*, August 16, 1862.

38 *British Colonist*, October 27, 1862.

39 *British Colonist*, December 25, 1862, to January 7, 1863.

40 *British Columbian*, October 27, 1862.

41 Ibid., February 25, 1860.

42 Zane S. Lewis, "Nelson, Hugh" *Dictionary of Canadian Biography*, vol. 12 (Toronto: University of Toronto, 2003.

43 A.G. Doughty and Gustave Lanctot, eds., *Cheadle's Journal of a Trip Across Canada 1862–1863* (Ottawa: Graphic Publishers, 1931), September 19, 1863.

44 Colonial Correspondence, Ballou to Commissioner of Lands and Works, August 8, 1862.

45 Ibid., Ballou and Kwong Lee & Co. to Col. Moody, November 27 and December 6, 1862. Lee Chang was referred to as "Kwong Lee" but only worked for the company.

46 *British Colonist*, July 28, 1863.

47 Bancroft, *History of British Columbia*, 352.

48 *British Columbian*, October 18, 1862.

49 Colonial Correspondence, Barnard to H.P.P. Crease, Attorney General, November 5, 1862.

50 Colonial Correspondence, Barnard to Young, January 1, 1862. Given the subject matter and circumstances, it is clear that this letter was misdated and should read "January 1, 1863."

51 Deaville, *Colonial Postal Systems*, 86.

52 Colonial Correspondence, Barnard to W.A.G. Young, May 18,, 1863.

53 RBCM, PR-1090, Barnard family fonds, Scrapbook, letter, F.J. Barnard to George Gowdie, July 5, 1863.

54 Ibid.

3 · BRITISH COLUMBIA'S FIRST STAGECOACHES

1 *British Columbian*, July 1, 1863.

2 Ibid., August 17, 1863.

3 Colonial Correspondence, Barnard to Douglas, February 5, 1864.

4 BC Archives, PR-0730 Steve Tingley fonds, diary for 1868, January 4.

5 Mark S. Wade, *The Cariboo Road* (Victoria: Haunted Bookshop, 1979), 85.

6 Richard Wright, *Barkerville, Williams Creek, Cariboo,* (Duncan, BC: Friends of Barkerville and Cariboo Historical Society 2003), 100.

7 Noel Robinson, "The First Whip of the Cariboo Road." *McLeans Magazine,* (April 1, 1925)

8 University of Victoria, *Government Gazette,* Vol. 2, No. 43, March 26, 1864.

9 Deaville, *Colonial Postage Systems,* 114.

10 *British Colonist,* June 9, 1864.

11 "Government Gazette," 2, no. 50, May 14, 1864, Official Gazettes of British Columbia, University of Victoria.

12 Ibid., November 4, 1864.

13 Ibid., November 18, 1864.

14 RBCM, PR-1090, Barnard family fonds, Scrapbook, letter, F.J. Barnard to George Gowdie, July 5, 1863.

15 F.W. Howay, *British Columbia from the Earliest Times to the Present,* vol. 2 (Vancouver: S.J. Clark, 1914), 137.

16 RBCM, Barnard family fonds, Scrapbook, letter, F.J. Barnard to George Gowdie, July 5, 1863.

17 *British Columbian,* September 14 and 17, November 12 and 25, 1863.

18 *British Colonist,* March 24, 1864.

19 Colonial Correspondence, Barnard to Douglas, February 11, 1864.

20 Ibid., Barnard to Colonial Secretary Birch, May 31, 1864.

21 *British Colonist,* August 8, 1864.

22 *British Columbian,* May 4, 1864.

23 *British Colonist,* January 6, 1865.

24 November 23, 1863, Doughty and Lanctot, *Cheadle's Journal,* 365.

25 *British Colonist,* April 22, 1865.

26 *Daily Province,* March 8, 1921.

27 Branwen Patenaude, *Trails to Gold* (Victoria: Horsdal & Schubart, 1995), 31.

28 Ibid., 34.

29 Ibid., 37.

30 F.W. Laing, "Notes on the Colonial Farm Settlers on the Mainland of British Columbia," MS-0700, BC Archives, William Liang fonds (PR-1691), 234.

31 Patenaude, *Trails to Gold,* 44.

32 Cheadle, *Journal,* October 16, 1863.

33 Branwen Patenaude, *Trails to Gold,* vol. 2 (Surrey: Heritage House, 1996), 225.

34 *Daily Province,* March 8, 1921.

35 Ibid.

36 *British Colonist,* May 1, 1865.

37 Ibid., April 2, 1865.

38 Ibid., August 14, 1865.

39 Ibid., December 4, 1865

40 *Yale Tribune,* April 23, 1866.

41 Ibid., April 30 1866.

42 Ibid., June 18, 1866.

43 *British Colonist*, June 6, 1866.

44 *Tribune*, July 30, 1866.

45 *British Colonist*, April 30, 1866.

46 Ibid., February 26, 1866.

47 Colonial Correspondence, BC Archives, Ball to W.A.G. Young, December 28, 1869 (BO1305, 11, F100).

48 William Winstanely Bilsland, "A History of Revelstoke and the Big Bend," masters thesis (University of British Columbia, 1955), 32.

49 *Cariboo Sentinel*, October 14, 1865.

50 *British Colonist*, March 22, 1866

51 *British Columbian*, June 2, 1866.

52 *Cariboo Sentinel*, May 24, 1866.

53 Ibid., October 29, 1867.

54 Ormsby, *British Columbia*, 221-222.

55 *British Colonist*, January 14 and 24, 1867.

56 Ibid., May 11, 1867.

57 *Sentinel*, June 6, 1867.

58 Ibid., July 8, 1867.

59 Laing, "Notes on the Colonial Farm Settlers," 308.

60 *Cariboo Sentinel*, June 20, 1867.

61 *British Colonist*, December 17, 1867.

4 · STAGECOACHES, DRIVERS, AND HORSES

1 G.C. Tomkins, *Compendium of the Overland Mail Company on the South Route, 1858-1861, and the Period Surrounding It* ([United States]: Talina Corp. 1985), 183.

2 Ibid., 197-203.

3 Willis J. West, *Stagecoach and Sternwheel Days in the Cariboo and Central B.C.* (Surrey: Heritage House, 1985), 19; Ormsby, "Barnard," *Dictionary of Canadian Biography*.

4 *British Colonist*, October 22, 1862.

5 Ibid., November 6, 1863.

6 Ibid., January 4, 1865.

7 Ibid., May 31, 1873.

8 Much of what follows is from Tomkins, *Compendium of the Overland Mail Company*, 183-194.

9 Walker A. Tompkins, *Stagecoach Days in Santa Barbara County* (Santa Barbara: McNally & Lofton, 1982).

10 William Banning and George Hugh Banning, *Six Horses* (New York: The Century Company, 1928), 362.

11 Ibid., 363–64.

12 West, *Stagecoach and Sternwheel Days*, 16.

13 *British Colonist*, January 16, 1862.

14 Colonial Correspondence, Barnard to Trutch, October 24, 1866.

15 Jean Barman, *The West Beyond the West: A History of British Columbia* (Toronto: University of of Toronto Press, 1996), 379, Table 5.

16 *British Colonist*, October 9, 1861.

17 Colonial Correspondence, Barnard to Colonial Secretary, December 12, 1864.

5 · BARNARD'S EXPANDING VISION

1 Wade, *Cariboo Road*, 94.

2 BC Archives, Barnard family fonds, Scrapbook, Letter from FJ Barnard to Mr. Crawford, December 1, 1867.

3 Howay, *British Columbia from the Earliest Times*, 547; J.B. Kerr, "Early Days in Priest's Valley," The Sixth Report of the Okanagan Historical Society, 1935 (Vancouver: Wrigley Printing, 1936), 284; Mabel Johnson, "The BX Ranch," *The Twentieth Report of Okanagan Historical Society, 1956* (Penticton: Herald, 1956), 86.

4 BC Archives, Barnard family fonds, Scrapbook, copy of letter from F.J. Barnard to S. Tingley, December 6, 1867.

5 BC Archives, PR-0730, Steve Tingley fonds, diary for 1868.

6 Ibid., February 9, 1868.

7 Walker A. Tompkins, *Santa Barbara's Royal Rancho:* The Fabulous History of Los Dos Pueblos (Berkeley: Howell-North Books, 1960), 190.

8 BC Archives, PR-0730, Steve Tingley fonds, diary for 1868, February 12.

9 Ibid., March 17, 1868.

10 Ibid., June 18, 1868.

11 Ibid., July 19, 1868.

12 Ibid., July 20, 1868.

13 Colonial Correspondence, Barnard to Colonial Secretary, March 11, 1868.

14 Ibid., Colonial Secretary to Barnard, March 16, 1868.

15 Ibid., Barnard to Colonial Secretary, April 18, 1868.

16 BC Archives, PR-0730, Steve Tingley fonds, diary for 1868, August 24.

17 Howay, *British Columbia from the Earliest Times to the Present*, Vol. 2, 597.

18 BC Archives, MS-0700, Laing, "Notes on the Colonial Farm Settlers," 462.

19 *British Colonist*, March 7, 1868.

20 Ibid., March 9, 1868.

21 Colonial Correspondence, Barnard to Colonial Secretary, February 4, 1868.

22 Ibid.

23 *British Colonist*, March 16, 1868.

24 *Colonial Dispatches*, Seymour to Buckingham, November 31, 1868.

25 Ibid., Begbie to Crease, August 5, 1867.

26 *British Colonist*, April 1, 1867.

27 Walter N. Sage, "The Critical Period of British Columbia History, 1866–1871" *Pacific Historical* Review 1, no. 4, (Dec. 1932): 429.

28 *British Columbian*, March 20, 1867.

29 Ormsby, *British Columbia: A History*, 241.

30 Walter, "The Critical Period of British Columbia History," 430.

31 BC Archives, Barnard family fonds, Scrapbook, Letter from FJ Barnard to Mr. Crawford, December 1, 1867.

32 Kamloops Museum, *Fort Kamloops Journal*, June 11 and 19, 1868.

33 Ormsby, *British Columbia: A History*, 226.

34 *Pacific Rural Press* (San Francisco), January 14, 1871.

35 Colonial Correspondence, Barnard to Musgrave, October 1, 1870.

36 Ibid.

37 Colonial Correspondence, Barnard to Colonial Secretary, November 8, 1870; Colonial Secretary to Barnard, December 7, 1870.

38 *British Colonist*, January 31, 1871.

39 Ibid, February 14, 1871.

40 Ibid., April 22, 1871.

41 Ibid., April 23, 1871.

42 Ibid., May 2, 1871.

43 Ibid., February 9, 1872.

44 Ibid., May 21, 1876.

6 · F.J. BARNARD & COMPANY

1 Adapted from Rev. Arthur Browning, "Steve's Last Ride," *Methodist Magazine and Review* 577, no. 3 (1903): 258–59.

2 Ibid., October 21, 1870.

3 Ibid., February 14, 1871.

4 Ibid., March 14, 1871.

5 Ibid., May 27, 1871.

6 Ibid., January 13, 1872.

7 BC Archives, MS-0056, Crease Papers, private letterbook, Crease to C.W. Franks, November 13, 1871.

8 Ibid., Alston to Crease, July 19, 1871.

9 Ibid., Macdonald to Crease, April 5, 1873.

10 Ibid., January 20, January 23, February 3, 1872.

11 Ibid., February 29, 1872.

12 Ibid., March 21, 1872.

13 Ibid., May 11, 1872.

14 *Cariboo Sentinel*, May 4, 1872.

15 *Journals of the Legislative Assembly*, vol. 1, March 6, 1872.

16 *British Colonist*, June 6, 1972.

17 Ibid., August 10, 1872.

18 Linda Peterat, "Searching for Alexander Vance," *83rd Report of Okanagan History*, 2019, 73.

19 Kamloops Archives, *Fort Kamloops Journal*, March 17, 1870.

20 *British Colonist*, November 6, 1872.

21 BC Archives, MS-0700, Laing, "Notes on the Colonial Farm Settlers," 462.

22 BC Archives, GR-0868, 948-73, letters, Marat Wilson & Robert Irving, June 19, 1873.

23 *British Colonist*, January 16, 1862.

24 Ibid., February 17, 1862.

25 BC Archives, PR-1090, Barnard family fonds, scrapbook.

26 *Victoria Daily Standard*, January 23, 1874. Note: these issues are no longer available; I am using clippings from the scrapbook in the Barnard family fonds at the BC Archives.

27 Ibid.

28 BC Archives, PR-1090, Barnard family fonds, scrapbook.

29 *Victoria Daily Standard*, December 4, 1872.

30 Ibid, January 31, 1874.

31 *British Colonist*, February 15, 1874.

32 *British Colonist*, February 24, 1874.

33 *Mainland Guardian*, March 7, 1874.

34 *Victoria Daily Standard*, March 6, 1874.

35 *Cariboo Sentinel*, May 25, June 6, 1874.

36 Ibid., August 21, 1875.

37 *British Colonist*, November 6, 1872.

38 Alexander Mackenzie, speech at Sarnia, quoted by Ormsby, *British Columbia: A History*, 261.

39 *British Colonist*, September 18, 1874.

40 Ibid., October 10, 1874.

41 BC Archives, PR-1090, Barnard family fonds, Scrapbook, letter F.J. Barnard to James Barnard, July 5, 1863.

42 City of Vancouver Archives, unpublished typescript by Frank H. Barnard.

43 *B.C. Tribune*, June 26, 1866.

44 BC Archives, PR-1090, Barnard family fonds, Scrapbook, letter F.J. Barnard to Mr. Crawford, December 1, 1867.
45 Ormsby, "Barnard, Francis Jones."
46 Statutes of the Province of British Columbia, 1878, Victoria, p.4, c.2, "An Act to Incorporate the British Columbia Express Company."
47 BC Archives, PR-1105, BC Express Company Business Records, minute book.
48 *British Colonist*, April 4, 1880.
49 Ibid., April 25, 1880.
50 Scholefield and Howay, British Columbia, vol. 3, 40–43.
51 British *Colonist*, September 23, 1873.
52 Ibid.
53 *Ottawa Citizen*, April 7, 1881.
54 *British Colonist*, October 4, 1883.
55 Ibid., February 1, March 30, 1878.

7 · THE BC EXPRESS COMPANY CARRIES ON THE TRADITION

1 Hariot Georgina Blackwood, Marchioness of Dufferin and Ava, *My Canadian Journal, 1872-8: Extracts from My Letters Home While Lord Dufferin Was Governor General* (London: John Murray, 1891), 273–82.
2 *British Colonist*, September 11, 1879.
3 BC Archives, PR-1105, BC Express Company Business Records, minute book.
4 *British Colonist*, April 12, 1881.
5 Douglas V. Parker, *No Horsecars in Paradise: A History of the Street Railways and Public Utilities in Victoria, British Columbia before 1897* (Vancouver: Whitecap Books, 1981), 74.
6 *British Colonist*, June 15, June 20, 1877.
7 HBC Archives, Letter John Tait, Kamloops, BC to William Charles, HBC Victoria, BC, February 27, 1875.
8 Ibid., April 11, 1876.
9 A.J. Hiebert, "District of Okanagan Assessment Roll, 1879," *Forty-first Annual Okanagan Historical Society Report, 1977* (N.p.).
10 HBC Archives, Letter John Tait, Kamloops, BC to William Charles, HBC Victoria, BC, July 6, 1874.
11 Ken Mather, *Frontier Cowboys and the Great Divide: Early Ranching in BC and Alberta* (Victoria: Heritage House, 2013), 45–51.
12 *British Colonist*, May 6, 1882.
13 John R. Craig, *Ranching with Lords and Commons, or Twenty Years on the Range* (Surrey, BC: Heritage House, 2006), 37.

14 High River Pioneers and Old Timers' Association, *Leaves from the Medicine Tree* ([Lethbridge]: Lethbridge Herald, 1960), 357.

15 BC Archives, PR-1090, Barnard family fonds, private letterbook, letter to Muir, Superintendent NPR, dated May 17, 1883.

16 High River Pioneers, *Leaves from the Medicine Tree*, 274.

17 BC Archives, PR-1090, Barnard family fonds, private letterbook, F.S. Barnard to Davies, dated September 10, 1883.

18 Ibid., F.S. Barnard to F. White, September 15; to F. Stimson, October 1; to G. Levigne, October 9 and 23, 1883. "Ranche" was the preferred spelling in the 1880s.

19 *Inland Sentinel*, November 27, 1884.

20 High River Pioneers, *Leaves from the Medicine Tree*, 355.

21 BC Archives, GR-0686 – 552/80 – J. Trutch to G.A. Walkem Chief Commissioner of Lands & Works, June 14, 1880.

22 *British Colonist*, June 6, 1882.

23 Ibid., August 9 and 29, 1882.

24 Ibid., August 22, 1880.

25 Ibid., May 25, 1881.

26 Ibid., June 20, 1884.

27 Wade, *Cariboo Road*, 245.

28 Ibid., November 5, 1884.

29 BC Archives, PR-1090, Barnard family fonds, private letterbook, F.S. Barnard to E.H. Wood, May 20, 1886.

30 Ibid., F.S. Barnard to H. Smith, Commissioner of Lands & Works, October 30, 1883.

31 Ibid., F.S. Barnard to Davies, dated Sept. 10, 1883.

32 Ibid., F.S. Barnard to Chief Commissioner of Lands & Works, November 3, 1883.

33 BC Archives, PR-1105, BC Express Business Records, minute book.

34 Ibid.

35 Ibid.

36 Ibid.

37 *Cariboo Sentinel*, May 4, 1872.

38 BC Gold Rush Press, "Russian Jack, The Stagecoach Trip with Steve Tingley," online at bcgoldrushpress.com/2013/12.

39 Patenaude, *Trails to Gold*, vol. 1, 110.

40 Ibid., 40, 100.

41 BC Archives, PR-1105, BC Express Business Records, minute book.

42 *Inland Sentinel*, September, 1883.

43 "Golden Cariboo," *Weekly World* (Vancouver), December 27. 1894.

44 Ibid.

45 West, *Stagecoach and Sternwheel Days*, 37.

46 *British Colonist*, July 4, 1897.

8 · HOLDUPS AND ACCIDENTS

1 Adapted from Wade, *Cariboo Road*, 218.
2 *British Colonist*, July 16, 1890.
3 Ibid., July 17, 1890.
4 Ibid.
5 BC Archives, PR-1105, BC Express Company Business Records, minute book.
6 *Inland Sentinel*, January 5, 1891.
7 Ibid., June 14, 1891.
8 West, *Stagecoach and Sternwheel Days*, 25.
9 BC Archives, PR-1105, BC Express Business Records, minute book, September 14, 1891.
10 Wade, *Cariboo Road*, 214.
11 West, *Stagecoach and Sternwheel Days*, 26.
12 Wade, *Cariboo Road*, 216.
13 *British Colonist*, July 1, 1894.
14 Wade, *Cariboo Road*, 216.
15 West, *Stagecoach and Sternwheel Days*, 29.
16 Ibid.
17 Ibid.
18 BC Archives, Leighton Papers, M-706, 1929.
19 *British Colonist*, September 12, 1864.
20 *Inland Sentinel*, March 7, 1881.
21 Mark S. Wade, *The Cariboo Road* (Victoria: Haunted Bookshop, 1979), 92.
22 Ted Kay, "Transporting Bees by Stagecoach: The Beginnings of the Honeybee Industry in BC," *British Columbia Historical News* 35, no. 2 (2002): 26–27.

9 · THE BC EXPRESS UNDER NEW OWNERSHIP

1 By the early 1900s, "Quesnelle Mouth" had been shortened to "Quesnel" and "Quesnelle Forks" to "Quesnel Forks."
2 Based upon Patenaude, *Trails to Gold*, Vol. 1, 95.
3 Willis J. West, "The 'B.X.' and the Rush to Fort George," *British Columbia Historical Quarterly* 13, nos. 3–4 (July 31, 1949): 132–34.
4 Ibid., 134–35.
5 BC Archives, MS-0548, BC Express Business Records, minute book.
6 Ibid., stock register.
7 Ibid., minute book.
8 W.K.L., "James Buie Leighton: 1851–1946," *British Columbia Historical Quarterly* 10, no. 1 (January, 1946), 86.
9 Ibid.

10 *Vancouver Province*, 1929, Kamloops Archives clipping file.

11 BC Archives, MS-0548, BC Express Business Records, Minute book.

12 *Vancouver Province*, 1929, Kamloops Archives clipping file.

13 *Ashcroft Journal*, May 19, 1900.

14 BC Archives, MS-0548, BC Express Business Records, Minute book.

15 West, *Stagecoach and Sternwheel Days*, 21–22.

16 West, "The 'B.X.' and the Rush to Fort George," 136.

17 *Vancouver Province*, n.d., Kamloops Archives clipping file.

18 Wade, *Cariboo Road*, 218–19.

19 BC Archives, MS-0548, BC Express Business Records, minute book.

20 Art Downs, *Paddlewheels on the Frontier*: The Story of British Columbia and Yukon Sternwheel Steamers (Sydney, BC: Grey's Publishing, 1972), 52–55.

21 West, *Stagecoach and Sternwheel Days*, 43.

22 Ibid., 50–51.

23 Ibid., 60.

24 Ibid., 67.

25 Downs, *Paddlewheels on the Frontier*, 58.

26 West, *Stagecoach and Sternwheel Days*, 54.

27 BC Archives, MS-0548, BC Express Business fonds, minute Book.

28 "When They Changed to Autos on the Cariboo Road," Kamloops Archives clipping file.

29 Patenaude, *Trails to Gold*, vol. 1, 194.

30 West, *Stagecoaches and Sternwheel Days*, 55–56.

31 *Ashcroft Journal*, September 13, 1913.

32 BC Archives, MS-0548, BC Express Business Records, minute book, meeting January 31, 1914.

33 BC Archives, MS-0548, BC Express Business Records, correspondence.

34 Ibid., balance sheet, Dec. 31, 1914.

35 Ibid., Agreement, Jan. 24, 1921

36 Eric Hutton, "Charlie Millar's Million Dollar Joke," *Maclean's Magazine*, June 15, 1952, 18–19, 26, 28.

BIBLIOGRAPHY

Akrigg, G.P.V. and Helen Akrigg. *British Columbia Chronicle, 1847–1871: Gold and Colonists.* Vancouver: Discovery Press, 1977.

Bancroft, Hubert H. *History of British Columbia 1792–1887.* San Francisco: The History Company, 1887. archive.org/details/historybritishco4bategoog/.

Banning, William, and George Hugh Banning. *Six Horses.* New York: The Century Company, 1928.

Barman, Jean. *The West Beyond the West: A History of British Columbia.* Rev. ed. Toronto: University of Toronto Press, 1996.

Barrett-Lennard, Charles Edward. *Travels in British Columbia: With the Narrative of a Yacht Voyage Round Vancouver's Island.* London: Hurst & Blackett, 1862. archive.org/details/travelsinbritishoobarr/.

Begbie, Matthew Bailie. "Journey into the Interior of British Columbia." *Journal of the Royal Geographical Society of London,* 31 (1861): 237–48. archive.org/details/jstor-1798264/.

Begg, Alexander. *History of British Columbia From Its Earliest Discovery to the Present Time.* 1894 ed. Toronto: Ryerson Archive Series, 1972.

Bilsland, William Winstanely. "A History of Revelstoke and the Big Bend." Masters thesis, University of British Columbia, 1955. open.library.ubc.ca/cIRcle/collections/ubctheses/831/items/1.0107145.

Browning, Reverend Arthur. "Steve's Last Ride." *Methodist Magazine and Review 577,* no. 3 (March 1903).

Carr, Dr. R.V.C. *British Columbia Express Covers from 1858 to 1900.* British North America Philatelic Society Ltd, no. 436, 1997.

Champness, W. *To Cariboo and Back—An Emigrant's Journey to the Gold Fields of British Columbia.* From the "Leisure Hour," 1862. catalog.hathitrust.org/Record/100257380

Cornwallis, Kinahan. *The New Eldorado; or British Columbia.* London: Thomas Cautley Newberry, 1858. archive.org/details/neweldoradoorbroocorngoog/.

Coutant, Frank Raymond. *Yankee steamboats on the Fraser River, British Columbia; A Story of Yankee Participation in Building and Operating Paddlewheelers during the Cariboo Hold Rush 1858-1871.* Monroe, Conn.: [The Author], n.d. archive.org/ stream/yankeesteamboatsoocout/yankeesteamboatsoocout_djvu.txt.

Craig, John R. *Ranching With Lords and Commons, or Twenty Years on the Range.* Surrey, BC: Heritage House, 2006.

Deaville, Alfred Stanley. *The Colonial Postal Systems and Postage Stamps of Vancouver Island and British Columbia.* Lawrence, Mass: Quarterman Publications, 1979.

Doughty, A.G. and Gustave Lanctot, eds. *Cheadle's Journal of Trip Across Canada 1862-1863.* Ottawa: Graphic Publishers Ltd., 1931. open.library.ubc.ca/ collections/bcbooks/items/1.0375749#p5z-6r0f.

Downs, Art. *Wagon Road North: The Story of the Cariboo Gold Rush in Historical Photos.* Quesnel: Northwest Digest Limited, 1960.

——. *Paddlewheels on the Frontier: The Story of British Columbia and Yukon Sternwheel Steamers.* Sydney, BC: Grey's Publishing Ltd., 1972.

Dufferin and Ava, Hariot Georgina Blackwood, Marchioness of. *My Canadian Journal, 1872-8: Extracts from My Letters Home While Lord Dufferin Was Governor-General.* London: John Murray, 1891. archive.org/details/mycanadianjournaooduffuoft/.

Elliot, Gordon R. *Barkerville, Quesnel & the Cariboo Gold Rush.* Vancouver: Douglas & McIntyre, 1958.

Elliot, Marie. *Gold and Grand Dreams: Cariboo East in the Early Years.* Victoria: Horsdal & Schubart Publishers Ltd, 2000.

Forsythe, Mark and Greg Dickson. *The Trial of 1858.* Madeira Park, BC: Harbour Publishing, 2007.

Fradkin, Philip L. *Stagecoach: Wells Fargo and the American West.* New York: Free Press, 2002.

Gosnell, R.E. *A History of British Columbia.* Victoria: The Lewis Publishing Co., 1906.

Grant, George Munro. *Ocean to Ocean: Sanford Fleming's Expedition Through Canada in 1872.* Toronto: Rose Bulford Publishing Co., 1877. archive.org/details/ oceantooceansano1grangoog/.

Hacking, Norman. "'Steamboat 'Round the Bend': American Steamers on the Fraser River in 1858." *British Columbia Historical Quarterly* 8, no. 4 (October 1944): 255-80. library.ubc.ca/archives/pdfs/bchf/bchq_1944_4.pdf.

Hiebert, A.J. "District of Okanagan Assessment Roll, 1879." *Forty-first Annual Okanagan Historical Society Report 1977.* N.p.

Higgins, D.W. *The Mystic Spring and Other Tales of Western Life.* Toronto: W. Biggs, 1904. archive.org/details/mysticspringotheoohigguoft/.

High River Pioneers and Old Timers' Association. *Leaves from the Medicine Tree.* [Lethbridge]: Lethbridge Herald, 1960.

Hill, Beth. *Sappers: The Royal Engineers in British Columbia*. Ganges, BC: Horsdal and Schubart, 1987.

Hills, Bishop George. *Columbia Mission, Annual Reports, 1860–1870*. London: Rivington's, 1862.

Howay, F.W. *British Columbia from the Earliest Times to the Present*. Vol. 2. Vancouver: S.J. Clark, 1914. open.library.ubc.ca/collections/bcbooks/items/1.0355314#p13z-4rof.

Howay, F.W. "The Early History of the Fraser River Mines." Archives of British Columbia, Memoir No. VI, 1926. Victoria: Charles F. Banfield. open.library.ubc.ca/collections/bcbooks/items/1.0347560#p0z-3rof.

Hutchison, Bruce. *The Fraser*. Toronto: Clark, Irwin, 1950.

Hutton, Eric. "Charlie Millar's Million Dollar Joke." *Maclean's Magazine*, June 15, 1952, 18–19, 26, 28.

Jackson, W. Turrentine. "Banking, Mail, and Express Service in British North America: The Role of Wells, Fargo and Company on Vancouver Island." *The Pacific Northwest Quarterly* 76, no. 4 (Oct. 1985): 137–47.

Johnson, Mabel. "The BX Ranch." *The Twentieth Report of Okanagan Historical Society, 1956*. Penticton: Herald, 1956.

Kay, Ted. "Transporting Bees by Stagecoach: The Beginnings of the Honeybee Industry in BC," *British Columbia Historical News* 35, no. 2 (2002): 26–27.

Kerr, J.B. *Biographical Dictionary of Well-Known British Columbians*. Vancouver: Kerr & Begg, 1890.

Kerr, R.D. "Early Days in Priest's Valley." *The Sixth Report of the Okanagan Historical Society, 1935*. Vancouver: Wrigley Printing, 1936.

Legislative Assembly of British Columbia. *Journals of the Legislative Assembly*. archives.leg.bc.ca/civix/content/leg_archives/legarchives/1973118582/1879_52983 3291/343082351/?xsl=/templates/browse.xsl.

Lewis, Zane S. "Nelson, Hugh." *Dictionary of Canadian Biography*, vol. 12. Toronto: University of Toronto, 2003. biographi.ca/en/bio/nelson_hugh_12E.html.

Mather, Ken. *Frontier Cowboys and the Great Divide: Early Ranching in BC and Alberta*. Victoria: Heritage House, 2013.

Mayne, Richard. *Four Years in British Columbia and Vancouver Island: An Account of Their Forests, Rivers, Gold Fields, and Resources for Colonization*. London: John Murray, 1862. archive.org/details/fouryearsinbritioomayn.

Milliken, A.C. "The Forgotten Expressman Billy Ballou." *Canada West Magazine* 4, no. 4 (1972): 16–22.

Moberly, Walter. "History of the Cariboo Road." *Art, Historical and Scientific Association Session 1907–8, Historical Papers*. Vancouver: Clark & Stewart.

Moore, James. "The Discovery of Hill's Bar in 1858." *British Columbia Historical Quarterly* 3, no. 1 (1939): 215–20. open.library.ubc.ca/collections/bch/items/1.0190731#p69z-3rof.

Morton, James. *In the Sea of Sterile Mountains: The Chinese in British Columbia*. Vancouver: J.J. Douglas Ltd, 1979.

Ormsby, Margaret A. *British Columbia: A History*. Vancouver: Macmillan, 1958.

——. "Barnard, Francis Jones." *Dictionary of Canadian Biography*, vol. 11. Toronto: University of Toronto Press, 1982. biographi.ca/en/bio/barnard_francis_jones_11E.html.

Parker, Douglas V. *No Horsecars in Paradise: A History of the Street Railways and Public Utilities in Victoria, British Columbia before 1897*. Vancouver: Whitecap Books Ltd., 1981.

Patenaude, Branwen. *Trails to Gold*. Victoria: Horsdal and Schubart, 1995.

——. *Trails to Gold, vol. 2*. Surrey: Heritage House, 1996.

Peterat, Linda. "Searching for Alexander Vance." *Okanagan History*, 83rd Report, 2019, 71–77.

Pethick, Derek. *Men of British Columbia*. Saanichton, BC: Hancock House, 1975.

Robinson, Noel. "The First Whip of the Cariboo Road." *Macleans Magazine*, April 1, 1925.

Sage, Walter N. "The Critical Period of British Columbia History, 1866–1871." *Pacific Historical Review* 1, no. 4 (December 1932): 424–43. open.library.ubc.ca/collections/bcbooks/items/1.0374757.

Scholefield, E.O.S., and F.W. Howay. *British Columbia from the Earliest Times to the Present*. 4 vols. Vancouver: S.J. Clark, 1914.

Scott, Laura Elaine. "The Imposition of British Culture as Portrayed in the New Westminster Capital Plan of 1859 to 1862." Master's thesis, Simon Fraser University, 1983. summit.sfu.ca/item/5945.

Smith, Dorothy Blakey, ed. *The Reminiscences of Doctor John Sebastian Helmcken*. Vancouver: UBC Press, 1975.

Splawn, A.J. *Ka-mi-akin, Last Hero of the Yakimas*. Portland: Kilnam, 1917.

Tomkins, G.C. *A Compendium of the Overland Mail Company on the South Route, 1858–1861, and the Period Surrounding It*. [United States]: Talina Corp., 1985.

Tompkins, Walker A. *Santa Barbara's Royal Rancho: The Fabulous History of Los Dos Pueblos*. Berkeley: Howell-North Books, 1960.

——. *Stagecoach Days in Santa Barbara County*. Santa Barbara: McNally & Lofton, 1982.

Wade, Mark S. *The Cariboo Road*. Victoria: Haunted Bookshop, 1979.

West, Willis J. "Staging and Stage Hold-ups in the Cariboo." *British Columbia Historical Quarterly* 12, no. 3 (1948): 185–210.

——. *Stagecoach and Sternwheel Days in the Cariboo and Central B.C.* Surrey, BC: Heritage House Publishing, 1985.

——. "The 'B.X.' and the Rush to Fort George." *British Columbia Historical Quarterly* 13, nos. 3–4 (July 31, 1949): 129–230. open.library.ubc.ca/collections/bch/items/1.0190657#p4z-3r0f.

[W.K.L.] "James Buie Leighton: 1851–1946," *British Columbia Historical Quarterly* 10, no. 1 (January, 1946), 86–87.

Wright, Richard Thomas. *Barkerville, Williams Creek, Cariboo: A Gold Rush Experience.* Rev. ed. Duncan, BC: Winter Quarters Press / Friends of Barkerville and Cariboo Goldfields Historical Society, 1993.

Young, B.F, "Early Days in British Columbia." *Sixth Report of the Okanagan Historical Society, 1933.* Vancouver: Wrigley Printing. open.library.ubc.ca/collections/ohs/items/1.0132249

ARCHIVAL SOURCES

Bancroft Library, MSS P-B 1, "Adventures of W.T. Ballou."

City of Vancouver Archives
  · Unpublished typescript by Frank H. Barnard, 1858

Greater Vernon Museum and Archives

Hudson's Bay Company Archives, Winnipeg, Manitoba

Kamloops Archives, clippings files and Fort Kamloops journals

Library and Archives Canada, Photographs

Royal BC Museum, BC Archives, Victoria
  · GR-0868 – Colonial Correspondence
  · GR-1054 – Department of Land and Works, Lytton Gold Commissioner's records
  · GR-1182 – Department of Lands and Works, Cariboo, Lytton, and Lillooet pre-emptions
  · GR-1372 – Colonial Correspondence, 1857–1872
  · PR-1691 – Frederick William Laing fonds, F.W. Laing, Notes on the Colonial Farm Settlers on the Mainland of British Columbia, MS-0700
  · PR-0730 – Steve Tingley Fonds, diary for 1868
  · PR-1090 – Barnard family fonds
    · Private letterbook
    · Scrapbook
    · Diary
    · Correspondence
  · PR-1105 – British Columbia Express Company fonds

University of British Columbia, Vancouver and Okanagan, Special Collections
  · BC Historical Photographs Collection

ONLINE SOURCES

BC Gold Rush Press. "Russian Jack: The Stagecoach Trip with Stephen Tingley."
    bcgoldrushpress.com/2013/12.

Canadiana Online. *Report of the Select Committee on Chinese Labor and Immigration.*
    Journal of the House of Commons, vol. 13, 1879. eco.canadiana.ca/view/
    00cihm.9_07171_13/2?r=0&s=1.

Colonial Despatches. "The Colonial Despatches of Vancouver Island and British
    Columbia 1846–1871." bcgenesis.uvic.ca/.

University of Victoria BC Gazettes collection. "Official Gazettes of the
    Province of British Columbia." vault.library.uvic.ca/collections/
    d9265b4b-b757-4508-bc7d-85bd3ae91ddc.

Journals of the Legislative Assembly. catalog.hathitrust.org/Record/006302398.

NEWSPAPERS

Ashcroft Journal
Kamloops *Inland Sentinel*
New Westminster *British Columbian*
Vancouver *Mainland Guardian*
Vancouver *Sunday Province*
Vancouver *Weekly World*
Victoria *British Colonist*
Victoria *Daily Standard*
Victoria *Gazette*
Yale *Tribune*

INDEX